Teaching for Thoughtfulness

Teaching for Thoughtfulness

Classroom Strategies to Enhance Intellectual Development

JOHN BARELL

MONTCLAIR STATE COLLEGE

Longman

New York & London

Teaching for Thoughtfulness: Classroom Strategies to Enhance Intellectual Development

Longman, 95 Church Street, White Plains, N.Y. 10601

Associated companies:
Longman Group Ltd., London
Longman Cheshire Pty., Melbourne
Longman Paul Pty., Auckland
Copp Clark Pitman, Toronto

Excerpts from Franklin in the Dark: *Text copyright © 1986 by Paulette Bourgeois. Reprinted by permission of Kids Can Press Ltd., Toronto, Canada.*

Figure 4.1 (pages 41–43). J. Edwards, "The Direct Teaching of Thinking Skills" in G. Evans (ed.) Learning and Teaching Cognitive Skills. *Melbourne, Australia: A.C.E.R., 1991. Reprinted by permission.*

Figure 5.3 (page 82). J. Bellanca and R. Fogarty, Blueprints for Thinking in the Cooperative Classroom. *Palantine, IL: Illinois Renewal Institute/Skylight Publishing Inc., 1990. Reprinted by permission.*

Thinking Journal Summary by Donna M. Sparacio. Reprinted by permission of the author.

Senior editor: Naomi Silverman
Production editor: Linda W. Witzling
Cover design: Susan J. Moore

Library of Congress Cataloging-in-Publication Data

Barell, John.
   Teaching for thoughtfulness : classroom strategies to enhance
intellectual development / John Barell.
     p. cm.
   Includes bibliographical references and index.
   ISBN 0-8013-0620-5
   1. Creative thinking. 2. Thought and thinking—Study and teaching
(Secondary) I. Title.
LB1062.B38 1991
370.15'2—dc20   90-22285
                                          CIP

2 3 4 5 6 7 8 9 10—AL—95 94 93 92 91

For Izzy and Emily and all the teachers and parents who have encouraged them to reflect and pose good questions.

Contents

Foreword

A breath of fresh air runs through the pages of this book. It breaks free of two marked tendencies—laying out a heavy theoretical overlay about education which is detached from the realities of the classroom and blaming teachers for failures in our educational system—rampant in the field of educational reform today.

Teaching for Thoughtfulness celebrates the work of teachers and their students. It shows us what can be achieved in the thoughtful classroom by teachers dedicated to helping students make the best of their potential as thinkers and learners. The descriptions provide paradigms of what education can be. Their authenticity shows us that classrooms which foster good thinking and learning are within our reach. The spirit of John Barell's work is uplifting, visionary, and at the same time wonderfully realistic.

The book's fundamental message is that the forms of thinking and the basic attitudes of thoughtfulness that are so important in our lives can be nurtured and taught effectively to students. Drawing from the best understanding and articulation of what this means, John Barell's comprehensive and deeply insightful synthesis advances our understanding of what it means to teach good thinking to students. *Teaching for Thoughtfulness* is not merely a collection of classroom stories. The commentary enhances our understanding of these classrooms and helps us get a rich sense of how we can incorporate the methods into our own teaching. More than any other work that has come out of the efforts to make thinking a primary emphasis in classrooms across this country, this book brings it all together. I delight in reading it and recommend it to anyone who has despaired of the ability of an institution like our public schools to restructure itself so that it makes education what it should be.

ROBERT SWARTZ

Acknowledgments

For thoughtfulness to become a characteristic of our classrooms, we need to work and learn together, collaboratively. The same is true of bringing a book such as this to fruition: In many ways this has been a cooperative project involving many people with wide diversity of experience, and I should like to acknowledge their contributions.

Many teachers, some of whose names are mentioned here, have shared their classrooms with me and been willing to experiment with ideas that seemed to meet a need. Beth Friedman and Doreen Guzo have invited me to work with their students on numerous occasions, and I have learned from the strategies and projects they have undertaken. Were it not for the high-spirited interest of Sylvia Mathis, I would never have been introduced to the children and teachers of Wasatch Elementary School and to their imaginative and reflective thoughts about wait time, a wide variety of thought processes, and their personal growth. Rosemarie Liebmann provided a working laboratory in her classroom, and several of the strategies—for example, goal setting and thinking journals—originated in our attempts to help her students gain more control over their own learning. In addition she read early drafts of this manuscript, and for her insightful comments and friendship I am always thankful.

For many years Irving Sigel has been a good friend and counselor on matters that affect how children grow and inquire. I am deeply indebted to him for open conversations that have always left me wondering about the nature of things. David Perkins's work on transfer, his studies of informal reasoning, and his proactive view of thinking have influenced the writing of this book significantly. Robin Fogarty has been most encouraging in her support for this project, and I appreciate her substantive and editorial assistance. Arthur Costa has publicly modeled many of the classroom strategies outlined here, and without his leadership many of us might have been unable to create the pathways toward school change that we have. He made important suggestions about the nature of inquiry and was incisive in his comments on the manuscript. Over the years I have shared many enriching conversations with Esther Fusco about children's marvelously inventive ways of thinking and being; I think some of her enthusiasm is reflected in these pages, which she also carefully read and for which she made valuable suggestions. And Robert Swartz read the entire manuscript not once but twice, and it was his personal interest in this project, spinning out graphic organizers over the dining room table, as well as the depth of his knowledge about the subject that helped me refine my thinking on the nature of thoughtfulness, and for his assistance and friendship I am deeply grateful.

Production editor Linda Witzling has provided incisive, caring, and thoughtful support as the manuscript became a book.

Naomi Silverman has not only excelled as an editor in refining the language of this document, she also provided the initial, professional encouragement for its development. She has posed significant questions that have helped me clarify my thinking and, throughout, has been excited about encouraging change in our classrooms.

Finally, a project such as this is like setting off on an expedition into virtually unknown territory, and such an endeavor is really inconceivable without the assurance of a strong, supportive home base. Nancy Ann has provided that with her love and encouragement, throughout the four years of work on this book.

About This Book

My intention in this book is to help us, teachers, administrators, teacher educators, and parents to empower all our students to take more control of their own education and their lives. We need to consider ways of challenging our students to pose and resolve some problems on their own. This suggests that we need to help these students to set goals and design strategies to reach those goals, both for academic and life achievement. Furthermore, it means we need to teach our students something about the nature of thinking, what makes a thoughtful person, and how one can improve one's intellectual performance by learning different ways of figuring things out.

I am not, however, interested in teaching our students to become so *self-directed* intellectually that they neglect to consider empathically the ways of thinking and feeling of other people. To be open to the ideas of others is one way in which we grow, and to respond to the feelings of others creates a trusting relationship necessary if people are to communicate and collaborate productively. This union of thought and feeling within the term *thoughtfulness* is one of the major themes of this book.

Some of you might be saying, "Students already know a lot about thinking. They do it all the time." I agree, in part. Students are thinking all the time, but experience teaches us that, without reflection on what we do, we are not likely to benefit from our good thinking. One of our challenges, then, is to create settings where students' thinking is encouraged as a natural process in school. As one student said, "I think outside school. Here [in school] I memorize stuff." We can change this perception and help students become more thoughtful as they are learning school subjects.

And, finally, this book is about creating the climate or classroom environment wherein our students feel invited to think productively. I call this kind of environment " invitational" because a colleague of mine, Judith MacDonald, always refers to the excellent teachers she has known as inviting students to think, to challenge, to question. An invitational environment, then, is one wherein students feel comfortable expressing their ideas, where they do not fear being wrong, are willing to challenge established points of view, and can risk asking, "What if?" and "Why not?"—kinds of questions that reflect their curiosity about the world. (See also Purkey 1978.)

An invitational environment does not, as Dewey said about thinking, occur spontaneously, of its own accord. It is carefully constructed, designed, and fashioned by the kind of teacher who challenges students to reflect on their lives in school and outside. Teachers like these, some of whom I will introduce to you in this book, have set themselves the goal of creating a flexible structure that nurtures the growth of their students' intellectual and emotional capacities.

Thoughtfulness, as I define it in these pages, is the guiding concept for this book, because it unites the head and the heart, thinking and feeling, the cognitive and the affective dimensions of living in our world. To separate one from the other does a disservice to the complex nature of living.

PLAN OF THE BOOK

My goal is to enhance the quality of students' lives in their classrooms. Toward this end I have laid out the chapters in the following way.

Chapter 2 presents a definition of the thinking process: the search for *meaning* (make sure problems "make sense"); the *adventurous* pursuit of alternative solutions, meanings, and perspectives; the attempt to base decisions or selections upon *reasonableness* (considering evidence); and the *reflection* metacognitively (thinking about thinking) on these processes to make them more conscious and bring them under our control. Thinking is conceived as creating one's own pathways, not following in others' footsteps.

Chapter 3 presents a classroom episode that demonstrates how teachers have used specific lessons to challenge students to think productively. Chapter 3 also pursues in more detail one of the underlying issues in the constant quest for more thoughtfulness within classrooms: Who controls the thinking and learning in the classroom?

Chapter 4 provides criteria and instruments for assessing the quality of our students' thinking and behaving.

Chapter 5 presents strategies for the creation of the invitational environment, and it identifies those teaching behaviors that research indicates are important if we want students to risk thinking productively.

Chapter 6 elaborates upon Chapter 5, to explore teacher modeling, sense of inquiry, and willingness to experiment as key processes in creating the invitational environment.

Chapter 7 presents models and sample lesson and unit plans for daily and long-range planning.

Chapters 8–11 present what some call macro thinking processes: problem solving, creative and critical thinking, and metacognition. I present these in separate chapters, but, in dealing with the kinds of ill-structured and messy problems we will face in the future, it becomes evident that we must engage in them as a whole, not in separate, distinct packages.

Chapter 12 provides some insights from teachers about what to do when students say, "Thinking gives me a headache!" In other words, what to do when the plans go awry.

Chapter 13 provides some suggestions for how schools themselves can work collaboratively to establish good staff development plans for the improvement of intelligent behavior within classrooms.

In Chapter 14 I share with the reader the personal testimony of two teachers who have taken up the challenge of modeling, inquiring, and experimenting with various instructional plans in their own classrooms. Here we focus on how teachers have learned to share some of their control with students in order to achieve the empowerment and self-direction they both desire.

In conclusion, this book is about helping all our students, from kindergarten through high school and on into college, become more thoughtful and thereby more like pioneers of the unknown and pilots of their own ships, and less like mindless memory machines.

THINKING JOURNALS

One of the major reflective strategies suggested herein involves maintaining a journal, in which we record our thoughts and feelings as we work through problems or reflect upon them later on.

I suggest to the reader that you keep such a journal as you engage the ideas presented here. In many places you will find what I call Points to Ponder. These are questions I have posed to you so you more actively engage the text; such questions, I hope, will become part of your own self-talk. I suggest you jot down your responses in your Thinking Journal *before reading on.* In the text following these Points I have discussed some of the ideas that might have occurred to you. This is one way of engaging you, the reader, interactively in your construction of meaning.

Here are other stems you might use for your more leisurely reflections:

"I wonder . . ."
"What puzzles me . . . What I am curious about . . ."
"This reminds me of [or relates to] . . ."
"What interests me here . . ."
"I feel . . ."
"What would happen if . . . ?"

In Chapter 11 you will read about how students have used such journals to enhance their own thinking and feeling. Your journal can then be the place where you conduct the inquiry and mental experimentation described in Chapter 6.

TEACHER RESOURCES

Many teachers are mentioned in this book, people who have taught me a great deal about challenging students to do more than take in and recite information.

With their permission I have listed their names in an appendix to this book in the hope that you, too, will learn from their inquiry and experimentation by corresponding directly with them. This book can serve thereby as a means for curious educators to communicate with each other.

RESPONDING TO THIS BOOK

The editors have included a Reader Response Survey on the last page of the book (facing the back cover) to enable you to communicate to me how you have used this book. I am most interested in your ideas and experiments, the thoughts and feelings that might have originated with reading something of value here. Please let me know what has made a difference in the development of your own thoughtfulness as well as that of your students.

All journeys like the ones described in this book involve risks, but I hope you will find some comfort in the stories of those who have already embarked upon the often uncharted waters of inquiry and experimentation.

REFERENCES

Purkey, William, and John Novak. 1978. *Inviting School Success*. Belmont, CA: Wadsworth.

Teaching for Thoughtfulness

CHAPTER 1

"Beam Me Up, Scotty!"

OVERVIEW

This chapter presents information from personal observations and national studies to support the conclusion that educators need to spend more time creating environments that foster thoughtfulness.

POSING GOOD QUESTIONS

Isidor I. Rabi was a nuclear physicist who won the Nobel Prize in 1944 for his work on atomic nuclei. When someone asked him how he grew up to be a physicist, he told this story:

When all his friends growing up in Brooklyn came home from school their mothers asked them, "So, what did you learn today?" But not his mother. When he came home his mother asked, "Izzy, did you ask a good question today?"

By Rabi's account, his mother's persistent question had a very strong influence upon the development of his inquiring mind.

One of my major goals in this book is to nurture the disposition in our students to pose and resolve good questions. In this way, we create the conditions that foster thoughtfulness.

Whole School Change

For all of us, the effort to pose good questions pushes us to explore new territories, to forge new pathways to thoughtfulness. These pathways will lead us to redesign not only our classrooms but our schools as well, a project undertaken not in isolation but in cooperation with our colleagues. The entire school, through its various goals, routines, and rewards, must profess the values of inquiry, experimentation, risk taking, and openness to change. (Chapters 5, 6, 7, and 13 focus upon these different kinds of environment.)

The inquiring mind can be nurtured within this kind of supportive environment, but it will not blossom where we teach various "thinking skills" in isolation from one another or from the integrative concept of thoughtfulness.

THE NEED FOR THOUGHTFULNESS

A Definition of Thoughtfulness

Langer (1989) has used the concept of "mindfulness" as meaning conscious, deliberate thought about goals, strategies, and options. The mindful person is open to new ideas and willing to move beyond stereotypes, therefore liberating him- or herself from routine and asserting more control over the thought processes. This is a very valuable concept for our work.

But I have chosen to focus most of my attention upon a different concept: thoughtfulness. This word combines two aspects of our lives: intellectual or cognitive operations plus feelings, attitudes, and dispositions. Thoughtfulness, therefore, calls upon us as educators to help students recognize the attitudes they have toward themselves as thinkers—Do I have confidence I can solve most problems?—and their attitudes toward others—Am I open to other people's ideas? Without both cognitive and affective components, we in schools too often focus upon the one aspect of intelligent behavior that is more easily measurable and planned for.

For some the essence of thoughtfulness will be seen in those intellectual operations that so often form the only focus of attempts to effect change within schools. For me these cognitive operations can be summarized as attempts to search for meaning in complex, nonroutine situations, being adventurous with solutions or interpretations, and the attempt to be reasonable in our choices and judgments. Surrounding each of these processes is the attempt to be reflective by gaining metacognitive awareness and control of our thinking.

Thoughtfulness, therefore, integrates thinking and feeling, a union of heart and mind too often overlooked. Because thoughtfulness is more complex than the teaching of specific "thinking skills," we must expand our explorations to the horizons of entire classroom and school cultures.

I should now like to share with you several observations that suggest to me that we need to spend more of our time creating environments in which we invite students to be thoughtful.

Emily's Story

During many years of working with and listening to students, one student's concerns have had a significant effect on my thinking. When Emily was in tenth grade, her teacher asked her to identify a problem she was trying to solve. Emily wrote the following:

I guess I could call myself smart. I mean I can usually get good grades. Sometimes I worry though, that I'm not equipped to achieve what I want, that *I'm just a tape recorder repeating back what I've heard.* [Emphasis added.] It scares me. . . . I do my work, but I don't have the motivation. I've done well on Iowa and PSAT tests but they are always multiple choice. I worry that once I'm out of school and people don't keep handing me information with questions and scantron sheets I'll be lost.

School is kind of unrealistic that way. Kids who do well often just repeat what the teacher has said. It just seems like time moves so quickly. There are so many things that already I'm too old to do. I'm fifteen and I feel old. There are so many things that I should be doing, but instead I watch T.V. and read books. As a matter of fact I believe I will depart now and watch "Star Trek." I guess that's my really only major problem, insecurity. I have no self-confidence really or at least at the right times. Fortunately, I'm very easy to please. An hour of bad TV programming will perk me up wonderfully. Beam me up, Scotty!"

Emily has captured my imagination, and I have been touched by the honesty of her feelings and observations. In an important way, Emily's reflections have provided the reason for writing this book. Let's consider her statement.

POINT TO PONDER: What do you think are the important points she is making about her education? (Please use your Thinking Journal to reflect upon Emily's statement.)

Some of you might focus upon the kinds of problems she has had to work through in school, on tests she takes and her fear that they will not prepare her for the world beyond the classroom, where problems are not easily identifiable and gradable on Scantron sheets. Emily knows that life in the world beyond classroom walls is composed of situations very different from the ones she has been prepared to respond to, composed of "well-formed" problems, to which there is a specific correct answer. Life, as Schon (1987) notes, consists of "messy, indeterminate situations," which we must recognize as problems to solve. She may be lost in burgeoning amounts of seemingly unrelated information, about which she must ask, What does it all mean? What's important and what's irrelevant? How do you go about figuring out complex situations where there are few, if any, rules?

Others of you might see evidence of the hidden curriculum: that Emily has, for some significant amount of time, been asked to memorize stuff and to repeat it back like a tape recorder. We could infer some of the teaching strategies she lives with in her classes: lecture; question and response; discussion where one point of view seems to prevail.

Another element that emerges from Emily's statement concerns the affective domain of thoughtfulness: There is no conscious processing or reflection on the information she has been taking in. Emily does not feel she exercises much control over her own education, and this, I think, is a point worth spending a lot of time thinking about. Without knowing it, Emily has used a metaphor that captures the essence of Langer's (1989) definition of "mind*lessness*": "blindly follow[ing] routines . . . acting like automatons . . ." (p. 4). Tape recorders mindlessly copy; they exercise no independent control.

Still others might focus upon her feeling "old" at fifteen. How sad that seems! We can wonder about the extent to which ten years of schooling might have contributed to this feeling. How do the teaching and learning strategies we experiece as students (and teachers) contribute to our feelings of well-being? To our images of ourselves?

Emily's teacher, Rosemarie Liebmann, reflected upon her student's thoughts and saw all the above and something else: Emily's desire to transcend this world she feels trapped in. "Beam me up, Scotty!" suggests this interest in growing beyond what is expected of her in traditional classrooms. Perhaps she envisions situations and environments where she can better fulfill the promises she feels growing within her.

Why do I accept Emily's conclusions as honest? Partly because Rosemarie knew Emily through classwork and numerous journal entries; Emily was not a "teacher pleaser" and she was very active in extra academic opportunities. Partly because at the end of her high school career I asked her to reflect on her role (see Conclusion); she used a similar metaphor to describe her status.

I wonder how many of us have experienced such thoughts of bewilderment and powerlessness? How do we feel under such circumstances? When I am in such situations, I feel depressed, and the only way out of the depression is to exercise some control. This means I must set a goal and work toward it on my own or in collaboration with others. I also need to have some practical strategies with which to approach very complex situations.

These two themes in Emily's reflection form the focus of this book: taking more control of one's educational and personal destiny, and learning specific strategies that help us confront the complexities of life. This book is about helping all the Emilys in our schools take more control of their education, helping them gain more self-direction so that they become originators rather than pawns in someone else's game (de Charmes 1968).

Now, where does Emily fit within the larger canvas? Is there any evidence that she is not alone in her sense of powerlessness and frustration with problematic situations? I think there is.

Beyond Emily's Story: Documenting the Need for Thoughtfulness

Consider, first, some of Goodlad's findings (1984), based on research in over 1,000 elementary and secondary school classrooms.

> Students in schools seldom engage in setting goals and making decisions about their own learning.
> Less than 1 percent of all classroom dialogue involves "reasoning" or forming opinions.

What do we make of these conclusions? Obviously some students are used to the kinds of routine that reserve decision making to the teachers. Some students spend very little time making judgments and being asked to defend them with evidence. Do we have any evidence that some students are not learning good problem-solving strategies? The National Assessment of Educational Progress (NAEP) reported (1981) that

> Students seem satisfied with their initial interpretations of what they have read and seem genuinely puzzled at requests to explain or defend their points of view. As a result, responses to assessment items requiring explanations of criteria, analysis of text or defense of a judgment or point of view were in general disappointing. Few students could provide more than superficial responses to such tasks, and even the "better" responses showed little evidence of well-developed problem-solving or critical-thinking skills. (p. 25)

Some of you may recognize observable behaviors here: the tendency to give short, one-word answers that avoid the more difficult challenge of thinking about concepts and issues in greater depth. What happens if our students continue to deal with the "messy, indeterminate situations" of life in such a superficial fashion?

In a more recent report on students' writing (1986) NAEP found among students in grades 4, 8, and 11 that

> only 25 percent of 11th graders could satisfactorily engage in comparing and contrasting
>
> only 28 percent of 11th graders could satisfactorily provide evidence for their conclusions
>
> and only 18 percent "wrote adequate responses to the task requiring them to project themselves imaginatively into a scene and to provide a lively and interesting description of what was going on around them." (p. 42)

Now, what do we make of all this? One way of interpreting the results is to notice that the skills measured—comparing, using evidence, and projecting ourselves imaginatively into strange situations—are all ones Emily can use in attempting to solve life's problems. They are all ones that call upon her to do far more than behave like a tape recorder. Evidently there are more Emilys in our classrooms.

Well, you don't have to take my word or that of these researchers. Just look at your own students. Are they good at analyzing complex situations to discover what they mean, to generate alternative solutions or interpretations, and to select from among them using criteria such as reasonableness? Do they believe in their own ability to solve most problems, and are they empathic, cooperative, persistent, good at listening, and deliberate in their thinking? If not, then maybe this book will be of some help.

CONCLUSION

One significant element in the growth of thoughtfulness within our schools and within society is the question Izzy's mother asked: "Did you ask a good question today?" From the inquiring mind flows the willingness to look at problems from different points of view, to generate alternative solutions by asking "What if?" and to weigh the consequences of each.

When we start asking such questions we call the whole world of patterns into question—those within our own classroom as well as those within the school. And if we wish to nurture Emily's growth as well as that of future Izzys, we shall have to consider redesigning the environments in which all our students may experience the frustration that led to the transcendent wish: "Beam me up, Scotty!"

REFERENCES

de Charmes, Richard. 1968. *Personal Causation: The Internal Affective Determinants of Behavior*. New York: Academic Press.

Goodlad, John. 1984. *A Place Called School*. New York: McGraw Hill.

Langer, Ellen. 1989. *Mindfulness*. Reading, MA: Addison-Wesley.

National Assessment of Educational Progress. 1981. *Reading, Thinking, and Writing*. Princeton, NJ: Educational Testing Service.

National Assessment of Educational Progress. 1986. *The Writing Report Card*. Princeton, NJ: Educational Testing Service.

Schon, Donald. 1987. *Educating the Reflective Practitioner*. San Francisco: Jossey-Bass.

Schrag, Francis. 1988. *Thinking in School and Society*. New York: Routledge.

CHAPTER 2

Creating Our Own Pathways: Toward a Definition of Thinking

OVERVIEW

In this chapter I define thinking as a search for meaning and understanding that can involve the adventurous generation of options, the attempt to arrive at logical, reasonable judgments, and reflection on the process. Several examples are given to illustrate these different facets of thinking.

TOWARD A DEFINITION

Thinking is the essential component of thoughtfulness. However, our thinking not only helps us figure out what to do in our lives but also to empathize with our friends and other members of the community.

Do you believe Emily was thinking when she described her life in school as being like a tape recorder? Are we thinking when we say the following?

I'm just trying to figure out how to redesign my garden.
How do we improve our tennis game?
Is it reasonable to believe this fellow?
What questions do you have about the meaning of this poem and how would you propose answering them?

I believe these questions and statements involve thinking, as they involve us in several processes illustrated in Figure 2.1.

First, we are trying to figure out some complex phenomenon, because it is significant to us and because there are no rules we can follow as simply as ABC. In all of the above situations, we are attempting to make a difficult situation more meaningful. We are searching for understanding and clarity. For example, Emily

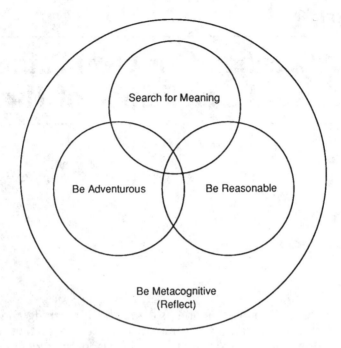

Search for Meaning

Be Adventurous

Be Reasonable

Be Metacognitive
(Reflect)

Figure 2.1

confronted her position in school, and initially it didn't quite make sense. As she worked through it, she clarified her role with the image of the tape recorder, an image that makes her dilemma more meaningful to us as well as to her.

Second, we are generating alternative perspectives, solutions, and meanings that may make our thinking "adventuresome" (Bartlett 1958). That is, we may create new mental pathways (Ryle 1979) that help us out of the ruts of conventional thinking. I note here that this was Einstein's favored domain of thinking: "Fantasy" meant more than "absorbing positive knowledge."

Third, we arrive at a judgment, a plan of action, or a decision that we select because it meets our criteria for reasonableness. Seeing oneself as a tape recorder is a reasonable metaphor given our knowledge of how many classrooms are conducted, and the frequent "fit" between classroom and machine.

Finally, all these dimensions of thinking will be enhanced by reflectiveness, which helps us gain more awareness and control of our thought processes and related feelings. Knowledge of ourselves, our attitudes, and perceptions of self all contribute to metacognitive awareness (Marzano 1988).

Thinking as a Search for Meaning

The thought processes mentioned above all involve some kind of problem, but not one narrowly perceived as belonging within a specific discipline, such as math and science. In those disciplines, and in others, we often think of a problem as something for which there is a "right answer" and a specific set of steps (an algorithm) that leads to it.

I am instead defining a problematic situation as any one that involves "doubt, uncertainty or difficulty" (Random House Dictionary 1967). Thus, we encounter problematic situations everywhere, in school and in our personal lives. They may, for example, involve gardens, sports, the believability of claims or statements or interpretation of prose and poetry. In attempting to figure out what to do or believe in these areas, we are attempting to interpret or make more meaningful something within our experience. Hannah Arendt (1977) defines thinking, not as the acquisition of knowledge, but as a "quest for meaning" (November 28, p. 121). This suggests to me that the search for verifiable truth is one dimension of intellectual behavior, but perceiving relationships among ideas, concepts, principles, and people is another and perhaps more significant dimension.

When do we commence this search for meaning? Let me give you two examples that illustrate our points of departure:

Example One. Recently a colleague of mine and I were driving toward a nearby town to conduct a workshop. We had a road map and had been there twice before, so it appeared to be a relatively routine journey. As we neared the town line, we noticed a roadblock just before a bridge over a major highway. A sign said "Detour," and I stopped the car. Here is a reconstruction of my mental processes:

All right, now what do we do? The detour sign says take a right and get onto Route 17 heading south. But we are in a hurry, and if we get lost, we'll be late. What should we do to ensure that we don't waste any time?

A trooper was parked a few feet away. I got out and asked him where the detour led, and he told me to follow the sign, and soon I'd see another sign for a turnaround, and it would be very simple, really.

"Is anything really simple?" I asked myself and proceeded to follow his directions, which turned out to be inaccurate, and we *were* late.

Example Two. Unlike an encounter with an unexpected roadblock, setting out to write this book was an act I undertook with the realization that it would involve many opportunities to think through difficulties that I *chose* to resolve. Perhaps my most compelling problem has been determining the major concepts and ideas I want to communicate. I have a tendency to be an "associational" thinker. This means that it is very easy for me to relate one idea to many other ideas and to seek out a lot of different examples to illustrate it. This is fun and meaningful, but in writing this book I realized that all these associations were getting in the way of the essential message. In other words, the main ideas began to get lost in a welter of details and related ideas. What do you do in this situation? In my case, I had to spend many hours asking the question, "What is really important here, and how can I communicate it directly?" It wasn't always easy to figure out what to do; my pathways through these difficulties were not always clear. But it seems that I was involved in a process of establishing priorities in accordance with a set of criteria, intense analysis of a segment of the educational scene, and synthesis of ideas and examples. Throughout the whole process I kept asking myself, "How am I doing? Am I conveying the message I want to?" Of course, I was aided in this process by many friends who read the text and pointed out areas that needed attention.

POINT TO PONDER: What do these two situations have in common?
Use your journal to record similarities you perceive and then
compare them with those below.

First, both created within me an uneasy feeling of not knowing what to do. Second, there were obstacles in my pathway. In the first instance, it was the detour sign, blocking my normal route. In the second instance, I had too many ideas and examples in the book. Both situations represented an interruption of the normal course of events, where expectations were upset.

Third, I had to become actively "involved in the mental *process* with a specific direction" (Bartlett 1958) if I wanted a successful resolution of the difficulty. I couldn't just sit back, relax, and follow a predetermined pathway to the workshop, or to focusing and textual error. I had to figure out what the situation meant, decide on an approach, make decisions based on prior experience, and put some plan into effect. Such action would, I hoped, remove the ambiguity. In order to understand the situation and make it meaningful, I had to become mentally and emotionally involved.

Fourth, I had encountered a situation where there were multiple options. In the first case, I could follow the detour, ask directions, turn around, or find another way. In the second case, I made a decision to cut a lot of text and add other sections, but every step of the way I kept asking myself, "Is this the best way to go? Are there other options I should consider?"

Fifth, each situation forced me to make a choice—a reasonable conclusion or resolution in the form of effective action. After considering all the options, I ultimately had to carry out a plan, which would restore the situation to a recognizable pattern of events, one more meaningful to me.

Sixth, as a result of such action, I could then reflect on the choices I personally made and evaluate this experience in order to learn from it. It is this reflection— to see causes and effects as Dewey describes in *Experience and Education* (1963) as the essence of having "an experience"—which made the events meaningful to me. If one does not engage in reflection, the danger is that these actions and responses become an undifferentiated mass of information without significant relationships. Finding these relationships is one way of creating and disclosing to ourselves and others the "meaning" of experiences and of determining the extent of our personal control over the situation.

The foregoing characterize some of our activities and experiences with thinking. Thinking in these two instances was stimulated when I encountered some kind of doubt or perplexity; Dewey (1933) likened it to coming to a fork in the road: "reflective thinking . . . involves (1) a state of doubt, hesitation, perplexity, mental difficulty, in which thinking originates, and (2) an act of searching, hunting, inquiring, to find material that will resolve the doubt, settle and dispose of the perplexity" (p. 12).

Dewey expands this description to include a definition of the word *problem* as anything—"no matter how slight and commonplace in character—[that] perplexes and challenges the mind so that it makes belief at all uncertain" (p. 13). This is the definition of *problem* that we are using in this text: Problem is *not limited to* well-structured situations often presented in mathematics and science. Rather, problem encompasses that "doubt, uncertainty or difficulty" we encounter in any human endeavor or subject of inquiry.

Problems are often those "messy" situations where we do not clearly see a path toward resolution and cannot simply use a formula to achieve our goal. Obviously, these can and do occur within any subject. As educators, however, we often give our students clearly defined problems without providing them with opportunities to define what is problematic for them. We can ask students, "What puzzles you? What questions do you have about this situation?" We want our students to define the problems for themselves.

One of the major themes of this book is that education for thoughtfulness is fostered whenever problems presented by teachers and/or students mean something to the participants. We must begin working on them; we must own them, make them ours. In the two instances above, I owned the problems in different ways.

How does the foregoing illustrate my definition of thinking as a search for meaning that is adventuresome and reasonable? In each situation I had to undertake certain activities in order to understand what was going on. As I describe in Chapter 8, making a mental representation or image of the geography around the roadblock, or trying to picture the nature of my book in its final form, are very productive ways of arriving at the meaning of an ambiguous situation by finding or creating a structure within seeming disorder (Hayes 1981). In other situations, such as understanding a poem or deciding whether or not to believe someone's statement, I must identify and understand the elements in each instance: words, ideas, concepts. Often we ask for definitions and examples if we are dealing with a complex concept—for example, consumerism, ergonomics, or abstract expressionism.

Once I have such a picture, I am in a much better position to create my own pathway through the brambles of uncertainty. Some of these paths could be quite adventuresome—for example, rethinking the book from an entirely different point of view—but to be successful I would hope that any course of action would be reasonable and in accordance with the best information at hand.

Thinking Involves Problem Solving

Now I can hear some of you asking questions like these: Am I thinking when I daydream and just have images floating around in my mind? Is it thinking if I am driving down the road and see a lovely sunset and say, "Isn't that beautiful!" Is thinking involved when I just see myself in a new job with more challenging responsibilities?

The answer to these questions may be no. These actions, by themselves, might not constitute thinking as defined above. These examples seem more like random concepts, images, ideas, anticipations, or other elements of thinking. We can be driving along immersed in creating a host of such conceptions that might appear as single unrelated slides on a screen. But when we take one—for example, noticing that the sunset is "beautiful"—and ask, "Why is it so beautiful?" this might be the wonderment, the puzzle or uncertainty that would set off a chain of purposeful steps in search of an answer. (Actually, the statement "Isn't this beautiful?" is a form of judgment or claim; we might ask ourselves to look for reasons to support such a statement.)

The words *persistent* and *deliberate* and *purpose* can be used to differentiate what is idle and random from the type of thinking defined in this volume: Picking any one of the random thoughts described above and trying to figure something out will constitute thinking. Real thinking would result in something akin to a longer slide show, consisting (not necessarily in logical sequence) of a number of different steps (or slides) that reflect your attempting to achieve a specific purpose (to reach a conclusion, solution, meaning). The conclusions and interpretations we work toward when we think represent for Bartlett (1958) the "direction" of our thought processes.

Why do we wish to pursue a particular direction or course of action? Probably some question or matter interests us at the moment. Perhaps we wonder about a perplexity that we have uncovered, and through thinking we pursue a deliberate course of mental action to arrive at a conclusion. We might be engaging in what Einstein called "combinatory play" with ideas (Barell 1980). Playing with ideas was Einstein's adventuresome way of becoming productive, and this preceded his more logical, reasonable kinds of thought. Combining and relating ideas is fun, and this is a form of thinking we often engage in even if the purpose seems rather fleeting.

A very interesting exercise is to attempt to catalog our thinking during a day's activity.

POINT TO PONDER: Stop at some point and ask yourself, What have been my thoughts within the past few moments?

Try to identify those sudden flashes, those images that are unconnected to one another: the pictures of yourself doing something tomorrow or a recollection of someplace you were yesterday. Instead of images, you might think in words and hear them spoken.

Then try to identify any succession of thoughts that occurred as you tried to make some situation more meaningful by searching for a solution, different perspective, conclusion, or the like.

In attempting this exercise often I find that I have a very hard time maintaining my focus on one situation I wish to think through. It is easy to become distracted by something in the environment or another thought (or, in my case, another visual image). So thinking is not always an easy adventure, because it takes deliberateness, persistence, and a strong sense of purpose to see ourselves through to whatever our purpose is—a conclusion, for example.

Thinking Involves Confronting Uncertainty

Thinking as defined in this volume is caused by encountering some sort of conflict or perplexity, something that brings with it uncertainty about what to do. To use Dewey's metaphor, thinking begins at a fork in the road, "a situation that is ambiguous, that presents a dilemma, that proposes alternatives" (1933, p. 14). This fork can be passively encountered (the roadblock) or actively sought (writing this book).

Irving Sigel et al. (1984) use similar language to refer to the detour problem described above. They call such incidents "violated expectations" or "discrepant experiences." The discrepancy resulted from the conflict between my expectations (my goals)—that the route would be routine and clear of roadblocks—and the given realities (obstacles). Sigel's distinction between a "task" and a "problem" may be helpful here. A task is any operation that we can perform without much or any thought, a routine operation; but a "problem" requires a search or inquiry to resolve some doubt or uncertainty. For example, a task for me as I write would be to insert a word in the preceding sentence. It is an operation I have done innumerable times. However, if the insert key on my computer malfunctions, or if something happens to the spacing operations within the word-processing program, I then have a problem.

Francis Schrag (1988) describes thoughtfulness as akin to embarking upon an expedition, an operation that is purposeful and deliberate. My second example is very much like this "territorial exploration," because "no matter how rigorous the preparation, [we are] bound to meet the unexpected, to be tested by challenges [we] could not precisely anticipate" (p. 6).

Thinking Involves "Self-Talk"

Once we recognize that we are in a situation characterized by "doubt, uncertainty or difficulty," most of the time we will attempt to remove the sources of these feelings. Gilbert Ryle, the philosopher, describes this process as one of creating a pathway, not following in someone else's footsteps:

> Thinking is trying to better one's instructions; it is trying out promising tracks which will exist, if they ever do exist, only after one has stumbled exploringly over ground where they are not. (1979, p. 78)

Thinking, therefore, is a process involving exploration and experimentation, with no guarantee of success. When we think, we are taking a calculated risk that might or might not turn out successfully. We must begin to figure things out for ourselves—even, as Ryle suggests, if it is attempting to spell the word *cat*. "Path-finding is not and cannot be path following. Pondering is precisely *not* knowing what steps to take but taking tentative steps all the same in order to learn something from their fate" (p. 92).

Thinking involves being tentative—sort of like setting up many little hypotheses and testing them out. "Thinking, then, can be saying things tentatively to oneself with the specific heuristic intention of trying, by saying them, to open one's own eyes, to consolidate one's own grasp, or to get oneself out of a rut . . ." (p. 92).

Thinking involves what we will later refer to as self-talk, a process of proceeding through the underbrush of the problem in order to find a solution or resolution. "Self-talk" is saying things to ourselves such as "What is my problem? How will I get out of it? What can I try? What or who can help me? Where have I seen a situation like this before? I can solve this problem if I really persist at it." All these statements will eventually become internalized and part of a repertoire for confronting difficult situations. As one seventh grader told me recently, "Thinking is talking to yourself when you have a problem."

Upon leaving Rosemarie Liebmann's high school class at semester's end, Tom said: "Thank you for helping me figure out what to do when I didn't know what to do." How, she asked, had this been accomplished? "It never occurred to me," he said, "to ask questions when I'm lost." This is the kind of self-talk that we can all engage in to begin the process of real thinking. Tom witnessed sufficient modeling of self-questioning and was asked enough times to write down his own questions in his Thinking Journal so that, at the end of the semester, he could realize that his teacher had helped him learn to think, to figure out some things on his own. Part of this figuring out is coming to understand the complexities of the "messy, indeterminate situations" (Schon 1987) we are in.

These self-instructions can be thought of as the series of steps we take to find the pathway and the series of slides we throw up on our mental screen that reflect our "tentative steps." I emphasize self-talk and pathways in this definition of thinking because they make a major point: *In thinking, we are in control of the processes.* Being mindful, being thoughtful means, inherently, that we are taking personal control of situations—ourselves and with other members of the community.

Thinking as Self-Regulation

Lauren Resnick (1987) has given us a framework within which to ponder the nature of thinking. She describes "higher order thinking" as having the following characteristics:

> *Nonalgorithmic.* The path of action is not fully specified in advance.
> *Complex.* The total path is not "visible" (mentally speaking) from any single vantage point.
> Characterized by *nuanced judgment* and interpretations.
> Involves the application of *multiple criteria,* which sometimes conflict with one another.
> Involves *uncertainty.* Not everything is known that bears on the task at hand.
> Means *self-regulation* of the thinking process. We are thinking only when we are calling the plays.
> "Higher order thinking involves *imposing meaning,* finding structure in apparent disorder." (Resnick 1987)

Resnick's formulation is much like Ryle's even though she approaches thinking not from the philosophic point of view but from that of cognitive psychology.

They use similar terms to describe following a path that is fraught with uncertainty and involves multiple possible interpretations and solutions. One of the key phrases she uses is "imposing meaning." Thinking is, indeed, very much a process of making something meaningful on our own. Processes involving rote memory and routine operations at someone else's direction are not thinking. This is exactly what Mary Mulcahy's first grader, Evan, noted about his working through a problem one day: "My thinking was not good today, because I was copying other peoples' thinking." It is also what Emily was doing as she thought through her high school situation; employing the adventuresome metaphor of being a tape recorder reflects her ability to figure out for herself the meaning of her situation.

Johnson (1975) has defined "meaningfulness" as creating a network of "referential associations." Thus, we make something more meaningful as we take control and search ourselves for the ever-widening sets of relationships among facts, ideas, concepts, and similar situations. To think is to be in control of meaning.

Thus, we have definitions of thinking from three different professions, philosophy (Arendt, Dewey, Ryle), cognitive science (Resnick), and science (Sigel). All of them refer, at least in part, to this characteristic, noted by Resnick, of attempting to impose or create structures for giving meaning to experience. Thinking as a search for meaning is quite possibly one of the defining characteristics of being human.

As Greene notes (1973) this search for meaning is liberating: "To make sense is to liberate [oneself] . . ." (p. 163). She is talking about calling all of life into question and, by this act, reflecting upon its very nature, purpose, and consequences. Heidegger notes that when we think, we very likely cause some things to be "unthought." To unthink something means to uncover and disclose preconceptions, assumptions, and myths that may no longer hold true (1972). Arendt makes a similar point when she says that thinking "unfreezes" what language has frozen into consciousness. "The word 'house' is something like a frozen thought that thinking must unfreeze to get at the original meaning of the notion" (p. 178). Langer (1989) speaks to this point when she notes that "mindlessness" often consists in overreliance on meanings no longer valid or useful.

In these ways thinking can be liberating and simultaneously disturbing to both the thinker and those with whom he or she interacts. Some teachers have a great deal of difficulty with this kind of intellectual behavior when practiced by students who raise their hands to question the teacher's conclusions and/or patterns of behavior in class. But this is one theme of the book: *Thinking is liberating; thinking empowers us to take more personal and shared control of our own destinies.* These notions will be threatening to those who insist upon maintaining a status quo without question.

THE PROCESSES OF THINKING

If thinking involves creating a pathway, what does this look like when we encounter a dilemma or difficulty? In the instances cited above, it means engaging in any of the following processes.

These questions seek meaning and structure amid disorder.

Do I have a problem? Is it important to solve?
What kind of problem is it? (Define, clarify, classify.)
Do I recognize any feelings associated with this situation?
How can I create a visual/mental representation of the situation?
Can I reduce this dilemma to several important elements or parts (e.g., causes, concepts, ideas, principles, feelings)?
How can I relate this situation to any I have seen before? How can I relate it to my prior experience/knowledge?
How can I reflect upon unstated assumptions, beliefs, biases, definitions of terms, concepts?
Can I redefine it, look at it in a different way?
What can help me? What kinds of resources do I need?
What do I want to do? What is my objective?

Here our thinking can become adventuresome.

What will my overall strategy be?
What alternatives can I think of? What are my options?

Here our thinking must seek reasonableness.

Which ones are best and why? What evidence supports one alternative over another? Is there counterevidence to suggest a different approach?
What action will I take and why?

Here our thinking is reflective.

How will I know if I succeed?
How well am I doing?
How well did I do? What might I do differently next time? Why?

These processes would not be followed in a lockstep fashion, but would probably be found in any good problem-solving situation. What is important is that the search for meaning and structure is present from the beginning of the thinking process. Here is where good problem solvers differentiate themselves from novices (Sternberg 1985): They spend more time figuring out what a problematic situation means by asking, "What does this mean to me?" As we move through the process, we can also be more or less adventuresome and more or less reasonable. All four aspects of thinking are present at various times.

If we follow steps like this, it is very likely that we will create our own pathway: We will reach the workshop without getting lost, and we will discover and solve the problems standing in the way of completing the book. In fact, I followed several of these after encountering difficulty.

I realized I had a problem when my routine structures were suddenly filled with ambiguity, and I didn't know what to do.

I compared each situation to others with similar problems—in doing this I realized that I would need help. I sought other resources in pursuit of an objective. In writing this book, I reached out to others who are knowledgeable in the field. I related this experience to previous ones of writing a book and articles, and I created a clear image of the finished product that helped organize my thoughts.

These problem-solving processes are analyzed in greater detail in Chapters 8 through 11.

Once I have deliberated on the meaning of the situation and set a goal, I am in a position to generate alternatives. In writing this book, many alternatives have come to mind to help clarify the ideas presented herein: making outlines, sharing the writing with students and colleagues, revising and attempting to use graphic organizers.

Ryle speaks of saying things to ourselves "with the specific heuristic intention of trying, by saying them, to open one's own eyes. . . . To get oneself out of a rut" (p. 92). This is part of the adventurous pursuit of alternatives, to see life's situations from different perspectives and thereby to be creative or inventive. The use of the graphic in Figure 2.1 has helped me focus and organize the major cognitive processes presented in subsequent chapters. Chapter 9 discusses adventurousness in greater detail.

Resnick notes that "higher order thinking" involves "nuanced judgment," often about the options we have generated. To make a judgment that is reasonable, sound, and logical, we collect evidence, challenge assumptions, define terms, identify biases, check the reliability of sources, examine counterexamples and evidence contrary to preferred solutions. In a word, part of finding our pathway through the brambles of information is a critical process discussed at length in Chapter 10. The evidence I collected in following the state trooper's directions indicated that he was wrong, and I felt even more lost. I am still learning that all persons in authority are subject to being questioned.

While I was creating this pathway, I was engaging in what Resnick calls self-regulation. I was continually asking myself, "What am I doing now? Is this the best course of action? Am I pleased with what is happening? Am I reaching my objective?" and at the end, "How well did I do in this case?"

By engaging in this kind of self-talk, we are practicing what some call metacognition, or reflecting on our own thinking processes. Chapter 11 deals very extensively with this reflective process, which seems to be one of the keys to productivity not only in schools but in problem solving in our personal and professional lives: Better thinkers, problem solvers, and readers are in control of their own thinking and make strategic decisions about what they know and don't know, where they are going, why and what they expect to find when they get there (Pressley et al. 1987).

Feelings toward Self and Others

As should be evident by now, thoughtfulness involves both thinking and feeling. Many times these feelings are ones of frustration that accompany the difficulties we are experiencing. Emily's eventual comparison of her life in the classroom to a tape recorder may have involved feelings about *herself* that transcended frustration to encompass the hope for a better tomorrow—"Beam me up, Scotty!" Our confidence in our own ability to think and be effective is a significant element of thoughtfulness.

At any point along the pathway, we might be concerned with the needs and feelings of *others:* those who would be inconvenienced if we didn't solve the roadblock quickly and those who would eventually read this book. Especially in the latter case, I have spent a lot of time (with some success, I hope) imagining the real situation of the reader and attempting to determine if my problem resolutions—or attempts at clarity—are successful. Problem solving in both cases involved being thoughtful—literally full of thought and feelings about ourselves and for the interests of others.

Those of us involved in education need to realize that thinking involves feeling along all the pathways we set out to create and maintain. We need to establish an environment that is invitational not only for thoughts but for feelings as well. We need to help students recognize, identify, and perhaps cope with their feelings about themselves, us (their teachers), and the subjects we teach. Perhaps too many of the difficulties both students and teachers have in school stem from this unnatural dichotomy between thought and feeling, and between the subjects we teach and the needs, feelings, and aspirations of our students. Bridging these gaps is one of the goals of this book.

CONCLUSION

There are certainly other ways of defining thoughtfulness and thinking in particular, ones different from my focus upon meaningfulness, adventurousness, reasonableness, and reflectiveness. (Schrag's [1988] incisive critique focuses upon the long-term dispositions of a thoughtful person to value thinking and persist, and is very close to my own analysis.) This is the structure that seems to work for me. It helps me organize my own thinking, how I work through difficult dilemmas (both alone and with others), and how I can help others reflect upon their own mental processes. I suggest it as one perspective among many.

Thinking, then, as I define it, involves responding to problems and perplexities, some of which will be thrust upon us unexpectedly and others of which we will consciously seek out for the fun or adventure of it. Either way, we begin to think when we recognize such an uncertainty and decide to do something about it. In such ill-structured situations we seem not to follow any one process in a straight line. We move in varieties of direction, often by fits and starts, until we reach our objective. Thinking is, as Shrag notes, very much like territorial exploration. And, of course, it isn't always easy.

John Steinbeck (1961) once compared thinking with the movement of an animal: "It's always hard to start to concentrate. The mind darts like a chicken, trying to escape thinking even though thinking is the most rewarding function of man" (p. 28).

And this is the way it seems to go when we are engaged in creating our own pathways, trying out steps, tentatively and exploringly, until we reach a conclusion or change our minds and go exploring in other territories.

It must be evident now that the processes described herein all have one more idea in common: personal control of our own lives. Creating our own pathways is inherently a self-directed experience, not one where we follow blindly and/or willingly someone else's direction. Thinking and thoughtful behavior by the definitions shared in this chapter are processes that empower persons to take more control of their own lives, and this is one of our goals in life as well as in schools.

REFERENCES

Arendt, Hannah. 1977. "Thinking." *The New Yorker,* November, December.

Barell, John. 1980. *Playgrounds of Our Minds.* New York: Teachers College Press.

Bartlett, Sir Frederick. 1958. *Thinking, An Experimental and Social Study.* New York: Basic Books.

Dewey, John. 1933. *How We Think.* Lexington, MA: D. C. Heath.

———. (1963). *Experience and Education.* New York: Collier Books.

Greene, Maxine. 1973. *Teacher as Stranger.* Belmont, CA: Wadsworth.

Hayes, John. 1981. *The Complete Problem Solver.* Philadelphia: Franklin Institute Press.

Heidegger, Martin. 1972. *What Is Called Thinking?* New York: Harper & Row.

Johnson, R. 1975. "Meaning in Complex Learning." *Review of Educational Research* 45:425–460.

Langer, Ellen. 1989. *Mindfulness.* Reading, MA: Addison-Wesley.

Marzano, Robert. 1988. *Dimensions of Thinking.* Alexandria, VA: Association for Supervision and Curriculum Development.

Perkins, David. 1981. *The Mind's Best Work.* Cambridge, MA: Harvard University Press.

Pressley, Michael, et al. 1987. "What Is Good Strategy Use and Why Is It Hard to Teach? An Optimistic Appraisal of the Challenges Associated with Strategy Instruction." May. Paper presented at the annual meeting of the American Educational Research Association, Washington, DC: 121, 182.

Resnick, Lauren. 1987. *Education and Learning to Think.* Washington, DC: National Academy Press.

Ryle, Gilbert. 1979. *On Thinking.* Totowa, NJ: Rowan & Littlefield.

Schon, Donald. 1987. *Educating the Reflective Practitioner.* San Francisco: Jossey-Bass.

Schrag, F. 1988. *Thinking in School and Society.* New York: Routledge.

Sigel, Irving, Carol Copple, and Ruth Saunders. 1984. *Educating the Young Thinker.* Hillsdale, NJ: Lawrence Erlbaum.

Steinbeck, John. 1961. *Sweet Thursday.* New York: Bantam.

Sternberg, Robert. 1985. *Beyond I.Q.: A Triarchic Theory of Human Intelligence.* Cambridge: Cambridge University Press.

CHAPTER 3

In the Classroom: A Conceptual Overview of Teaching for Thinking

OVERVIEW

In this chapter I present a model lesson that illustrates my definition of thoughtful behavior, and offers instructional planning and teaching practices that productively engage students. I conclude with a brief discussion of the issue "Who controls the thinking and learning in classrooms?"

"FRANKLIN IN THE DARK": A MODEL LESSON

Not too long ago I had the pleasure of observing a second-grade class engaged in reading a story. After the observation and discussion with the teachers, it occurred to me that this episode illustrates some aspects of thinking and thoughtfulness. It provides a structured overview of what two teachers did to challenge their students to figure out a course of action that involved searching for meaning, the adventurous creation of alternatives, and the selection of the ones most reasonable. It also suggests ways we have of creating an environment that invites students to take risks—something that always involves feelings about ourselves and others. Without a positive and warm, supportive setting, these students would not have participated as they did in this learning experience.

Embedded within this episode is the question, Who controls our thinking and learning? This curricular issue has been present within the nature of schooling for a long time. My purpose here is to present our current efforts to improve the quality of intelligent behavior within classrooms, not as an isolated phenomenon but as one inextricably linked to and evolved from long experience.

Classroom Episode

Karen Guidera and Mary Ellen O'Donnell are second-grade teachers who work primarily with students who have learning difficulties, who are below average in achievement, and might be termed by some as at-risk students (Mirman, Swartz & Barell 1988). These students leave their own classroom at appointed times during the day to receive special, individualized attention. On this occasion, I entered their room to see Karen sitting in one corner of the room in a rocking chair with the words *Author's Chair* affixed to the head rest. Eight students were seated around her on the carpet the two teachers had obtained in order to make a linoleum-covered floor more inviting in this corner of the room. To Karen's right was a bookcase full of children's stories, and behind her Mary Ellen was standing near the chalk board listening to the story.

As I entered, Karen had just begun to read a delightful story called *Franklin in the Dark,* by Paulette Bourgeois and Brenda Clark (1986). She read the following:

> Franklin could slide down a riverbank all by himself. He could count forwards and backwards. He could even zip zippers and button buttons. But Franklin was afraid of small, dark places and that was a problem because . . .
>
> Franklin was a turtle. He was afraid of crawling into his small, dark shell. And so, Franklin the turtle dragged his shell behind him. [Illustration of disgruntled turtle dragging by rope an empty turtle shell alongside a stream full of smiling frogs.]
>
> Every night, Franklin's mother would take a flashlight and shine it into his shell.
>
> "See," she would say, "there's nothing to be afraid of."
>
> She always said that. She wasn't afraid of anything. But Franklin was sure that creepy things, slippery things, and monsters lived inside his small, dark shell. [Illustration of light shining into empty shell as creepy, slippery, gobliny animals lurk about.]
>
> So Franklin went looking for help. He walked until he met a duck.
>
> "Excuse me, Duck. I'm afraid of small, dark places and I can't crawl inside my shell. Can you help me?"
>
> "Maybe," quacked the duck. "You see, I'm afraid of very deep water. Sometimes, when nobody is watching, I wear my water wings. Would my water wings help you?"
>
> "No," said Franklin. "I'm not afraid of water."
>
> So Franklin walked and walked until he met a lion.
>
> "Excuse me, Lion. I'm afraid of small, dark places and I can't crawl inside my shell. Can you help me?"
>
> "Maybe," roared the lion. "You see, I'm afraid of great, loud noises. Sometimes, when nobody is looking, I wear my earmuffs. Would my earmuffs help you?"
>
> "No," said Franklin. "I'm not afraid of great, loud noises."

And so on as Franklin encountered a bird and a polar bear that gave him no helpful suggestions. As she read the story, Karen showed the children the colorful illustrations.

At this point Karen stopped telling the story.

POINT TO PONDER: Instead of finishing the story, what do you think she did?

Some of you might have said she asked the children to describe or summarize what had already occurred. Some others might have thought she asked them to think ahead, to predict what might come next. Both are excellent practices depending upon our purpose. But Karen did something different. She then posed this question: "If you were Franklin you would be in a difficult situation. What do you think his problem is?"

Students responded with unanimity: "Franklin was afraid of going into his shell because it was dark." Mary Ellen wrote this with a magic marker on a large piece of flip chart paper affixed to the chalk board. Can you think of other ways of identifying the problem? Usually, when asked this question, adults come up with a number of different identifications of Franklin's problem: Fear of the unknown; search for identity; how to live outside a shell; how to live with fear.

Then Karen asked, "Now what would you do to solve this problem if you were Franklin?" Why don't you think of a number of different solutions to Franklin's problem:

POINT TO PONDER: Jot down how you would solve this problem if you were Franklin.

As they were generating their alternatives, Karen left the chair and her students informally moved about on the rug and climbed into the rocking chair. Here's what the second graders thought of:

Bring in a flashlight.
Keep a flashlight shining into his shell.
Try to squeeze in Mom's shell with her.
Sleep on top of Mom.
Put two shells together.
Put a television in his shell.
Try to sleep in his shell when it was light out.
Practice sleeping in sunlight so he'd like his shell.
Get a bigger shell and sleep with his friends.
Sleep with a stuffed animal.
Get embarrassed and just go in.
Sleep in the shell with his head in and his feet out.
Trick Mom into thinking he had slept in his shell by putting a stuffed animal
    in his place.

How did your solutions compare with these? Were they as extensive?

Karen and Mary Ellen accepted each suggestion without judgment, since they had told the children on previous occasions, "When we are thinking up solutions, we don't criticize anybody's idea. We write it down and then discuss it later." So the children listened to each other's ideas as their teachers wrote them down for everybody to see. Each child's name was clearly written beside his or her suggestion for all to see and later refer to. Sometimes the students raised hands, but at other times they just waited until someone was finished and offered a different idea.

The bell then rang, and the children were supposed to return to their regular classes, but the teachers decided this was too important a point in this lesson to interrupt it. One of them went down the hall to ask if they could keep the children another few minutes, and with that permission Mary Ellen asked her students a question.

POINT TO PONDER: What would you ask or say to the children at this point?

Here's what she asked, "Now, which solution do you think is best?" How does your response compare with Mary Ellen's? Which do you prefer?

Immediately hands shot up, and as each student gave a reply she or he went to the paper and pointed out the best solution and gave the reason.

Tim was first up, "I think the first one is the best!" he said proudly.

"Why?"

"Because it's mine," he replied, smiling.

Beth then said she felt that Jane's was best. "Why?" "Because he might get used to sleeping inside the shell." And Jimmy said he liked Billy's idea: "Because like Beth said, he might get used to his shell."

Then a very quiet girl who usually did not contribute during these sessions raised her hand. Jennifer got up and pointed to the solution that suggested Franklin just get embarrassed and go in. "Why?"

"Because then he can learn to like small, dark places and not be afraid," she said.

Jennifer was the last student to respond, and then Karen read the story's ending before students returned to class:

Well, Franklin knew what he had to do. He crawled inside his small, dark shell. He was sure he saw creepy things, slippery things, and a monster. But he said a brave "Good night." And then, when nobody was looking, Franklin the turtle turned on his night light.

Teachers' Perceptions of This Episode

After the class we discussed the teachers' perceptions of the class session. A few of the points we made in our discussion merit our attention here.

1. The students were genuinely *interested* in solving the problem and analyzing their solutions. How did we know? From the extent of their participation; they generated thirteen alternatives without needing any prompting. And, finally, they did not want to return to their own classroom immediately.

2. They *listened* to each other's solutions. It seemed as if students were getting more ideas from listening to their friends. How did we know? Because they waited for one person to finish before making another suggestion, and when evaluating the solutions, they responded directly to what a previous student had said. They showed respect for and interest in what their friends were saying, two very positive feelings.

3. The students had improved during the weeks that Karen and Mary Ellen had been experimenting with new intellectual challenges. When they first began, students would hear a solution like "Bring in a flashlight" and say, "Oh, you couldn't fit one of those inside that small shell!" But now they listened patiently to each others' ideas and often built upon them. The students were perhaps becoming more empathic.

4. If you analyze the solutions, they may show some developmental changes from first to last. The first solution ("Bring in a flashlight") and the seventh ("Try to sleep in his shell when it was light out") show some difference in terms of using external means of keeping the darkness out and attempting to grow accustomed to a small (if not dark) space. The eleventh suggestion ("Get embarrassed and just go in") shows more internal resolve and locus of control than the first, certainly. Thus, these responses seem to illustrate what we know about good problem solvers: They go to the heart of the matter and identify what the real problem is. Jennifer selected the solution that helps Franklin overcome his fear and, perhaps, one that reflected her feelings about herself.

5. Each student could give a reason for her/his choice. We noted the differences in Tim's and Jennifer's reasoning: One is very egocentric whereas the other seems to focus upon just what would solve the problem best (according to Jennifer, that is).

6. We mentioned alternatives to the question, "Which do you think is the best solution and why?" When appropriate, you might see if your students can find similarities and differences among the solutions and then decide. For example, solutions 1, 2, 6, and 10 require the use of some outside source of comfort: flashlights, TVs, and animals. Like Charles Schulz's Linus and his security blanket, these solutions provide external reinforcers. By contrast, solution 11 ("Get embarrassed and just go in") is inner-directed. This task of comparing and contrasting sometimes reveals criteria for choice. Which solution is better (or more effective): one relying upon some mechanical device or one where you have to rely upon your own resources?

7. Finally, we discussed the possibility of asking the children a question such as, "How did you come up with all those answers?" or "How did you decide which was the best?" Such questions challenge students to

think about their own mental processes as a way of helping them take more control of their own learning and thinking. Mary Mulcahy tried this with her first and second graders after spending a lot of time solving problems, and they were able to say that good problem solvers, for example, "take parts out of the problem that you don't really need—get to the main problem. . . . Make the problem littler and littler. . . . Look at the problem from a different angle." So even young children can reflect on how they go about doing such things.

Analysis of This Classroom Episode: Major Concepts and Processes

Next, let us briefly analyze this episode in terms of the major concepts and processes that we will be discussing at greater length in the ensuing chapters:

The nature and causes of thinking (Chapter 2).
The environment for thinking (Chapters 5 and 6).
Pedagogical moves that enhance thinking (Chapters 5 and 6).
Staff development processes that focus upon organizational change (Chapter 13).
Curriculum and instructional planning (Chapter 7).

The Nature and Causes of Thinking.   Usually, students hearing the story of *Franklin in the Dark* sit quietly and listen. They might think ahead to what the story would be about, considering the title and the picture on the cover (Franklin sitting in a darkened room leaning on his empty shell surrounded by blocks and toy turtles). What Karen and Mary Ellen did, however, was to challenge their second graders to do more than listen attentively. They challenged them to use their imaginations and identify with Franklin in his predicament.

Then they asked students to figure out what Franklin's problem was. In answering this question ("If you were Franklin, you would be in a difficult situation. What do you think his problem is?") the students conveyed an understanding of the situation. They probably could picture in their minds Franklin's being fearful of all the demons he thought were inside his shell. This was probably not a doubt or perplexity for most students.

But then the teachers asked, "How would you go about solving it if you were Franklin?" This, indeed, might present some students with a difficulty: imagining yourself as an animal and then thinking of a number of different pathways to follow. Here students started out with rather obvious solutions: bring in a flashlight or TV. But eventually some of them became a little more imaginative, original, and adventuresome: Trick Mom, practice sleeping in sunlight.

Finally, Mary Ellen asked the children to select the best solution. Here she challenged them to think comparatively: to decide which solution met their criteria for *best*. This is the act of making logical and reasonable judgments, ones that can then be discussed in terms of the reasons for our choices (our criteria, evidence available, etc.). We know what Jennifer's criteria were, in part: whatever solves the real problem. Flashlights and TVs, in Jennifer's mind, do not deal directly with Franklin's fear of "small dark places."

Had Karen and Mary Ellen asked students to attempt to identify the processes used to solve the problem, the students would have reflected on their thinking and might have acquired some metacognitive control over their thinking—something more difficult for these children than for older ones.

The Environment That Invites Thoughtfulness.   While she was reading *Franklin in the Dark,* the teacher sat in a rocking chair with her students comfortably electing to sit on the rug around her. How we arrange space to provide for maximum of input and interaction is not something to be left to chance.

Both teachers communicated certain *dispositions* by their very decision to present ever more complex problems to students with lower than average achievement levels:

"You can succeed. Believe in yourself!"
"If you persist, you will be able to resolve difficult situations."
"Listening to each other is important because you can add onto somebody else's ideas!"
"In this classroom we not only listen to each other, we cooperate with them in solving problems."

All these statements are meant to communicate specific messages that students can internalize as "scripts" of their own; "scripts" are those words we repeatedly say to ourselves that promote specific dispositions such as good listening, cooperation, and empathy. They were presented by the teachers' modeling specific behaviors for the students.

These messages are vital if we wish to establish, from the very first day, that thinking and concern for others are important in this classroom. Without these messages, students would not risk expressing their ideas; they would not be as willing to share with others.

Pedagogical Strategies That Enhance Thinking.   In presenting the lesson, the teachers identified a specific objective: "Students will generate and critique options within a story." Thus, they focused upon significant mental processes related to problem solving and decision making, and they did it within the context of a story they would normally read with their students. They could just as easily have focused their intentions on significant concepts, such as fear, comfort, or friendship.

At the beginning of the lesson, Karen and Mary Ellen might have done what they did when they introduced other lessons on problem solving: that is model the process for their students. "Here is a problem I am confronting and here is how I go about thinking it through." Obviously, we learn a great deal from the models we encounter in and out of school, and their modeling is one factor that enabled these students to think of so many solutions.

But what they actually did was to present a significant problem to solve by posing the question: "What was Franklin's problem and how would you solve it?'' They waited for thirteen responses, because figuring things out takes time, and we see the benefit of waiting: more and perhaps better answers. We know that intellectual growth is fostered by continually confronting complex problems that are of interest and significance for us.

Karen and Mary Ellen did not probe or explore each alternative by asking such questions as "How did you arrive at that? Can you tell us more about it? How would that help? What if you didn't have a flashlight?'' They didn't because their objective was different. But in asking, "Which solution do you think is best and why?'' they provided for critical analysis and for the kind of peer interaction that fosters improved thinking. Students did not respond to each others' answers verbally, but Jennifer's final assessment seems to indicate some disagreement with the previous speakers.

Perhaps the next day Karen and Mary Ellen asked students how they might transfer their thinking abilities to situations outside the classroom and where they have used them before. (How might you use such problem-solving skills at home? On the playground?) They might also ask a metacognitive question: "How did you figure out your solutions, and which one was best?''

These pedagogical strategies: specifying an objective, modeling, problem posing, waiting, quality responding, peer interaction, transfer, and metacognitive questions are all important if we wish to provide students with opportunities to figure out ever more complex situations.

Instructional and Curricular Planning.   It is evident that Karen and Mary Ellen planned this lesson to emphasize certain skills: mainly problem identification and resolution processes. They were engaged in what some (Costa 1985) call "teaching for thinking.'' They were not engaged in what Beyer (1987) calls teaching the specific problem-solving skill of generating alternatives. Chapter 7 provides an instructional format for incorporating a broad spectrum of teaching activities that will enhance thinking. Chapters 8–11 will discuss teaching some of these processes more directly.

You will remember that when the bell rang, one of the teachers went to the students' next teacher to ask if they could extend class time just a little. Why did they do this? Because the processes they were focusing upon were sufficiently important to take the time. The question "What is most worth spending time thinking about?'' is a traditional curriculum question that continues to be significant. For example, Karen and Mary Ellen could follow this lesson with a discussion of feelings of fear and insecurity, or with a discussion of the concept of identity. Either way, they must make a conscious decision about how to spend their valuable time.

Finally, what this episode illustrates is how we can identify the problematic within our subject areas. To read the story straight through serves a purpose. But Karen and Mary Ellen chose to present students with a problem, because they know that a problem-centered curriculum is one that challenges us to think and thereby grow intellectually and emotionally.

Staff Development Processes that Focus on Organizational Change.   What is not evident from this episode is the planning that went into it—not just Karen and

Mary Ellen's decision to present a story and interrupt it just before the end to challenge students' thinking, but also the planning that was undertaken by the district and by an instructor who led a ten-week after-school session attended by the two teachers.

In Chapter 13 I present various models of how to commence a long-term staff development plan that meets local district needs. Karen and Mary Ellen were part of an introductory program that helped them identify needs and develop strategies to meet these needs. During the course of the ten-week session, these teachers, as well as ones from the local high school, examined their own thinking and set goals. They also brought to their classrooms informal means of assessing their students' thinking. One conclusion Karen and Mary Ellen reached was that students had real difficulties solving problems; they relied on the teachers for far too much: "Tell us what to do!" was the common response to questions like "How would you solve this problem?" Like so many other teachers, Karen and Mary Ellen realized that many of their students have an external locus of control as evidenced by such statements as "Why did you give me this grade?" "I haven't got a clue about how to solve this!" and "Show me!" The lesson described above was one move in a longer-range plan to help students become empowered to pose and resolve their own problems, to set some of their own goals, to take more responsibility for their own learning, and to see problematic situations as challenging opportunities to figure out the many different pathways toward a resolution.

It is probably evident to you that the lesson and the staff development plan have this in common: a focus on problem identification and problem solving. To empower students, in the first instance, and staff (teachers and administrators) in the second, to identify needs and design strategies to meet them.

THINKING AND FEELING

Throughout this episode I have attempted to illustrate how students' and teachers' feelings played a role in working through a problematic situation. Even though neither teacher said, as she might have, "Tell me how you feel about Franklin . . . about your solutions . . . about what we did this morning," it was evident that through their modeling, the openness of their communications and their commitment to taking risk, Karen and Mary Ellen have paid a good deal of attention to creating a setting in which students feel comfortable in exploring the unknown, unafraid of not always being "right." Students here express, in their willingness to generate alternatives and evaluate them, a confidence in their own abilities as well as an openness to others' ideas—the dispositional core of thoughtfulness.

WHO CONTROLS THINKING AND
LEARNING IN THE CLASSROOM?

Karen and Mary Ellen's episode illustrates the fundamental issue: Who controls the thinking and learning of our students? Who controls the educative process? This is an important issue, because without some degree of sharing control not much independent or collaborative thought is possible. If we want Emily and her younger friends to feel confident in acting independently we must find ways to allow them to experiment with controlling classroom decisions.

Historically, our schools have fostered a vision of very tight adult control. David Tyack's *The One Best System* (1974) provides us with ample illustrations of how strictly some adults controlled the behavior of their students during the nineteenth century.

In 1878 one superintendent of schools made this observation: "If teachers have advice to give their superior, it is to be given as the good daughter talks with the father" (Tyack 1974, p. 60). Most teachers at that time were unmarried women, and the men who ran the schools valued them because of their docility and willingness to obey rules established by their patriarchal, authoritarian principals and superintendents.

At about the same time William Torrey Harris, one of the nineteenth century's foremost educators and one-time superintendent of schools in St. Louis, noted that "the first requisite of the school is order: each pupil must be taught first and foremost to conform his behavior to a general standard, just like the running of the trains" (Tyack, p. 42).

Another superintendent, Frank Rigler, personally instructed his teachers on "what questions to ask and what answers to accept" (Tyack, p. 48).

We certainly have come a long way since these folks ran schools, but sometimes I wonder if their ancestors (or their ghosts) are not lurking about the corridors of schools where everyone sits in rows, few questions are encouraged, and often only one point of view is acceptable.

The question of who controls our thinking and learning is accompanied by another question: For what reason? Rigler and Harris perhaps felt they needed such control in order to refine the large immigrant populations they had to deal with. What are the reasons now for such tight control? You can think of many: Adults desire to do things their way; this is how we all were taught, to a degree; it is much easier to be directive most of the time; what will occur if we share control? Still other observers have pointed to possible reasons behind such adult control of thinking: the desire to perpetuate a socioeconomic way of life, where certain people lead and others follow, where some of us tell and others listen. (Apple 1982; Spring 1990.)

Why is the issue of control so important right now? Why is it important to empower students and teachers to take more control of their own lives in and out of school?

POINT TO PONDER: Why do you think control is an important issue now?

I suggest one reason is that if life continues, as it always has, to present us with those "messy, indeterminate situations" Emily recognizes beyond classroom walls, we are going to need persons who have the strength of heart and mind to confront, analyze, and deal with them. Certainly, tape recorders are not going to help much here.

Some of you might be thinking that we want students to exercise some control over their own destiny, because schooling, like any undertaking, is more productive when it is the result of a collaborative effort. In other words, if businesses can improve their productivity by working with employees to identify and solve problems (Peters 1987; Waterman 1987), why wouldn't schools that function the same way become just as effective?

Still others of you might be thinking that it is important to share control because only by doing so do we learn more about how our children think. There is an abundance of research today suggesting that students have unique ways of solving problems (Peterson, Fennema & Carpenter 1989) and only by being open to what students do have some control over (if we encourage them), their own thinking, can we learn how well they perform on complex problems. What always results from "making thinking visible," is that we all learn about the richness of other peoples' ways of creating their own pathways.

Let me just add one more thought: We want to empower our students to take more control of their lives because it seems to be our destiny as persons: to be self-directing, to be in control of our destinies, and not to grow up to be path followers all the time. We have noted the comparison between thinking and exploration (Ryle 1979; Schrag 1988), and if we view human beings as posers of questions and potential explorers of the unknown, it is vital that they learn how to set and achieve goals, both alone and in collaboration with others.

One excellent way of encouraging this kind of growth and maturity is by cooperatively working through a problem-posing curriculum. Karen and Mary Ellen presented a nice balance between teacher and student control, and thereby they, and so many of the teachers mentioned in this volume, illustrate what Freire (1974) means when he talks about teachers being taught in dialogue with our students, who in turn teach us.

CONCLUSION

In this chapter I have taken one classroom episode to show how two teachers posed a significant problem for students, challenging them to identify the problem, generate solutions, and select the best one. This episode illustrates the nature of thoughtfulness, the kind of environment and pedagogical practices that invite thoughtfulness, and the issue of who controls the schools.

REFERENCES

Apple, Michael, ed. 1982. *Cultural and Economic Reproduction in Education: Essays on Class, Ideology and the State.* London: Routledge & Kegan Paul.

Beyer, Barry. 1987. *Practical Strategies for the Teaching of Thinking.* Boston: Allyn & Bacon.

Bourgeois, Paulette, and Brenda Clark. 1986. *Franklin in the Dark*. New York: Scholastic, Inc.

Costa, Arthur. 1985. "Teaching for, of, and about Thinking." In *Developing Minds,* ed. A. Costa. Alexandria, VA: Association for Supervision and Curriculum Development.

Freire, Paolo. 1974. *Pedagogy of the Oppressed*. New York: Seabury Press.

Mirman, Jill, Robert Swartz, and John Barell. 1988. "Teaching At-Risk Students to Think." In *At-Risk Students and Thinking,* ed. B. Presseisen. Washington, DC: National Educational Association and Research for Better Schools.

Peters, Tom. 1987. *Thriving on Chaos, Handbook for a Management Revolution*. New York: Alfred A. Knopf.

Peterson, Penelope, Elizabeth Fennema, and Thomas Carpenter. 1989. "Using Knowledge of How Students Think about Mathematics." In *Educational Leadership* 46, 4:42–47.

Ryle, Gilbert. 1979. *On Thinking*. Totowa, NJ: Rowan & Littlefield.

Schrag, F. 1988. *Thinking in School and Society*. New York: Routledge.

Spring, Joel. 1990. *The American School 1642–1990: Varieties of Historical Interpretation of the Foundations and Development of American Education*. White Plains, NY: Longman.

Tyack, David. 1974. *The One Best System*. Cambridge, MA: Harvard University Press.

Waterman, Robert. 1987. *The Renewal Factor, How the Best Get and Keep the Competitive Edge*. Toronto: Bantam Books.

CHAPTER 4

Assessment of Students' Thinking

OVERVIEW

In this chapter I present an overview of an essential first step in instructional planning: conducting a needs assessment. Several different means of assessing the quality of students' thinking are described: teacher observation, informal written assessments, analysis of student products and portfolios, partner observations, asking students themselves, and using videotapes. I pay special attention to fostering self-evaluation of their own performances on authentic tasks.

CLASSROOM EPISODE

Mary Mulcahy engaged her first graders in thinking through the problem Sarah found herself in: She had broken her arm over the weekend. At the end of the activity, Mary asked students to evaluate their own thinking. I would like us to listen as Mary's students solve this nonroutine, authentic problem.

"Before we solve it, can anyone expand upon Sarah's problem?" Let's try to define the extent of her dilemma.

"She can't go out and play. . . ."

"She won't be able to do her homework. . . ."

"And she will have a hard time doing her school work."

Then Mary asked for solutions.

"Learn how to write with her left hand, and then when the cast is off, she will be able to write with both hands. . . ."

"Her Mom can teach her how to use her left hand."

"But what if Sarah's Mom can't write with her left hand?" observed John.

Irene replied, "Then she can ask a friend of her Mom's who writes with her left hand." "Or she could ask Laura to teach her, because Laura's a lefty." Lisa then said, "You could write with both hands on the computer." "Aha!" exclaimed Mrs. Mulcahy. "She can use a computer!"

Several students then questioned what would happen if Sarah did not have a computer. John said, "You could use one at a friend's house." Matthew said, "What if her friend does not let her use the computer?"

Then Mary asked her students to recall all the solutions suggested and decide upon the best:

"Computer, because you can use either hand."

"Use a typewriter."

"Ignore your arm—don't look at it."

"Which is the best solution and why?" Mary asked.

"Typewriter, because nearly every house has a typewriter, but not all houses have a computer."

"Does everyone agree with these reasons?"

"Computer is best, because you don't have to press so hard."

"Computer costs more, and what if you have no disks or printer?"

Up to this point Mary had provided her students with an opportunity to help Sarah solve a real problem. Notice how she asked students to expand upon it or identify its many parts, then she asked them to generate solutions. While solutions were being suggested, students began to comment upon each other's ideas, showing how they, like those second graders doing *Franklin in the Dark,* were listening to each other and cooperating. Finally, Mary asked her students to select one and give good reasons.

Her final question challenged students to evaluate their thinking: "Think about your thinking today. Were you a good thinker today or not a good thinker?"

"I don't think I was a good thinker today, because I usually think of more ideas," said Thomas.

"Whenever we do this, other people come with solutions, and I can add on or make comments. . . ." John observed.

Then Evan noted that his thinking was not too good, "because I was sort of copying other peoples' ideas." Another student agreed with him that, when you are copying others' thinking, you are not really thinking for yourself."

Notice how Evan's self-reflection reminds us of Ryle's definition of thinking: *Thinking occurs when we create our own pathway* (not when we follow someone else's footsteps), and when we say things to ourselves tentatively in order to figure something out. Evan seems to realize that sometimes he is depending upon others to do the thinking.

CONDUCTING A NEEDS ASSESSMENT

An Overview of the Process

Here is what the assessment process can look like:

Establish criteria for assessment. (What knowledge, skills, attitudes, and ways of thinking are important? and why?)

Observe students in accordance with these criteria.
Make judgments about students' strengths and areas requiring further development.
Set goals—short- and long-term.
Design strategies to foster intended outcomes.
Continually monitor and evaluate.

What to Look For: Characteristics of Thoughtful Persons

The characteristics of a thoughtful person are drawn from research on teaching and cognitive development. The objectives of your assessment could very well be different, but this list provides a start.

Characteristics of Thoughtful Persons

They have confidence in problem-solving abilities.
They persist.
They control their own impulsivity.

They are open to others' ideas.
They cooperate with others in solving problems.
They listen.
They are empathic.

They tolerate ambiguity and complexity.
They approach problems from a variety of perspectives.
They research problems thoroughly.
They relate prior experience to current problems and make multiple connections.
They are open to many different solutions and evidence that may contradict favored points of view.
They pose what-if questions, challenging assumptions and playing with variables.
They are metacognitive: They plan, monitor, and evaluate their thinking.
They are able to transfer concepts and skills from one situation to another.
They are curious and wonder about the world. They ask "good questions."

Methods for Assessing Students' Thoughtfulness

Means of assessing the quality of students' thinking and their dispositions toward confidence and empathy include the following:

Teacher observation
Informal written assessments
Student products
Partner observations: teachers and supervisors
Students' own answers
Videotapes

We'll explore each of these in turn. But before we begin, look again at the above six steps that comprise the process of conducting a needs assessment, and keep in mind that this process is the same for each method of evaluating students' thoughtfulness.

Teacher Observation

Yogi Berra, former New York Yankee and Hall of Famer, is reputed to have said that you can do a lot of observing just by watching. And this is how we learn so much about our students—watching them as they interact with us, their friends, parents, and others. We need to find the time to watch and diagnose.

We observe certain dispositions, or habits of mind, that are developed over a long period of time and are thus different from ephemeral feelings that can be changed more easily. Listed below are dispositions toward self and others with guidelines for helping you determine from your observations whether or not your students meet these particular criteria. After reading this section, you should be able to create your own set of criteria. Use your Thinking Journals to make notes on your own students.

Observing Confidence in Problem Solving.   One of the two dispositions essential to thoughtful persons is the confidence in one's self that one's thinking makes a difference, that one can solve most problems. Research (Pressley 1987) indicates a connection between this confidence and the ability to achieve on standardized tests, and it stands to reason that if we don't believe we will succeed, we probably won't. Look for students who:

> Push their papers away and mutter, "I can't do this kind of thing. I'm never good at this stuff!"
> Avoid encountering any situation that is novel or slightly more complex than they are used to.
> Tend to get frustrated when situations are different from expectations and then cannot move beyond those feelings of frustration. Tend not to persist in the face of obstacles.

Jot down what you see in your students.

I shall leave to you, the reader, the task of figuring out what the positive side of each of these dispositions and behaviors is. For example, people with confidence in their own thinking will say, "I can do this!" and will accept challenges to engage in novel, complex tasks. They will persist when confronted with expected obstacles and eventually succeed.

Observing the Control of Impulsivity.   Thoughtful persons are often characterized by a lack of impulsivity. This means that when confronted with a complex problem such as a deteriorating relationship with a superior or loved one, we will take the time to reflect on the nature of the situation and not act precipitously without considering causes, alternative solutions, and possible consequences.

Sternberg (1985) notes that "better reasoners tend to spend more time encoding the terms of a problem than do poorer reasoners but tend to spend less time operating on these encodings than do poorer reasoners'' (p. 104). Thus, good problem solvers take time to think about the nature of the problem. They might ask such questions as "What are the key concepts here? Is this situation related to any others I know? Can I reduce it to several different parts?" In other words, people experienced in problem solving spend a lot of time thinking before they leap toward a solution. Look for students who:

> Immediately raise their hands, perhaps even before you complete the question.
>
> Quickly place pencil to paper and start writing. They may have identified a strategy or solution without much thought.
>
> Solve problems without spending much time researching to gather information.
>
> Give up without spending much time analyzing the situation.

I should note that some of these actions might reflect learning styles or dispositions to act quickly. It might also be true that some of us think more quickly than others. Young children are often viewed as more impulsive than older ones, thus revealing significant developmental differences.

Observing Persistence.   Persistence is that quality of sticking to a process, even though it appears at first glance that this might take some time. Physicist and Nobel Laureate Richard Feynman in his autobiography, *Surely You're Joking, Mr. Feynman* (1985), noted that when he was a child he offered to fix a neighbor's radio:

> I finally fixed it because I had, and still have, persistence. Once on a puzzle, I can't get off. . . . I want to beat [the] damn thing. I can't just leave it after I've found out so much about it. I have to keep going to find out ultimately what is the matter with it in the end. That's a puzzle drive.

Feynman's parents' friends were amazed at this ability: "'He fixes radios by *thinking!*' The whole idea of thinking, to fix a radio—a little boy stops and thinks, and figures out how to do it—[they] never thought that was possible."
Sternberg (1985, p. 104) notes that "Persistence and involvement in the problems was highly correlated with success in solution: The more intelligent individuals did not give up, nor did they fall for the obvious, but often incorrect, solutions." Look for students who:

> Have difficulty staying with a task. Who give up quickly and reflect an "I can't do this" attitude.
>
> Are quick to ask for help from you: "Mrs. Wright! This is too hard. Please help me!" This may be an example of giving up too soon. (It might also be an instance where the level of complexity is too much for students.)
>
> Quickly accept one solution without exploring other options. Piaget noticed while doing his experiments with adolescents (1958) that most of them were

satisfied with initial solutions to a problem. They lacked the persistence to see if there were other possibilities. Students who do persist can be heard to say in class, "Wait a minute! I'll figure it out." Or "Let's give her time, she'll solve it."

Cannot find examples in school or in their own lives of how they have persisted.

Observing Listening Skills.   Listening represents the second foundational element in thoughtfulness: our ability to be open to the feelings and ideas of others. Listening requires physically attending to what another person is saying, focusing upon the speaker, and attempting to create a mental picture (or model) of what she/he is saying. It requires that we hold in abeyance our own feelings and point of view. We grow intellectually as the result of listening to contrasting viewpoints, and the strength of our interpersonal relationships is very directly affected by our ability to receive the content and feeling tone of another's message. As one advertiser noted: "Nothing new ever entered the mind through an open mouth" (Wolvin & Coakley 1985, p. 15). Look for students who:

Continually ask for repetition of directions.

Can seldom repeat what another says in class discussions.

Have a hard time responding to a previous comment.

Always wave their hands with the answer.

Observing Cooperation.   Students who can cooperate with another person in problem solving can play the role of partner, watcher, evaluator, and proposer of alternative strategies (Forman & Kraker 1985). Much of problem solving is learned in this kind of social context, not simply by ourselves working alone.

By working collaboratively students learn how to coordinate their planning strategies. "In coordinating plans, children seem to learn about their own and each other's cognitive activities" (Rogoff, Gauvain & Gardner 1987).

As Waterman (1987) has noted about success in business, self-renewing companies place much more emphasis upon trust, team work, and collaborative problem solving than they do on competition within the organization. Citing Kohn, he notes that "Cooperation takes advantage of all the skills represented in a group as well as the mysterious process by which that group becomes more than the sum of its parts. By contrast, competition makes people suspicious and hostile toward one another and actively discourages this process" (p. 196). Look for students who:

Can play sports and games well together. Watch for those who might need to win at all costs.

Willingly share time, materials, and ideas with friends in and out of class.

Can work well in small groups, listening, offering suggestions, building upon others' ideas, praising good teamwork, etc.

Can organize an unstructured task with their friends such as moving chairs or cleaning up without having to be told.

Observing Empathy.   Students who are empathic are able, as Buber noted, to "imagine the real" situation of someone else, what that person is thinking and feeling. In a cooperative community of inquirers, students will make an attempt to see another person's point of view, to sense how he or she is feeling within a particular situation. Our ability to empathize improves with age; middle and high school students can be much better at it. Look for students who:

Say, "I know how you feel. I understand how you are arriving at your point of view."

Make an attempt to imagine how persons in literature or life think and feel. This might be done by active listening, posing questions, and responding with acceptance and not judgment.

Observing a Tolerance for Ambiguity and the Complexity of Problems.   Lois Granito (1990) teaches second grade, and during a research project on how students learn mathematics, she observed that her young students already seemed to have an attitude that, if they couldn't solve a problem almost immediately, they might as well give up. She noted also that they did not seem to have any tolerance for the different ways in which simple problems could be solved. They were looking for the one right way to do it.

A number of faculty assessed the quality of their students' thinking: "My students have a great deal of difficulty with problems that have no right or wrong answer. Whenever a problem is complex and can be analyzed or interpreted from a number of different angles, they immediately think that it's an either/or situation. They have tremendous difficulty beginning to see the nuances in some life situations—they want everything categorized into black and white."

We might expect this kind of black/white either/or thinking among younger children, in elementary and middle schools. But my colleagues were talking about college sophomores and juniors. These students by the ages of nineteen and twenty should be able to recognize the complexity of some issues and be able to analyze them from a wide variety of perspectives, but the truth is that many adults have difficulty with conceptual complexity, because we haven't been challenged to look for nuances of meaning or for multiple perspectives.

Baron and Glatthorn (1985) note that "Good thinkers welcome problematic situations and [are] tolerant of ambiguity . . . [while] poor thinkers search for certainty and are intolerant of ambiguity." There are, of course, developmental differences between Lois's second graders and our college students. We expect younger children to cling more to the black/white, yes/no analysis of situations. Look for students who:

Quickly dismiss complex problems and issues by saying, "I haven't a clue!"

Have real difficulty figuring out alternative ways of interpreting or analyzing a situation. They cling to one sure way of doing things or are stymied by

TABLE 4.1 Assessment of Students' Thoughtfulness

Thoughtful Behavior/Attitude: Controlling Impulsivity		
Observed Behavior	**Strategy**	**Intended Outcome**
1. "I can't do this!"	Outlaw "I can't" statements	Takes time to think
2. Raises hand quickly	TNT "Thinking Needs Time"	Deliberates
3. Goes for quck easy answer	Write down thoughts; pair with partner; share with group	Considers options
4. Plugs in formula without much thought	Write in Thinking Journal	Analyzes situations deliberately
5.		
6.		
7.		
8.		

Observational Record of Progress: Student Name:		
Date	Observed Behavior	Plan

our questions: "What other ways are there to examine this situation? What other solutions are there?"

Want above all else to be sure they are right! "But what's the *right answer?*" they importune.

Look baffled when we show them an alternative way of thinking about a problematic situation.

I think the foregoing is enough of a start for each of us to begin looking closely at our students to observe instances of various kinds of behavior. If we find that our students need to develop their ability to listen, persist, cooperate, and believe in their ability to solve problems with thought, then we can set these as our targets for a semester or a year and use Table 4.1 as a planning guide.

This will help you identify the behavior and monitor students' progress toward improvement.

The rest of the characteristics of thoughtful persons (page 34) are more or less related to good problem solving, being reasonable and inquisitive, and I shall now turn to other kinds of assessment instruments that might give us some clues about these kinds of behaviors.

Informal Written Assessments

Over the past few years, in conjunction with colleagues, I have developed several informal means of assessing students' thinking abilities that have helped teachers do two things:

Identify strengths and weaknesses of individual students in their classrooms. Assess overall schoolwide strengths and weaknesses.

These assessments, naturally, facilitate teachers' instructional planning, and they can provide the necessary basis for long-term curricular and staff development planning. One of the best informal assessment instruments was created by John Edwards (Edwards 1991). I have used his instrument (see Figure 4.1) with many teachers, and they find it a helpful way of assessing students' thinking as well as students' assessing their own. It can also be used to help us set individual and class goals for improvement.

The problems we have given to students are more or less *authentic*. That is, they reflect situations students might naturally encounter in their lives outside school. The more authentic the situations, perhaps, the more significant the thinking reflected therein. We need to focus more attention on such authentic problems because so much schooling involves drill and practice on nonauthentic, nonchallenging tasks.

Here are some tests I have devised over the years and used with many teachers who were assessing and designing curricula:

Assessing Problem Solving.   In order to assess students' problem-solving abilities I have used several varieties of an informal test designed by Irving Sigel of Educational Testing Service and myself. For upper elementary students we attempted to select a problem that, for them, would seem nonroutine, challenging, and authentic. For upper grades, teachers have modified the focus of the problem, a train.

Bobby received a new train for his birthday. It worked well for a few days and then just stopped. Please write a story about how you would solve this problem.

This test was designed to determine students' abilities to engage in a number of thinking processes:

Analyze a problem.
Search for causes.
Generate a number of hypotheses and solutions.
Test and evaluate their proposed solutions. Search for evidence.
Project possible consequences.
Imagine herself/himself within the problem situation.
Have confidence she/he can figure things out on her/his own.

In the River Edge, New Jersey, school district, we used this problem to conduct a general assessment of students' thinking abilities. During one summer, teachers read over 100 such essays and used the results to develop their own model of intelligent behavior. (See Chapter 13.) Let me share with you the two responses that for these teachers formed two ends of a continuum.

Student Name: _____

	Completely False	Mostly False	Partly False/ Partly True	Mostly True	Completely True
Response:					
Abbreviation:	CF	MF	PFPT	MT	CT
1. The student is very interested in ideas.	CF	MF	PFPT	MT	CT
2. The student works well in discussion groups.	CF	MF	PFPT	MT	CT
3. The student can express ideas clearly.	CF	MF	PFPT	MT	CT
4. The student is not good at using information.	CF	MF	PFPT	MT	CT
5. The student can think well about a wide range of things.	CF	MF	PFPT	MT	CT
6. The student cannot tell which ideas are more important.	CF	MF	PFPT	MT	CT
7. The student does not often have important ideas.	CF	MF	PFPT	MT	CT
8. The student can often combine many ideas into one idea.	CF	MF	PFPT	MT	CT
9. The student can easily recognize good ideas.	CF	MF	PFPT	MT	CT
10. The student often runs out of ideas quickly.	CF	MF	PFPT	MT	CT
11. The student finds it hard to tell if one idea is different from another.	CF	MF	PFPT	MT	CT
12. The student can often suggest ideas not mentioned before.	CF	MF	PFPT	MT	CT

Figure 4.1. Teacher Assessment of Student Thinking. (Continued on next page.)

41

Figure 4.1 (continued).

	Response:	Completely False	Mostly False	Partly False/ Partly True	Mostly True	Completely True
13.	The student's thinking is not well organized.	CF	MF	PFPT	MT	CT
14.	The student is a lazy thinker.	CF	MF	PFPT	MT	CT
15.	The student likes to try difficult problems.	CF	MF	PFPT	MT	CT
16.	The student finds it hard to apply thinking in real life situations.	CF	MF	PFPT	MT	CT
17.	The student cannot concentrate for long.	CF	MF	PFPT	MT	CT
18.	The student is not good at solving problems.	CF	MF	PFPT	MT	CT
19.	The student is good at coming up with ideas.	CF	MF	PFPT	MT	CT
20.	The student can find different ways of looking at the same problem.	CF	MF	PFPT	MT	CT
21.	The student gets confused easily.	CF	MF	PFPT	MT	CT
22.	Other people respect the student's ideas.	CF	MF	PFPT	MT	CT
23.	The student can change thinking approaches to suit the problem.	CF	MF	PFPT	MT	CT
24.	Most of the student's ideas are not clear.	CF	MF	PFPT	MT	CT
25.	The student knows how to tackle a problem.	CF	MF	PFPT	MT	CT
26.	If confused, the student asks questions.	CF	MF	PFPT	MT	CT
27.	The student thinks carefully about suggestions before rejecting them.	CF	MF	PFPT	MT	CT

28. The student rarely thinks about own thinking.	CF	MF	PFPT	MT	CT
29. The student is not as creative a thinker as most of the class.	CF	MF	PFPT	MT	CT
30. The student finds it hard to use knowledge in new situations.	CF	MF	PFPT	MT	CT
31. The plans the student makes are well thought out.	CF	MF	PFPT	MT	CT
32. The student asks good questions.	CF	MF	PFPT	MT	CT
33. The student gives up easily on difficult questions.	CF	MF	PFPT	MT	CT
34. The student does not consider the consequences before acting.	CF	MF	PFPT	MT	CT
35. The student is confident of thinking things through to a conclusion.	CF	MF	PFPT	MT	CT
36. The student can easily distinguish the most important part of a problem.	CF	MF	PFPT	MT	CT
37. The student can accept that there is often more than one right answer in a situation.	CF	MF	PFPT	MT	CT
38. The student can keep in mind where the student's thinking is heading.	CF	MF	PFPT	MT	CT
39. The student has trouble making decisions.	CF	MF	PFPT	MT	CT
40. The student can work things out independently.	CF	MF	PFPT	MT	CT

Here is Student A:

If I was in boby's case I would ask my dad for help with the train and if there was something I broke I would get it repaired but if it was broken when I brought [*sic*] it I would bring it back to the store for the owner to fix. But before that just in case I would look for a gaurantee. [*sic*] (Three minutes to write.)

Student B responded to the same assignment:

Suddenly, my train stopped moving. It just stopped where it was. I got up and checked the tracks to see if something was blocking the train. (Nothing was). I checked the train wheels, they were fine. I even checked the batteries and tested them in my walk-man [*sic*]. They worked perfectly. What could be wrong? I didn't know what to do. If I told my parents, they would have a fit about me being careless. But, maybe they wouldn't. My old man is a handy guy and maybe he would fix it. Yeah, he would or would he? I'm so confused. What can I do? I know, if my folks want me to show them how the train works (and it doesn't by then) I'll say, "I don't know what happened, I haven't touched it all day." Yeah, that's good. *No!* I can't do that. My folks don't lie to me, so I can't lie to them. I have to have courage 'cause it wasn't my fault. Or was it? My parents came home an hour later. During dinner I told them I was playing with my train set and it stopped working. My old man asked me if I did anything to it. I told him no, and that I checked everything and everything was fine. Then I asked him if he would look at it. He said he would and thanked me for telling the truth. Boy am I glad that's over. (By the way, I didn't do anything to the train, the manufacturer just has a bad way of making trains. We sent it back to the company.) (Sixteen minutes to write, all students having approximately twenty to finish.)

POINT TO PONDER: Before going on, try comparing these two responses. What differences do you notice?

Teachers selected these two, because they seemed to illustrate several themes in the essays in general: reliance upon oneself or upon another person; identifying the problem and working through a sequence of steps to figure out what was wrong; checking evidence for various hypotheses; reflecting on one's own thinking (metacognition); presence of emotional factors that often condition problem solving. Perhaps you noticed these elements as well.

One of the most evident aspects of problem solving—confidence in your own thinking—seems to be evident in Student B's thinking. This student seems to own the problem and, in not passing it on to her father immediately, tackles several possibilities first. She explores options, and when those are not fruitful, then she thinks of how her "old man" can help. Of course, given a different kind of problem, Student A might have done the same thing. We should also note, though, that Nick, Student A, didn't enjoy writing as much as did Jennifer, Student B.

As a result of reading these essays, the teachers constructed a model of intelligent behavior that included problem solving, critical and creative thinking, and metacognition. They also identified important attitudes that foster good thinking. Finally, and a little bit later in the year, they identified problem solving as the intellectual process they wished to make the focus of their staff development efforts.

What do these tests reveal? Various degrees of lack of impulsivity, persistence, and comfort with ambiguous situations. They further reveal various degrees of facility with analyzing problems and generating solutions.

One important caveat! Several teachers have given these tests in their classes without any introduction and rationale, and students have responded accordingly—by writing little or nothing. This demonstrates the need to provide students with reasons for asking them to engage in such processes. Some teachers have simply stated: "I want to learn more about how you think" and elaborated upon the importance of thinking. Others have said, "I am taking a graduate course, and you can help me do my work by responding as best you can to these problems." Quite interestingly, when students are given these tests, some have asked, "Why don't other teachers give us problems like these? *Why aren't other teachers interested in how we think?*" (Emphasis added.)

I have never made any attempt to undertake statistical analyses of these informal measures. At best, they give us a limited amount of evidence that must be related to other clues to arrive at tentative conclusions.

Assessing Reasonableness.   There is one test that I have administered to students from kindergarten through college. It poses the following problem:

> Suppose the principal (or president) came to your class and said that this was the best elementary, high school, or college in the entire state (or country). How would you respond? Why?

What I am looking for here is students' ability to assess the believability of a statement: What evidence is there to support it? What assumptions are being made? What biases does the speaker reveal? What is the other side of the coin?— for example, evidence to the contrary?

Some sixth graders responded thusly: "It would depend upon who told him, and whether he was trying to get you to stay or to do something."

Two eighth graders said, "Yes, we have smart kids in this school."

Another eighth grader said he "would respect the principal's right to his opinion but would not believe him until the principal had visited and evaluated all the other schools in Pennsylvania."

Other eighth graders responded: "No, did he see all the schools in New Jersey?" "No! We have too much homework . . . our lockers are too small . . . we have rotten food."

One high school sophomore said his school couldn't be the best in the state because he wasn't allowed to leave during his free time.

Several college students responded in the following fashion: "I disagree. . . . If I were going to an interview and sitting next to a Princeton graduate, who do you think would get the job?" "No, because the college does not have a lot of clubs and you don't meet anyone." ". . . he says it because it makes a good impression. . . ." "I would need some backing up, like information or surveys."

POINT TO PONDER: How would you evaluate these responses?

Here a varied range of abilities is reflected. As you have noticed, not too many students identify the speaker's possible bias. Only one college student recognized that the speaker is not the most reliable and objective source: "He says it because it makes a good impression."

The kinds of evidence that most students present are very narrow: "We have too much homework" (grade 8), and "The college does not have a lot of clubs" (college). As one teacher noted, his students "personalized" their reasons for rejecting the statement: It's not the best because I can't leave when I want to. As we will note later in this chapter, the ability to think abstractly depends on age, experience, and environment. These limited and concrete responses give evidence of something we need to help students with: generalizing from their own experience to a more global perspective. This is no easy task, and we have discovered students at several different age levels having difficulty with this task: abstracting specifics from their own experience with which to create a more general concept, rule, norm, or perspective. This, to me, suggests that these students need work in teasing out attributes from experiences and objects that can be generalized to all other experiences and/or objects. This ability matures with age and experience.

One need not be a "formal" (in the Piagetian sense) thinker, whether a teenager or a mature adult, in order to challenge the bias and lack of evidence in the principal's statement. For example, the only kindergarten class this problem was administered to had many students who, when asked this question, raised their voices in praise for the school: "Oh, yeah, it's the very, very best!"

But there was one little girl in this class, named Nancy, and when her teacher, Margaret, posed the question, she strongly disagreed: "But he hasn't seen all the other schools! He hasn't been to all the other schools!"

How did she come to evaluate this principal's statement by asking for the kind of evidence he used? Perhaps she learned this kind of response at home. This is very likely, but the point is that you needn't be a very advanced, complex thinker to ask to see the evidence or to question authority.

Newmann (1990) reports on the assessment of perhaps a more authentic problem for high school students: analyzing a Supreme Court case involving a locker search and the right to privacy. Students wrote essays reflecting the position they would take and their reasons for this choice.

Using Ennis's standardized test of critical judgment (1985) is another possibility that I have used with faculty during long-term assessment projects. This test focuses upon induction, credibility, observation, deduction, and assumption identification. The Ennis test, together with others, is thoroughly analyzed by Norris and Ennis (1989) in *Evaluating Critical Thinking*.

Assessing Cognitive Development.   There are many ways to assess cognitive development. All of the Piagetian tasks can be given to students at various stages of their development. Furth's *Thinking Goes to School* (1974) presents many possibilities for younger children as will *Educating the Young Thinker* (Sigel, Copple & Saunders 1984). The Arlin Test of Formal Reasoning has been used with adolescents (Arter & Salmon 1987) from grade 6 through adulthood.

The test I like the best is, perhaps, that one designed by Peel (1964)—the Careful Airman test. This one gives us an idea of whether or not students can engage in "contingency thinking"—that is, can they analyze a situation and see that we need more information and that there could be many possible reasons or causes for an event. Peel's test rather clearly separates those immature thinkers who look only for right/wrong answers from the more mature students who attempt to see if there are more complex elements involved. Here is the test item:

> Only courageous pilots are allowed to fly over high mountains. This summer a fighter pilot, flying over the Rocky Mountains, collided with an aerial sky ride cable and cut it, causing some sky ride cars to fall to the rocks below. Several people were killed and many others had to spend the night suspended above the rocks. Was this pilot a careful airman? Why do you think this? (Peel 1974)

Here is how some eighth graders responded:

> Student A: "No he wasn't because he would of been more careful if he was."
> Student B: "No because before you go flying anywhere you should know the rules of the sky and be careful at all times."
> Student C: "No because the pilot was probably going too fast and he could make it over the mountain."
> Student D: "No. But, their two side to every story . . . he mite have been a great pilot but their mite have been a storem. That push him of course . . ."[*sic*].
> Student E: "It depends on the situation he was in. Maybe he was being very careful but something happend to his plane. Then again he could have been very careless and wasn't looking where he was going. You can't really answer this without knowing more about the situation."

These responses fascinate me, and I would like to see if you notice the same kinds of things I do in rereading them.

POINT TO PONDER: What developmental differences do you notice?

This test was designed by Peel to determine a person's ability to engage in what he called "contingency" thinking. That is, Peel was interested in the transition between what Piaget called "concrete" and "formal" operations. In the former stage youngsters reason from concrete objects; they can also engage in multiple classifications, conservation of matter, seriation. But they have difficulty with those processes that adolescents and adults should be able to perform: thinking more in the abstract; projecting consequences into the distant future; seeing multiple causes, meanings, and inferences; engaging in nuanced judgment (Resnick); and becoming adept at "combinatorial reasoning." The latter ability means that older persons might be able to generate all possible combinations of several different variables, for example combinations of ice cream cones with four different flavors. Adolescents begin to see the relativity of situations, and you hear them say, "It depends on the situation," because they do not engage in the kind of black/white thinking of their younger brothers and sisters. The younger students are sometimes more authoritarian in their thinking: "Things are this way, and that's the way they are supposed to be." Therefore, these younger students (in the concrete stage of cognitive development) do not as readily see possibilities for modification and alteration. Older students are better able to think of possibilities in the abstract—for example, to see public institutions as one among many possible ways of organizing ourselves.

With this all too brief background, we can examine the responses to Peel's test to see that only students D and E seem to see the multiple possibilities that could have affected the pilot in this situation. The crash might have occurred because of mechanical failure ("something happened to his plane") or weather conditions ("their mite have been a storem [*sic*]"). Other students have noted that he could have suffered a heart attack, or the weather might have been a factor. Some have even hypothesized that this was a kamikaze pilot who intentionally crashed his plane.

Student A is engaging in what we might call circular reasoning: He wasn't careful because he wasn't. Students B and C attribute responsibility to the pilot for not knowing rules and/or going too fast. These are possibilities, but as Student E says, "You can't really answer this without knowing more about the situation." This is the "it depends" kind of response that might separate a "concrete operational" student from one who is beginning to think more abstractly.

Students B and C seem to be more absolute in their thinking, less able to infer possibilities or contingencies. There is a fixedness in their thinking that Schroder, Driver, and Streufert (1967) have detected in some of their informal tests. They asked students, for example, to write three or four sentences on a number of topics (the Paragraph Completion Test). For example, on the question "What I think of rules . . ." a younger and/or a more intellectually fixed, concrete person responded: "Rules are made to be followed. They give you direction and are not to be broken."

An older, more intellectually flexible person responded: "Rules are necessary for a society to function well. However, rules should not be so strictly adhered to that they cannot be modified when circumstances alter. The purpose or the effects of rules are more important than the rules themselves."

Obviously with the latter response not only do we see a student who sees what *is* as one of many possibilities, but we also see someone far more comfortable with thinking in the abstract—he/she speaks of society and rules in general, more abstract terms.

Assessing Adventurous Thinking. An assessment that I invented after using a number of Torrance's tests of creativity is: "What if it started snowing tomorrow and never, ever stopped? What would happen?"

My original intention was to test students' abilities to generate a number of possibilities that might reflect originality, fluency (number of ideas), and flexibility (approaching problems from different perspectives). Recent research (Perkins 1981) suggests that the latter criterion, flexibility, is really important in good problem solving. However, I also noticed, as you probably have already, that this little assessment will provide us with information on students' abilities to think abstractly, to project consequences into the near and far future, and to manipulate a wide number of variables.

Most elementary school students say things like the following: "We'd all die. . . . there'd be no school. . . . Daddy couldn't go to work. . . . we'd build snowmen all day. . . . there'd be no food. . . ." etc.

Here is one seventh grader: "At first all jobs and schools would be paralyzed. We would have quite a bit of snow. Scientists would have to come up with a heat ray to melt the snow. Could make a dome city with a heat ray to melt the snow. We would have to seek other places to live: ocean, moon, other planets. Lots of snowmen. If you were a driveway shoveler, you'd be in the money."

Compare these responses with that of an intellectually more mature twelfth grader named Amy:

> Simplistically, we'd die.
>
> Alternatively, there are many kinds of snow and many different degrees of snow. . . . if it were light snow that melted upon contact, survival is possible. . . . the result would be world-wide climate change. (Assuming, that is, that this snow is world-wide.) . . . If the snow were heavy, blizzard like, man at first . . . would manage. However, he would eventually become extinct. The food chain would be destroyed, and man would starve. Of course, the life cycle would then probably repeat itself—another ice age would prevail. Then, if it never stopped, the world would be forever frozen. If it were to melt, life as biological history demonstrates would repeat itself again—dinosaurs, apes, man, etc.
>
> Of course, this was a purely biological consideration. Philosophically, poetically, psychologically, mathematically, astrologically, or meteorologically, there are different considerations. We could analyze religiously, too. However, each person sees it as a different sign, a representative of something else, and many will read it as symbolism. . . . Nevertheless, does it really matter? Man is supreme only in his own mind and when we speak of consequences we deal only with what we know. Man must die in the end, and the means is a purely academic question. Life as we know it would end, but in a universal scheme, perpetual snow on that little rock called Earth is of no consequence. It changes nothing. . . . We see only what we want to see, and no more.
>
> P.S.! Ridiculous, isn't it? If you propose such questions, you should prepare for equally insane responses! Every person will answer as to his concerns: Musicians will sing only about snow—no more sun. Students will say—no more school. Religious individuals will belief [sic] in Noah's Ark II. Cinematographers will consider sets in snow. Painters will despair at no sunlight for painting. . . . Man is essentially self-centered, and he sees only what concerns him. All else pales in comparison. But remember—skiers will have a great time!

Take a few minutes to make your own comparisons about the differences and similarities you see in all three levels of thinking.

POINT TO PONDER: First, analyze them using the criteria of originality, flexibility, and fluency. What do you notice?

Perhaps you noticed that the younger students seem to have a number of good ideas from different perspectives.

Next, consider the developmental notions discussed in this section in your analysis:

Projection of possibilities into the near and far future.
Contingency thinking—what might be, possibilities not stated explicitly, "If this . . . then that" kind of thinking.
"It depends" thinking.
Use of prior or background knowledge.
Thinking in concrete-immediate and/or abstract terms . . . e.g., the differences between "Daddy" and "Man" and "Religious individuals."
Approaching problems from multiple perspectives.
Critical inquiry: identifying unstated assumptions.
Considering multiple variables simultaneously.

You have undoubtedly noticed the complexity of the responses increasing with age. Even though the youngest students approach the situation from a number of different perspectives, the thinking is quite limited to the here and now, the concrete, immediate consequences. The seventh grader begins to see the possibilities of living even under these conditions; he has hope because he can see beyond the immediate situation toward possible solutions.

One thing that teachers I work with always seem to notice is that, as students get older and more sophisticated in their thinking, they realize that such a condition, unlimited snow, does not necessarily mean extinction, as evidenced by the seventh grader. Neither does it necessarily mean that the snow accumulates to suffocating depths, as one student noticed: "Yes, it is always snowing but it melts when it strikes the ground." Thus, this little exercise also challenges students to see beyond their immediate assumptions of death and catastrophe.

One final note. Consider this eleventh grader's response: "Well if it snowed everyone would die because they would get trapped inside their houses and not have enough food to live."

Conclusions? There are many possibilities. Everyone does not mature intellectually in the same way and not every seventeen-year-old has the ability to reason as Amy, our twelfth grader, did. Then too, perhaps some students were not interested in, or bored with, the question.

How Can We Use Informal Written Assessments?   The action we take when we get a sense of students' intellectual maturity is to follow the lead presented in our definition of thinking—as problem solving, as recognizing and resolving "doubt, uncertainty or difficulty." And a way to go about that is by attempting to provide experiences wherein students will be challenged to expand or extend their thinking to consider alternate possibilities. This is why a problem-posing curriculum is so vital.

> Put problems before them. Make things difficult for them. . . . Produce things for them to think about and question their thinking at every stage. They are inventive and original. (Highet 1954, p. 40)

With *younger students:* We can use Sigel's distancing theory. Ask students, "How would you group these toy animals?" When she/he responds by putting all the two-legged in one and four-legged creatures in another pile, ask, "How else could you group them?" Help students seek alternative strategies: "How did you go to Grandma's house? How else could you have gone? What if there were snow [or other impediment]?" (See "Problem Posing" in Chapter 5.)

With *older students:* Engage in problem solving as described in Chapter 7. Problematic situations wherein we ask students to identify problems, generate alternatives, be active listeners to other persons' ways of seeing and solving will have the effect of opening their mind's eyes to alternatives. Mosher (1979) recommends such a curriculum precisely because it enhances students' cognitive development. What we want to do, suggests Meyers (1987), is to "set students' minds to pondering, for in such a context they will experience both curiosity to know more and disequilibrium that will challenge their old ways of thinking and prepare them for new modes of critical thinking."

These are some informal assessments that I have used over the years to help learn more about the quality of students' thinking. Of course, there are more formal tests. Piaget's tests of formal reasoning are fully described in his and Barbel Inhelder's 1958 book *The Development of Logical Thinking from Childhood to Adolescence.* All of these and many more are referenced by Arter and Salmon (1987) in a monograph entitled *Assessing Higher Order Thinking Skills.*

Analysis of Student Products and Portfolios

We certainly ought not to ignore all the assignments we give during the course of a year as potential assessment instruments. These too can be a source for making cumulative judgments on students' ability to see the complexities of situations, for example. Essays, lab reports, project activities, homework, test results, and in-class work can easily be assessed using any of the indicators mentioned in this chapter or those in Chapters 8–11.

Compiling such products into student "portfolios" (Brown 1989; Costa 1989) can become effective ways of assessing student growth along any of the dimensions suggested herein. Such student portfolios could become the focus of small-group teacher meetings, department meetings, and full faculty gatherings devoted to the objective of assessing the quality of students' thinking and how our grading system reflects our curricular goals of fostering thinking throughout the curriculum. Sylvia Mathis of Salt Lake City suggests asking students what products they wish to place in their portfolios. This gesture would involve them in exercising some degree of self-monitoring.

Here are some additional suggestions for starting with students' products:

Products within a Specific Subject.   Take the most recently concluded unit and examine some of its products—tests, homework, final projects, etc.—and at a leisurely pace examine several of them for evidence of good thinking. To begin you might look for these qualities:

Persistence, lack of impulsivity, openness to ambiguity, complexity.
Ability to identify a problem, search for alternative solutions or interpretations.
Ability to state a conclusion and present evidence to support it. Use the recent NAEP studies (1986) as evaluative criteria for students' products: Can they, for example, compare/contrast? Solve multistage problems? Hypothesize?
Ability to draw reasonable comparisons and contrasts between different kinds of situations (classifying by attributes, etc.).

Student Questions.   Every time a student asks a question, he/she is providing us with information about how they process information. Are they asking about important details that should be obvious? If so, they might be having difficulty with what Sternberg (1985) calls "selective encoding," or determining what is important.

They might also be having difficulty relating ideas and concepts, seeing patterns and connections. Their questions will reveal misconceptions, naive notions about how the world functions, and difficulties with analyzing problems. "I can't figure this out. Will you help me?" may mean the student has trouble analyzing a situation to discover its major concepts, breaking it into parts, and representing it graphically or visually. Our propensity for demanding the "right" answer has not left sufficient time to help students engage in these very significant processes.

Their inability to ask questions about a reading passage might, for example, indicate some difficulties with finding discrepancies or recognizing uncertainties in the plot. These are part of problem finding and might be the result of difficulty with taking ideas or information and relating it to what they already know. Only by making such comparisons can we discover that what we are reading or hearing does not square with what we think we know.

We can ask our students to read a passage and then generate questions about it. Then we can ask students to classify the different kinds of questions and generate a set of criteria for "good questions."

As a result, we will gain valuable insights into those concepts and ideas with which students are having difficulty. I have often observed that adolescents as well as adults have difficulty determining general principles, unless explicitly stated; they can work well only with the factual information, and this could very well reflect developmental differences.

Student Logs or Journals.   In subsequent chapters I shall present a wide variety of excerpts from student Thinking Journals, notably in Chapters 8 and 11. Let me just say here that if we get students in the habit of reflecting on their performance with such questions as "What was the problem? How did I solve it? Did

I do it well? What might I do differently next time? Where else can I use such thought processes?'' we can gather a lot of information about how they think they think and about their progress over time. Important observations can be of the kind where a student evaluates her own thinking. Here is one second grader's assessment: "How do you think we did? Bad becs [*sic*] I did not open my mind."

And a high school student used a journal entry after analyzing the writing of an essay on utopias: "I never realized that you make so many decisions while going through something like this."

You notice, I'm sure, that these students are, through the writing process, becoming aware of their own thinking. Eventually they will exercise more control over their thinking, thus becoming more metacognitive.

Partner Observations: Teachers and Supervisors

Invite a colleague to your classroom to observe students as they work on problems or projects. He or she can observe such dispositions as cooperation, listening/empathy, attentiveness, persistence, focus upon the task and specific skills such as problem solving. Such peer observations can be mutually reinforcing and the basis for good discussions about how to help students become better at any one of the attitudes or skills identified above.

Use your supervisor to help you do what you want. Ask him or her to look for specific evidences of students' thinking. You may have to share your concept of what thoughtfulness looks like, but with tact and patience you will be able to enlist this person's help during regular visits. You might also consider inviting him or her in at other times to help you work on students' thinking. It can be an exciting adventure for both of you. Ask the supervisor:

> To note such behaviors as lack of persistence or good cooperative spirit.
> To document what they see.
> To share with you their observations soon after the class.

Invite parents to look for evidence of the behavior you are concerned with. Good parent–teacher communications can be an invaluable source of support, for parents can play a significant role in supporting what we teachers do. After attending Sylvia Mathis's parent workshops in Salt Lake City, the parents report to teachers on their children's ability to "brainstorm" and use "wait time."

Asking Students Themselves

There are many different ways of assessing students' thinking. One that we haven't discussed is very simple: Ask the students. What do I mean? Students are excellent observers of your behavior as well as their own. They know if they are getting better at something.

> . . . we must constantly remind ourselves that the ultimate purpose of evaluation
> is to enable students to evaluate themselves. (Costa 1989)

> The goals of thoughtfulness are that students internalize capacities to evaluate their learning, do so as they learn, and so in ways that exhibit their capacity to be performing thinkers, problems solvers, and inquirers. (Brown 1989)

I have followed this sound advice in different ways. I once worked with high school students in problem solving. After one student solved one problem, I asked, "What did you do to solve it?" After he listed a few processes, I asked his classmates, "What did you see Chris do that reflects good thinking?" They mentioned a number of different processes and dispositions: "He identified the problem . . . looked for alternatives . . . showed persistence . . . checked his answer. . . ." I then asked students what they understood by "persistence." They told me, "Sticking with something . . . not giving up." Then I asked, "Now, how could I tell if someone in this class was being persistent?" They responded by generating a list of things I could look for: "There'll be a lot of work on the paper. . . . If there is a mistake you'll see cross outs and start overs. . . . they'll ask for help from others and not only the teacher . . . etc."

These high school students, in other words, were very good observers of their own ability to persist in problem solving. All we have to do is include them in the evaluative experience.

We return now to Mary Mulcahy. At the beginning of this chapter, we saw how she engaged her first and second graders in a wide variety of problem-solving activities over several weeks' time. After the last session, she decided she wanted to find out what her youngsters thought about their own thinking. She asked them: "Were you a good thinker today?" She wanted a record of these proceedings, so she brought her microcassette to school and passed it around to her students as they answered her question. Here are a few responses:

John said, "I was a good thinker, because whenever we do this I think more because other people are coming with solutions and I can add onto that or make comments. . . ."

Evan noted that he wasn't a good thinker, "because I was sort of copying other people's ideas. . . ."

And Bob reported, "Today I had lots of ideas because I understand the problem."

Mary asked Evan why he thought copying others' ideas was not good thinking, and he replied, "because it's like thinking the same thing."

Nicole added that her thinking on this occasion was good, "because I took time to think in between each idea."

And Matthew said with excitement, "I think we're doing so many of these things [problem solving activities] that I'm getting better and better at it."

Obviously these youngsters are able to compare their performance with each others' and with their own earlier in the sequence of these problem-solving experiences. Some of their criteria for "goodness" appear to be numbers of ideas, taking time to think, figuring things out for yourself and not copying, and understanding the problem.

At another point Mary asked her students, "How would you teach someone else to be a good thinker?" Once again she received clearly articulated responses:

NICOLE: You have to make the problem littler.

LISA: State your problem over and over again. . . . Get it down on paper before you talk to a group.

JOHN: To try to solve something you say it in your head. . . .

ANDREW: Take the problem and add new things to it . . . combine two things. . . .

From both of these examples you can see that Mary's first and second graders had become quite observant of their own thinking. What can we do with this information? Here are two suggestions:

Ask students periodically to evaluate their own thinking performance individually and in groups.

Develop a class list of thoughtful behaviors, then challenge the class to take one of the characteristics and set group or individual goals for improvement. After this kind of activity, one group of fifth graders decided that they wanted to rely more on themselves and not so much on others, especially the teacher, when they faced a difficulty. Consequently, they weren't so inclined to rush up to their teacher with questions they could perhaps answer themselves.

Of course, you run into some difficulties doing this. One high school student evaluated his own thinking and came to the conclusion: "I'm becoming too repulsive about my own thinking."

Sylvia Mathis used a somewhat different strategy to gather information from students grades 1 through 6. She asked all of them to write me letters because I was interested in what they were learning about their own thinking. "He is especially interested in wait time, but he would also like to know about anything else that might be helping you become a good thinker." Subsequently, I received in the mail a large batch of letters with students' assessments of what helps them think. Here are a few samples:

Hear is something about wait Time. you Stop your Bain and slow down. Matt, Grade 1.

Brainstorming. Like if you have a problem and don't know how to solve it, and then all of a sudden an idea pops into your head. Some people would probably take that first idea, but if you "brainstorm," and maybe take the sixth or seventh, that idea is more creative and unusual than the first. . . .Charlotte, Grade 5.

The building and surroundings of our school makes you think alot. The pictures and paintings on the walls that other classes did, make you think. Just changing classes make you think. For example, every school morning I change for math: I have regular Math on Monday and Wednesday, and Pre-Algebra on Tuesday and Thursday. When I change I think about:

What book am I going to have to bring?
Did I do my homework?
Are we having a test today? Maria, Grade 6.

Maria's questions seem quite reflective; they are the kind of metacognitive awarenesses that may result from the wide variety of thinking activities within Sylvia's school.

Reading the many letters children wrote gives one the impression that they have learned some very specific characteristics of teaching practices like *wait time,* thinking skills words like *brainstorming,* and the benefit of some of their special programs like Think About and the use of Thinking Hats (de Bono 1985). There is general agreement, for example, among all students' writings about the meaning of wait time and brainstorming. Sylvia, therefore, has done a good job in her various visits to these classrooms in helping students think through the meaning, value, and usefulness of these means for improving our thinking.

Sylvia's letters are another means of acquiring information on the question: "What are our students learning about thinking, about their thinking, and how it is useful in their lives?"

Using Audio- and Videotapes

John Erickson of Hopkinton, Minnesota, and Peter Johnson of Waukesha, Wisconsin, have for the past several years worked with teacher volunteers interested in learning about their questioning, waiting, responding, and ability to engage students in peer interaction. For this purpose teachers have made many audio- and videotapes, listened, and viewed them in order to learn more about their own teaching. Teachers have discovered that, "I asked good questions, but students didn't answer as I expected." "I learned [such and such] about my teaching."

We can show these tapes to students and ask them to reflect upon their own performance with the following kinds of questions:

What do you notice about your own behavior?
What instances of intelligence, thoughtfulness, good thinking do you see? Give specific examples.
What is facilitating our thinking here? (Elicit characteristics of the environment and our own teaching.)
What would improve your ability to think? (Elicit suggestions for improvement that become our goals.)

I have learned much from watching myself on videotape. The last tape I viewed showed that my ability to generate ideas was getting in the way of responding to a student's question. He posed the question, and I began associating his question with many different ideas that then spawned a brief discussion. After viewing this in class I asked him, "How did you feel about the discussion?" He responded, "I felt a little left out and wondered if my question were going to be answered."

So sometimes having a lot of ideas is good, but at other times it can be an impediment. After this I began to see my teaching as related to the way I write: Sometimes there are just too many ideas.

CONCLUSION

I have attempted to share with you ways in which many teachers have begun to focus upon the thoughtfulness within their classrooms: by assessing the strengths of their students and setting goals. Teacher observation, informal assessments in writing, students' portfolios, students' self-reflections, teacher and supervisor observations, and the use of videotapes are all possible ways of collecting information. Once we have done this, we can set modest goals and work toward one or two of them at a time.

Asking the kinds of questions of ourselves and of students suggested here often reveals the marvels of the inventive mind. Here is third grader Mike from Sylvia's school reflecting upon his thinking:

Dear Dr. Barell I think Waittime is a good and fair thing to do. I think it's such a good ting t do I do it evry single day use waittime to make a imaginary box to put troubles in.
                                   from
                                   Mike
                                   Mehr

Figure 4.2.

In the next chapters, 5 and 6, I shall ask us to think about how to create an environment that is invitational to the kinds of thoughtful behaviors discussed here, making specific suggestions for developing skills and attitudes. In Chapters 7–11 I shall attempt to deal with instructional and curricular planning that focuses upon stimulating thought as we did with the *Franklin in the Dark* episode: through problem identification and resolution.

REFERENCES

Arlin, Patricia. See Arter and Salmon, below.

Arter, J., and J. Salmon. 1987. *Assessing Higher Order Thinking Skills: A Consumer's Guide*. Portland, OR: Northwest Regional Educational Laboratory.

Baron, Jonathan, and Alan Glatthorn. 1985. "The Good Thinker." In *Developing Minds*, ed. Arthur Costa. Alexandria, VA: Association for Supervision and Curriculum Development.

Brown, Rexford. 1989. "Testing and Thoughtfulness." *Educational Leadership* 46 (April), 7:31–35.

Costa, Arthur. 1989. "Re-Assessing Assessment." *Educational Leadership* 46 (April), 7:2.

de Bono, Edward. 1985. *Six Thinking Hats*. Boston: Little, Brown.

Edwards, John. 1991. "The Direct Teaching of Thinking Skills." In *Learning and Teaching Cognitive Skills*, ed. Arthur Costa. Melbourne: Australian Council for Educational Research.

Ennis, Robert, and Jason Millman. 1985. *Cornell Critical Thinking Test. Level X*. Pacific Grove, CA: Midwest Publications.

Feynman, Richard. 1985. *Surely You're Joking, Mr. Feynman, Adventures of a Curious Character*. New York: W. W. Norton.

Forman, Ellice, and Myra Kraker. 1985. "The Social Origins of Logic: The Contributions of Piaget and Vygotsky." In *Peer Conflict and Psychological Growth: New Directions for Child Development*, ed. M. W. Berkowitz, No. 29, pp. 23–29. San Francisco: Jossey-Bass.

Furth, Hans, and Harry Wachs. 1974. *Thinking Goes to School: Piaget's Theory in Practice*. New York: Oxford University Press.

Granito, Lois. 1990. "Initial Research on Metacognition in Mathematics." Unpublished manuscript. Montclair State College.

Highet, Gilbert. 1954. *Man's Unconquerable Mind*. New York: Columbia University Press.

Meyers, Chet. 1987. *Developing Critical Thinkers*. San Francisco: Jossey-Bass.

Mosher, Ralph. 1979. *Adolescents' Development and Education, A Janus Knot*. Berkeley, CA: McCutchan Publishing Corporation.

National Assessment of Educational Progress. 1986. *The Writing Report Card*. Princeton, NJ: Educational Testing Service.

Newmann, Fred. 1990. *The Relationship of Classroom Thoughtfulness to Students' Higher Order Thinking: Preliminary Results in High School Social Studies*. Madison, WI: National Center on Effective Secondary Schools.

Norris, Stephan, and Robert Ennis. 1989. *Evaluating Critical Thinking*. Pacific Grove, CA: Midwest Publications.

Peel, E. A. 1974. "A Study of Differences in the Judgments of Adolescent Pupils." In *Adolescence: Studies in Development*, Z. Cantwell and P. Srajian. Itasca, IL: Peacock Publishers.

Perkins, David. 1981. *The Mind's Best Work*. Cambridge, MA: Harvard University Press.

Piaget, Jean, and Barbel Inhelder. 1958. *The Development of Logical Thinking from Childhood to Adolescence*. New York: Basic Books.

Pressley, Michael, et al. 1987. "What Is Good Strategy Use and Why Is It Hard to Teach? An Optimistic Appraisal of the Challenges Associated with Strategy Instruction." Paper presented at the annual meeting of the American Educational Research Association, Washington, D.C.

Resnick, Lauren. 1987. *Education and Learning to Think*. Washington, DC: National Academy Press.

Rogoff, Barbara, Mary Gauvain, and William Gardner. "Children's Adjustment of Plans to Circumstances." In *Blueprints for Thinking*, ed. Sarah Friedman, Ellen Scholnick, and Rodney Cocking. Cambridge: Cambridge University Press.

Schroder, Harold, Michael Driver, and Siegfried Streufert. 1967. *Human Information Processing, Individuals and Groups Functioning in Complex Social Situations*. New York: Holt, Rinehart & Winston.

Sigel, Irving, Carol Copple, and Ruth Saunders. 1984. *Educating the Young Thinker*. Hillsdale, NJ: Lawrence Erlbaum.

Sternberg, Robert. 1985. *Beyond I. Q.: Toward a Triarchic Theory of Human Intelligence*. Cambridge: Cambridge University Press.

Waterman, Robert. 1987. *The Renewal Factor, How the Best Get and Keep the Competitive Edge*. Toronto: Bantam Books.

Wolvin, Andrew, and Carol Coakley. 1985. *Listening*. 2d ed. Dubuque, IA: Wm. C. Brown.

CHAPTER 5

Designing a Classroom That Invites Thoughtfulness

OVERVIEW

In this chapter I explore ways of designing a classroom environment that invites students' thoughtfulness. Two components of the environment are addressed: dispositions to undertake problems and pedagogical processes such as questioning. I suggest strategies that involve self-coaching, using the concept of internalized self-talk to reach these objectives.

TWO CLASSROOMS THAT INVITE THOUGHTFULNESS

When we visit Mary Mulcahy's elementary school classroom not only do we observe the students posing and solving problems, but we also observe the conditions that foster these intellectual adventures.

If we were to visit Rosemarie Liebmann's high school classroom, we would observe not only that Emily and her friends write extensively about their thoughts in Thinking Journals, but also that, as in Mary's classroom, there is an environment that nurtures the risk taking these students feel comfortable with. In both, the teachers engage in specific, powerful pedagogical practices that communicate to students the essence of thoughtfulness: that their ideas are important and that being open to others' ideas helps us learn. In short, in both classrooms, you would notice teachers inviting their students to think.

What is it about these classrooms that invites thoughtful participation? First in importance, perhaps, are belief in one's ability to think and solve problems, the development of an internal locus of control, and the resultant disposition to persist. Second is openness to other persons' ideas, listening, and cooperation. Finally—an absolute essential element for the creation of an invitational environment—is control shared between students and teacher.

These are dispositions, or habits of mind, we encourage on the very first day of classes in September, to communicate this message: *In this classroom we use all our intellectual abilities to our utmost, we believe in ourselves, and we respect each others' ideas and points of view.*

PEDAGOGICAL STRATEGIES THAT FOSTER THOUGHTFUL BEHAVIOR

There are a wide variety of strategies that challenge students to risk thinking through complex and novel situations. In addition to knowing about such strategies, we should also be aware of the power of scripts that we have written and continue to write on the tableaux of our minds. Such scripts act as the documents that condition our actions. Scripts are one form of self-talk—we say things to ourselves (as Ryle noted) in similar situations.

For example, how often do we confront a certain problem or dilemma and exclaim, "Oh, I'm no good at doing this kind of thing!" This is a conditioned response, a script we have internalized over many years, perhaps as the result of early difficulties. Unfortunately, when it comes to certain problems—often in mathematics—students by the second grade have internalized such scripts. They feel "You know it or you don't." By high school the scripts are so embedded that we hear students telling us, "Look, why don't you just tell us the right answer!" As Langer (1989) notes, "The grooves of mindlessness run deep. We know our scripts by heart."

Where do these memorized lines of self-talk come from? From our experiences with parents, teachers, friends, and so forth.

The most important aspect of this situation is that our attitudes and consequently our performance are modifiable. In this sense, we can use scripts to conduct self-coaching—talking ourselves into or out of various kinds of behavior.

Mental health experts tell us that we can alter our behavior by changing the nature of our thinking. Langer (1989) quotes philosophers such as Marcus Aurelius, who said, "Our life is what our thoughts make it." We transform our lives by altering the kinds of thoughts and images we flood our minds with. We can, therefore, coach ourselves into the attainment of certain goals by analyzing and altering our self-talk from "I panic when I see such problems" to "I can do it if I persist."

Golf professional Hubert Green exhibited such self-coaching when during a tournament he was overheard talking to himself:

No, no, no, Hubie. You don't go for pars anymore. Amateurs go for pars. You're a pro now. You go for birdies and eagles. You forget about pars. *Birdies. Eagles.* You're a *pro.* (Hoff 1988)

Hubert Green walked all around the golf course "*constantly establishing his expectations for himself*" (Hoff, emphasis added). And this is what we want our students to learn to do in the invitational environment: coach themselves through all twelve years of school and well beyond. In order to accomplish this they need our help.

Frameworks for Modifying the Classroom Environment

In this chapter I am presenting frameworks for considering a number of different environmental concerns and instructional processes. Each framework acts as an organizer or a way of working toward the development of thoughtfulness. Here are the framework elements:

> Name of environmental concept or instructional process—Locus of Control or Quality Responding, for example.
> Research—evidence that such concerns are important.
> Teacher Self-Talk—what the teacher might say to him- or herself or to the class.
> Student Self-Talk—what students might learn to say to themselves as they become more thoughtful.
> Strategies to Effect Desired Change—experiences that help us reach our goals.

These frameworks can work in several different fashions. One way is for us to identify a need and strive to meet this need through our given curriculum. Lois Granito discovered that her second graders were giving up on math problems within a matter of a few seconds, saying, "I'm no good at this stuff." In other words, they were saying to themselves, "If I can't solve this in 15 seconds, I'll never be able to do it. I'm no good at numbers." This is a very self-defeating kind of script, especially at such an early age. She decided to make increased student confidence in their ability to solve most problems and student persistence in trying a variety of strategies her priorities. She used mathematics as her primary vehicle within which to work toward these objectives. She modeled more positive self-talk: "When I have a problem, I must be patient, think of all the information I know and try out different ways to solve it. I must persist." She also gave her students opportunities to engage in small group problem solving and large group discussion of varieties of strategies for problem solving. Eventually they wrote about their problem solving in their Thinking Journals. (See Vanessa's entry, Chapter 11.)

Here is how one teacher integrated a concern for belief in the power of thinking and persistence within her standard curriculum. These frameworks are meant to provide suggestions for your doing the same.

Lois further exemplifies the inquiring spirit (Chapters 6, 13, and 14) that identifies a need in terms of patterns of student and teacher behavior, seeks and selects reasonable alternatives to reach a goal, and then reflects upon her own practice.

Let's now look at the nature of the invitational environment. We will start with one of the most important elements of any designed setting.

Use of Physical Space.   The design of any environment begins with analyzing how we want to use the space. How should the elements within that space be arranged so as to reach our objective?

Research. Where students sit in the classroom has a direct effect upon their participation in class activities (Good & Brophy 1984). Teachers tend to call upon a select group of students found close to the teacher's desk. Those sitting in front tended to have positive attitudes toward learning; they "felt they had the capacity to succeed in school and reported working hard to get good grades." Those who preferred the rear of the room reported "negative attitudes toward school, studying, and their own capacity for success" (Weinstein 1987, p. 545, reporting on a high school study by Walberg).

Teacher Self-Talk. "I want to arrange the space in my room to give students maximum access to each other, to information, and to me."

Student Self-Talk. "It is important for me to sit where I can see and hear my friends and the teacher."

Strategies

>   Mary Mulcahy gathered her first graders around her as they discussed the problems mentioned above. Students sat in a semicircle on a small carpet around her. The seats in her classroom are formed into a U-shape, which facilitates discussion and mutual exchange of views.

>   When I begin my class I usually ask my graduate students to place themselves in a circle. A circular formation is the one that allows me access to everybody almost equally—whether I sit in the circle or use center stage. Since I conduct most of my classes as large group discussions, the circular formation is most suitable. Whenever we have problems to solve or case studies to examine, I use the small group formation.

These strategies focus upon seating arrangements, because they are one of the most important manifestations of our attitudes toward teaching and learning. We are all used to having students sit in rows where they are perhaps more easily controlled. Consider the circle: Here no one can hide behind Brenda's or Steve's head; everyone is equally open to inquiry, because everyone's face is visible.

In your Thinking Journal, jot down your own strategies. Continue to do so as you finish each of the succeeding elements.

Now we come to those dispositions that represent the core of our concept of thoughtfulness: our belief or confidence in our own ability to think.

Belief in Our Own Thinking Abilities

Research. Good thinkers "value rationality, believing that thinking is useful for solving problems . . ." (Baron & Glatthorn 1985). "Good strategy use is more likely to occur when people consider themselves to be agents who can control their own fates than if they think they are simply pawns in some impossible-to-control system . . ." (Pressley 1987).

Teacher Self-Talk. "When I uncover a problem or difficulty I enjoy trying to think of new and different solutions."

Student Self-Talk. "I like to think through situations that have some difficulty to them—some areas of uncertainty where I can think up different kinds of solutions. I believe that I can succeed if I try hard enough and work intelligently—using good strategies."

Strategies

TEACHER MODELING Practice presenting your own script to students. Communicate the enjoyment and frustration you feel in finding, analyzing, and working toward solutions to difficulties and uncertainties in your life and in your subject matter. (For this to work, obviously, we must be genuine in what we communicate: We *believe* that with time, persistence, and a lot of effort we can solve a lot of problems.)

GROUP PROBLEM SOLVING Form the class into small groups. After their work has been completed ask, "What did you contribute? What does this tell you about the power of your thinking? Of the group's working together? What are you especially good at? What did you learn by listening to others? What are you going to try to improve upon?" The point of this strategy is for students to see that they can make a contribution, even if, initially, it is small—for example, acting as recorder or the person who keeps everybody on task. Recording how they contributed to the small group in Thinking Journals will be advantageous for students if they reflect on them periodically.

BEST STRATEGIES In Mary Mulcahy's class, students developed their own list of the ways in which they like to solve problems. This list (prominently displayed in the room for all to see) included such strategies as "Take parts out of the problem you don't really need. . . . Look at the problem from a different angle. . . . Make sure the problem makes sense. . . . Add to someone's thinking . . . Have confidence in yourself." Whenever we solved a problem, Mary or I would ask, "Which of your strategies did we use today?" and students would point to ones they used. I think in this way we worked toward their having confidence in their own ways of thinking.

VISUALIZATION Have students actively practice visualization techniques. (Imagine yourself being successful solving problems. With that picture in your mind, talk to yourself: "I can succeed if I put my mind to it and persist.") Visualization is one of the most powerful thought conditioners, because it sets up specific expectations that we then work toward.

Locus of Control

Research. Persons with an internal locus of control attribute their success to their own effort and abilities. Persons with an external locus tend to attribute their performance to luck, chance, or characteristics of the task. Persons who attribute success to their abilities and efforts are more likely to succeed at what they want to do (Thomas 1980).

Teacher Self-Talk. "*I* am responsible for my own success—not luck! When I succeed and/or fail at a task, I must examine what I did to bring about this result: How was I acting responsibly here? What did I do to contribute to my success and/or failure? How will I act differently next time to improve?"

Student Self-Talk. "If I am to succeed, I should learn that I am responsible for my own successes—not the teacher, primarily. I must make sure I understand the task and use appropriate strategies, because the results I get will be largely the result of the persistence, effort, and ability I use."

Strategies

TEACHER MODELING Think aloud saying, "How did I learn to act responsibly? How and when did I learn that I was responsible for my own success and/or failures and not luck or chance? How easy and/or difficult was it to do this? How do I go about analyzing results to determine what I was responsible for?"

GROUP DISCUSSION Take any task or problem students have engaged in: doing chores at home, making money, succeeding in sports, making friends, settling arguments, etc. Ask some of the following questions to help them see the relationship between outcome and their effort:

> What did you have to do?
> Did you accomplish what you set out to? Did you reach your objective?
> What did you do to obtain these results? How were you responsible for your results? What didn't you do that would have altered the results more to your liking?
> What will you do differently in the future? Why?
> How do you feel about these results? Why?
> Why did you (or did you not) take responsibility? What does it mean "to take responsibility" for one's actions?
> What are you learning about taking responsibility for your own success and/or failure?

REPETITION OF ABOVE This time use examples from students' school work. Gradually, they will see the relationship between their efforts and the results observed.

VISUALIZATION AND SELF-TALK "What image do you create when you think of someone who is successful and feels responsible for his/her own success? (What words do you hear in your mind?) What do you need to say to yourself before, during, and after a task or problem to ensure that you take responsibility for the outcomes?"

Achieving the sense of being in control of your own life, being your own pilot, and not a tape recorder, is the essence of this book. It is not a task for one teacher in one classroom; rather, to become an originator and not a pawn is a lifelong task facing Emily and every one of us.

Persistence

Research. "Persistence and involvement in the problems [is] highly correlated with success in solution: The more intelligent individuals [do] not give up, nor [do] they fall for the obvious, but often incorrect, solutions" (Sternberg 1985).

Teacher Self-Talk. "If I keep at it, I can usually solve most problems. What I need to do is to keep on trying and to remember that persistence most often pays off."

Student Self-Talk. "I must learn that with persistence I can find an answer or solution to most situations. If I keep at it, I will succeed."

Strategies

TEACHER MODELING   Present as many examples as possible of how we have acted with persistence and the kind of results we obtain. What role did persistence play in our successes or lack thereof? What other attitudes were important to our achievement? Use professional as well as personal examples.

DEFINE THE WORD "PERSISTENCE"   Ask students to define the word and compare theirs with a dictionary definition: "To continue steadily or firmly in some purpose or course of action, especially in spite of opposition" (Random House Dictionary, 1967). It might be wise to ask students to define the word first. Discuss the sort of obstacles we all encounter as we face problems and strategies for overcoming them. Which of these strategies can we use here in school? Where? Which have you used and with what success? Cindy asked her fourth graders to define a number of characteristics of good thinkers (listening, cooperating, overcoming impulsivity, persisting, etc.) and to give an example. One student defined persistence and gave as an example Mozart's difficulties in publishing one of his sonatas; another student recalled Harriet Tubman's persistence in helping to free runaway slaves through the Underground Railroad.

DISCUSS PROBLEMS OUTSIDE THE CLASSROOM   "Where have you encountered a problem and kept at it until you resolved it? What helped you be successful? Why did you persist? [Seek underlying motivation.] What kinds of attitudes were required to solve these problems? What did that prove to you? How can you use these strategies here in school?" (The point here is to start with students' lives outside school, where they have no doubt persisted in the attainment of several different kinds of objectives, despite obstacles. *It might also be important for students to identify the kind of problem that does not yield easily to persistence: divorce, other people's selfishness, etc.* Students should develop a sense of those problems that lend themselves to their control (e.g., their attitudes and action) and those that do not so readily (e.g., other people's attitudes, beliefs, and actions).

REPEAT ABOVE   using situations in school.

RECORD RESULTS IN THINKING JOURNALS   Have students write a monthly summary of what they are learning about their thinking abilities and attitudes.

These attitudes and feelings about ourselves are so important because, without them, we are not likely to enjoy challenges of various kinds, and we shall be forever enslaved by scripts that say, "Oh, I'm no good at that sort of thing." We want to empower ourselves and our students with scripts that say instead: "If I persist, I know I can conquer this problem, that I can reach my goals." Remember the oft-cited challenge: "If you can imagine it, you can achieve it!"

Now we come to the enhancement of our respect for and attention to the thoughts and feelings of others. Without such feelings of respect and openness, we stand a chance of growing up to be more egocentric than thoughtful. Our openness to alternatives involves the disposition to want to hear what others have to say and to realize that we can learn a lot from listening to others' ideas. Remember the second grader who evaluated her own thinking as not very good, "becs [sic] I did not open my mind."

Openness to Alternatives

Research. "Openness, not only to new information, but to different points of view is also an important feature of mindfulness. . . . Once we become mindfully aware of views other than our own, we start to realize that there are as many different views as there are different observers. Such awareness is potentially liberating . . . change becomes more possible" (Langer 1989).

Teacher Self-Talk. "Am I open to all the possible solutions or interpretations? How do I ensure I'm maintaining an open mind about all possibilities in this situation?"

Student Self-Talk. "Have I considered all factors? How can I look at this another way?"

Strategies

TEACHER MODELING   By our own thinking through situations aloud, we communicate to students our degree of openness.

PRODUCTIVE THINKERS   Examine the works and thinking of persons within your school or community, or prominent in history who seem to reflect varying degrees of openness to different problematic situations. For example, Einstein welcomed others' pointing out errors in his thinking because this would bring him closer to the truth.

SMALL-GROUP PROBLEM SOLVING   Share with students some content-free problems, for example, "Your friend hit a ball through a neighbor's window" or "There is too much noise for the teacher in the classroom," in small groups and give them specific directions to "Examine these from as many perspectives as you possibly can." Ask students to "Think of as many different ways of looking at this problem as possible. How many problems do you see here?" Then compare results, not to find the correct one, but to see how flexible people are in their thinking.

THINKING JOURNALS   Using a model such as "What was the problem? How did you solve it? Did you solve it well? What would you do differently next time and why?" students will have an opportunity to reflect upon their openness.

Listening.   If we spent the better part of a year helping students listen to each other, we could do much to enhance their tendencies to question and respond to each other intelligently.

Research. Persons who listen well, who can receive another's message, who relate to what the other person knows, who understand the reasoning behind the message and put themselves in another's shoes are better able to respond thoughtfully in a discussion. Listening is a prerequisite to becoming more of an empathic person. Dillon (1988) notes: "It may surprise us to learn that both wrong and right answers and smart and dumb pupils bear listening to . . . you might prefer to stay a bit with both kinds of answer given by both types of pupil, until such time as you have appreciated the knowledge that led each pupil to give either answer."

Teacher Self-Talk. "What am I listening to? What is the topic about? What do I already know about it? What does it relate to? What do I think will come next? Do I understand the reasoning/story line? How well did I do?"

Student Self-Talk. "Do I understand what I am listening to? Can I identify the topic? What do I already know about this topic? Can I relate the topic to my experience? What do I think will happen or be presented next? Do I understand the reasoning involved? Was I right? If not, do I understand why not? How well did I do?"

Strategies

TEACHER MODELING   Share your listening strategies with your students: "I physically attend to the speaker [by leaning slightly toward the person]. . . . I attempt to establish and maintain eye contact [this is not always easy and takes concentration] . . . and, most important, I try to clear my mind of extraneous stuff while listening." This final point is extremely important, because too often we are preparing our next question, not listening.

ASK THE STUDENTS   "How do you know when someone is listening?" Benna Kallick uses this strategy effectively, and I have found that students are very good at telling us what is involved in listening: "looking at the person . . . being able to repeat, add on, or comment upon what someone else said."

GENERAL PRACTICE   Divide students into triads and assign three different roles: speaker, listener, observer. Give students one sentence, one paragraph, or a brief story to tell. Have the listener engage in the following: repeating word-for-word what was said, summarizing the major points, and then selecting one idea to add onto or comment upon. I have had a lot of fun with this kind of exercise, and students, mostly adults, find that listening requires more concentration than they usually provide in such circumstances.

MODELING WHAT NOT TO DO   Karen Mahn taught her first graders a valuable lesson about listening when she invited several fifth graders into her class to model poor small-group-interaction practices. "They're not listening to each other!" exclaimed Karen's students (among other observations), and, henceforth, her students were much more conscious of how to behave well in small-group problem-solving sessions (Mahn 1989).

ANALYZING   In a recent staff development meeting, Bill, a fifth grade teacher, said, "We need to get students not only accepting information but processing it." "How?" I asked. "By having them analyze and evaluate what they are hearing." Here is the kind of self-talk we want to encourage in our students while they are listening and then contribute to the discussion:

> Do I understand what the speaker is saying?
> Do I agree/disagree with what is being said?
> Can I relate this to anything in my own experience?
> What do I think will come next [if listening to a story]?
> What questions do I have about the subject? What am I curious about?

LISTENING   In Carol Cutrupi's fourth grade classroom, students are taught to listen to each other and to respond, "I agree [or disagree] with your idea, Robert, because—" Hand raising is discouraged, so students will look at and listen to the speaker.

Cooperation

Research. Cooperative interaction in schools leads to higher levels of achievement, improved self-esteem, and positive attitudes toward school (Johnson & Johnson 1986).

"The discussion process in cooperative groups promotes the discovery and development of higher quality cognitive strategies for learning more than does the individual reasoning found in competitive and individualistic learning situations" (Johnson & Johnson 1983, cited in Kohn 1986).

Teacher Self-Talk. "In this classroom we cooperate with each other. . . . This means that we listen to each other . . . we help each other whenever we can . . . try to ask for others' help before asking me."

Student Self-Talk. "I can learn more if I am willing to work with others. If I cooperate by listening and helping others, we all will learn better."

Strategies

TEACHER EMPHASIS   At the beginning of the year we should emphasize that in this classroom we all learn together—that we will use a variety of means to help students learn cooperatively. Listening to each others' comments will be very important.

TEACHER MODELING   "Here's what I have learned about cooperating with others in my life and this is how I have benefited."

COLLABORATION   Provide students with opportunities to work collaboratively with each other:

1. Pose a problem for students to think about. Then have them share responses and arrive at consensus or agreement. Emphasize listening, finding answers to questions from classmates, not the teacher, checking each other, and being responsible for knowing how others arrived at their answers (Daniels 1990). As a variation, challenge them to develop a response or solution collaboratively.
2. Cooperatively check homework for accuracy, conceptual understanding, and ability to describe another's way of thinking through a problem or issue.
3. In her high school math classes, Rosemarie Liebmann used small-group problem solving and "think aloud" strategies so often that at semester's end one student evaluated his class by saying, "We are like a family." Requiring more emphasis upon social skills of interdependence, these groups can learn to work collaboratively with good teacher nurturing and coaching on how to help each other figure out problems and not just give answers.
4. Composition pairs. "Student A explains what she or he plans to write to Student B [who] takes notes or makes an outline. Together they plan the opening or thesis statement." Then reverse the process, exchange outlines and use them to write essays (Johnson, Johnson & Holubec 1987, 1988).

THINKING JOURNALS   Ask students, "What are we learning about problem solving?" They will begin to respond as John Borchert's eighth grade science students did: "It is much easier to work as a group, because more is getting done. [I'm] also learning that even a very small group can make a difference."

Ask them to record instances where they worked collaboratively and to express what they learned from the process. Ask them how they can transfer those learnings to the classroom.

POSITIVES AND NEGATIVES   After group work discuss these. Be prepared to help students listen and ask questions so they can become good coaches, not just givers of information. Discuss how students feel about cooperative work.

The last strategy is very important because attitudes like openness to alternatives and a willingness to cooperate obviously involve feelings of safety, security, and comfort to varying degrees. Furthermore, a class discussion may be the best way to help students become better coaches; coaching requires the ability to pose questions and to listen, to determine what the difficulties are.

Sharing Control with Students.   *We, the adults, do more to stifle students' thinking than perhaps any other element I could identify.* We do this by the kind of problem we do not present students to solve and by the ways in which we respond to students' answers or comments. We control by making all the decisions about what is to be learned, how, when, where, why, and what grade to put on it after it is over.

It is, therefore, necessary to emphasize from the very first day of school that this is *our classroom:* Here we work together toward common goals. Here everybody has some responsibility for his/her learning and for that of others as well. Students will not and cannot feel empowered if everything is done for and to them. If they have no opportunity to set goals, design strategies, and feel responsible for these decisions, they will leave school with less than a feeling of confidence in their own ability to take control of their own lives.

Research

Students make very few decisions about their own learning (Goodlad 1984).

Persons will work more effectively and diligently within settings where they have exercised some personal control than in settings where they have no stake in the outcome. "If people think they have even modest personal control over their destinies, they will persist at tasks. They will do better at them. They will become more committed to them. . . . The fact . . . that we think we have a bit more discretion leads to much greater commitment" (Peters & Waterman 1982, p. 80).

Shared decision making can positively and directly affect teachers' "degree of energy, dedication and mutual support" (Ashton & Webb 1986, p. 121).

"When we are mindful, we see all sorts of choices and generate new endpoints. The opportunity to make choices increases our motivation" (Langer 1989, p. 85).

Teacher Self-Talk. "This is our classroom. What rules do we need in order to work well together? How should we arrange our space in order to listen to and work well with each other? How can each of us work collaboratively to learn what we must learn?"

Student Self-Talk. "How do I wish to participate in this class? What roles and responsibilities will I assume? How do I learn best, and how can I make decisions about my own learning?"

Strategies

USE OF CLASSROOM SPACE   Here is a relatively easy place to begin discussing how we can use our space so we all learn to the best of our ability.

CLASSROOM CONSTITUTION   Rather than have the teacher lay down the law on the very first day, some, like Carol Cutrupi, have asked, "What are rules? Why do we need them? What kinds of rules should we have in this classroom?" Students create some rules for their behavior, and then toward midsemester they evaluate them and revise as necessary. This is another opportunity to reflect upon our experience by planning, monitoring, and evaluating. (See Chapter 11.)

SUBJECT MATTER CONTENT   Here is a more difficult area for most of us to consider sharing control with students. But many teachers have identified areas wherein students can exercise some control over decision making:

1. How to study: alone, in pairs, small groups, etc.
2. How to acquire knowledge: books, tapes, working together on projects, etc. Here we can attune ourselves to some of the students' individual differences such as their auditory, kinesthetic, and visual abilities.
3. How to report about learning: individual reports, group efforts, speeches, role-plays, visual representations, etc. Again, another opportunity for students to reflect and act upon their individual learning preferences.
4. How to evaluate learning; students devise questions. Also let students participate in evaluating their own work: "How well do you think you did? What might you do differently next time? Why?"
5. There are also questions that focus upon our objectives: "What do you know about the beach? What do you want to know? How will we find out?" In Chapter 7 I shall describe how one first grade teacher used this strategy and how she was surprised at what her students transferred from one situation to another.

In Chapter 13, I will share with you the personal reports of two teachers who have experimented extensively and quite successfully with sharing control. Our goal is an improved sense of efficacy: "I can control my fate."

Some Frameworks for Instructional Processes

Concomitant with establishing a warm, supportive environment full of healthy, nurturing kinds of attitudes, we need to spend some time examining our instructional processes—those skills we use to present content or to disclose the nature of important concepts, ideas, skills, processes, and attitudes. Each of these processes has been selected because of the effect it will have upon facilitating the empowerment of students' thinking and behaving.

Goal Setting.   There may be no more important process in the development of empowered persons than goal setting. We know from the world of business that successful managers are ones who set reasonable, attainable goals for themselves and for their employees (Boyatsis 1982). Peters's (1987) and Waterman's (1987) books on excellence and organizational renewal stress the importance of goal setting. In their first joint effort (*The Pursuit of Excellence*, 1982) they identify some of the significant characteristics of excellent companies:

> Virtually all of the excellent companies are driven by just a few key values, and then give lots of space to employees to take initiatives in support of those values—finding their own paths, so making the task and its outcome their own. (p. 72)

Thus, the excellent companies these authors studied were ones that took advantage of "yet another very human need—the need one has to control one's destiny." In other words, they encourage employees to set goals for themselves, for their own productivity.

It seems that most successful people decide they want to do something, establish a reasonable goal, figure out how to get there and continually monitor their progress toward this goal. If this is so, why do schools spend virtually all of their time telling students what to do and how to do it, leaving almost nothing for them to figure out on their own?

Research. "Students in the classes we observed made scarcely any decisions about their learning, even though many perceived themselves as doing so" (Goodlad 1984).

"Students do not often get involved in projects where they and their classmates set and achieve goals that are important to them" (Goodlad 1984). The view that emerges, continues Goodlad, "is one of students increasingly conforming, not assuming an increasingly independent decision-making role in their own education."

When students do set goals for their own learning, they profit by improving their achievement levels, developing more of an internal locus of control, and becoming more aware of their own problem-solving capabilities. "The extent to which students see themselves as a cause of their own behavior may be the single most important determinant of continued motivation" (Thomas 1980).

Teacher Self-Talk. "I have learned that, if there is something I really want, I usually have to set a goal to achieve it. Often I write down these goals and list the ways or plans I will use to reach them. Periodically I must monitor my progress. Goal setting becomes easier and easier as you learn what you want and how you can get it."

Student Self-Talk. "What is my goal [what problems am I trying to solve]? What kinds of strategies [or plans] can I think of to help me solve this problem? How well am I doing? How well did I do? What helped me achieve my goal? What hindered my progress? What would I do differently next time and why?"

Strategies

TEACHER MODELING Show students how we set and achieve goals. Use examples first from our lives outside school and then, perhaps, refer to professional goals. Finally, demonstrate how every instructional task involves goal setting and deciding upon a plan of action.

GROUP DISCUSSION Give students opportunities to relate some of their own experiences with goal setting. "What have you wanted very much [the goal]? How have you attempted to get it [the plan or strategy]? How successful were you [evaluation]? What did you learn about yourself? Your planning? What kinds of feelings did you have at the beginning? The middle? Toward the end? How might you proceed differently next time?" Then pose this question: "How do these lessons apply to our classroom? How can we all learn from our collective experience with goal setting?"

STUDENT PRACTICE Give students opportunities to set goals for their lives in general or for work in your classroom. In Viola Stanley's sixth grade classroom, we spent two months helping students set and achieve personal goals. (See Figure 5.1.) This process grew out of an earlier social studies unit studying Columbus

INDIVIDUAL GOAL SETTING

NAME _____   DATE _____

OBJECTIVE _____
(State exactly what you wish to accompish; e.g., "To improve my grade in this class from _____
to _____"; "To improve my test results from _____to _____"; "To complete my homework on
time"; "To spend more time paying attention in class"; "To ask better questions to improve my
understanding.")

TIME _____
(Time by which you wish to accomplish this objective.)

REASON _____

_____
(State why the reaching of this objective is important to you.)

STRATEGY
(What is your long-range plan for reaching the objective? List specific steps you will take to
reach the objective that is important to you.)

    1.
    2.
    3.
    4.
    5.

                        SIGNATURE _____

Figure 5.1. Goals.

as a person who had a vision, who set goals and designed strategies to attain
them. Thus, students had a model of a real person who worked toward a long-
range goal. Students had little difficulty in setting some reasonable goals relating
to their personal lives: not biting fingernails, eating more fruits and vegetables,
becoming more organized, and not fighting with siblings and parents. We did not
stress academic goals, because our primary intention was for students to have a
positive experience with setting and achieving an attainable goal. We hoped this
experience, if treated reflectively, would transfer into their academic lives. Here
is some of what they noted upon completing this process:

1.   "In [using my] Thinking Journal and in goal setting I have learned how
to think of a goal and then go through the steps and strategies to accomplish that goal. I have learned to always follow something through. Never
quit in the middle of a goal or anything else in life . . . that you not only
use these strategies for goal setting, but also if you have a problem or
something you could think of ways to solve it, by breaking it up and
approaching it from all sides. . . ."

2. "I learned that you have to have strategies for your goals if you intend to accomplish them. You also have to concentrate on your goal so that you don't forget about it. Another step to reaching goals is to keep trying like Christopher Columbus. If he had given up, we would have never heard of him this day. . . ."

3. Goal setting was important for several reasons. "First, you learn how to set your goal and write strategies to complete your goal, you get that extra confidence sometimes when you complete or start to complete your goal, also cause everyone helps you complete it they tell you new strategies and tell you sometimes what your doing wrong. . . ."

STUDENT GOALS   Using the same format Rosemarie Liebmann and I have helped high school students set goals for the improvement of their own learning. In this instance we focused more upon academic achievement. Here are some of the lessons we have learned in the process of working with elementary and high school students:

1. Students often have difficulty identifying a worthwhile goal. Very often they select something very global, for example "to graduate with all A's" or "to become a rock star." These are fine for the long duration, and what we can do with them is to help students break them down into manageable parts so they are working toward something of shorter duration, where they think they have a chance at success. Students have difficulty here, because they have not had practice in writing down their own goals. It is definitely a skill they (and some of us) need to practice.

2. The next area of difficulty students encountered was determining a strategy. Most of the high school students' goals had to do with grade improvement. And how were they going to do this? "Study harder. . . . Study more. . . . Do more of the same." Well, doing more of the same is not going to help us become better. We spent a lot of time breaking down the idea that more of the same would result in improvement.

   Very often students just couldn't think of strategies, so we used a large group problem-solving format. For example, in Viola's classes one of her students wanted to stop fighting with and talking back to her parents. The initial strategy she came up with was "Just do what they tell me." But after some discussion, where other strategies were suggested, someone said, "Maybe you should talk it over with your parents." What was interesting here was that, given some time to think about strategies, students' thinking went from an immediate, somewhat impulsive response to one that might get at the source of the problem. (Just as Jennifer's solution did with Franklin: "Get embarrassed and go in.")

3. The second goal setting format (Figure 5.2) is the experiential record: "This is what you said you were going to do. What did you do and what did you learn from the experience? Now redirect your efforts toward your goal." Viola Stanley's students responded to the question "What have you learned about your own thinking, the effort you put into reach-

ing your goal?'' with new insights into themselves. Todd discovered that he was ''lazy'' and Megan that ''You can achieve if you try.'' Kate noted that even though she failed she ''never gave up,'' and Beth observed, ''Not everyone is perfect and everyone has their faults.''

A final word: All of what is written here relates to an instructional process without, so far, a word about the subject matter content. Obviously, goal setting is used in service of learning the subject matter and taking responsibility for one's success in that endeavor. Goals can be about improving grades, but they could also focus upon understanding and using key concepts, ideas, and skills within any subject. (''How are you going to master punctuation? How will you come to understand force vectors thoroughly?'')

Goal setting is a first step toward our own and student empowerment. What I want to see in classrooms is more of the entrepreneurial spirit that you so often find in successful business organizations. Isn't it just possible that we could look upon students as young entrepreneurs and ensure that they have opportunities to take control, to innovate, to carve out a tiny niche within the subject to learn

NAME _____   DATE _____

ORIGINAL OBJECTIVE (Restate your Original Objective):

INTENDED STRATEGY: Restate briefly your original plan for reaching this objective.

1.
2.
3.
4.
5.

ACTUAL STRATEGY: Describe here what you actually did to accomplish this objective.

OBSTACLES/FACILITATORS: What got in the way of your reaching the objective? Why? What will you do differently now?
What helped you reach the objective?

GROWTH: What did you learn from these experiences that can be applied to your plan for reaching objectives next week/month/semester/year?

1.
2.
3.
4.
SIGNATURE _____

Figure 5.2. Experience and Growth Report.

more about, to conduct a little research, do a little writing, explore some hidden questions, and follow their own curiosities? Seeing our students as entrepreneurs means we value their setting some goals of their own and giving them credit for doing so.

Setting High Expectations.   To expect "implies confidently believing, usually for good reasons, that an event will occur" (Random House Dictionary). Expectations refer to what we live up to—those self-imposed or externally presented ideals, values, or rules that we believe we will work toward or enact. Entrepreneurs are people who live by very high self-generated expectations for success and taking calculated risks. Schools are places, like the home and work, where we create environments that set certain kinds of expectations for behavior. What kinds of expectations are fostered within these academic settings?

Research

1. Many students "seem satisfied with their initial interpretations of what they have read and seem genuinely puzzled at requests to explain or defend their points of view" (National Assessment of Educational Progress 1981). Students, in other words, expect that we their teachers will accept their one-word, rather superficial responses. They are not used to being challenged to defend, extend, clarify, or explain how they derived their answer or idea.
2. "Low expectations combined with an attitude of futility will be communicated to certain students, leading to erosion of their confidence and motivation for school learning" (Good & Brophy 1986).
3. Teacher "efficacy," or the belief that all students can achieve was a contributing factor to student achievement and the attainment of project goals in various change efforts (McLaughlin & Marsh 1978).

Teacher Self-Talk.   "In our class everyone can do very well. . . . Everyone can succeed who tries and persists. I expect everyone to participate and to contribute to class."

Student Self-Talk.   "I will be about as successful as I make up my mind to become. If I try hard and persist in my efforts, I probably will succeed."

Strategies.   I shall group the strategies for communicating high expectations in four categories: (1) use of direct statements; (2) how we respond to students' comments; (3) using wait time; and (4) students' generating their own problems. The obvious means of telling others what we expect is to do just that, and this category is reflected in the Teacher Script above.

USING DIRECT STATEMENTS   Teachers, like Beth Via in first grade, make statements that set the tone and the level of expectations. On the first day in school Beth says to her youngsters, "You are all members of the First Raters Club. We will all learn to read either by ourselves or with the help of our friends." Here the message sets the level of expectation, and it clearly identifies two major possible strategies: independent work and collaborative problem solving.

RESPONDING TO STUDENTS' ANSWERS   Be sure to encourage all students to clarify, expand, or explain their answers or comments. As Dillon notes (1988), we should expect those with wrong answers to clarify their thinking just as much as those with correct responses.

When students of perceived lower ability respond, do not let them off the hook with silence. Brophy and Evertson (1978) found that in lower-ability classes, effective teachers spent more time working with individuals "especially attempting to elicit improved responses" (p. 117). This communicates to such students the message: "I am worth the teacher's spending time with." Over time this process will have a positive effect.

USING WAIT TIME   A friend of mine once noted about my teaching: "You very early on communicate high expectations."

"How?" I asked.

"Well, one of the things you do is wait for people to respond. You don't immediately go on to someone else if there is not an answer immediately forthcoming." If we wait upon people, that evidently tells them, "I am expecting that you have a response, and it is worth waiting for."

ENCOURAGING STUDENTS TO GENERATE THEIR OWN PROBLEMS   Goodlad reminds us that if students engage in creating their own problems to solve (as they do in Karen Mahn's and Mary Mulcahy's classes), there is a good possibility of their setting their own standards. After students have completed their work, we can ask them to evaluate their project in accordance with their own expectations.

Modeling.   A "model" is often referred to as an example or structure worth imitating. It is also used in science to refer to a visual representation of complex and often invisible phenomena (such as a model of the atom or the inner workings of a galaxy). Teachers model when they stand in front of the classroom or behind the desk or sit in a circle with their students. Here we are exemplifying attitudes and ways of perceiving that are important. We can also model our thinking by speaking about it, voicing our thoughts in front of students, and creating pictures of how the human mind functions.

Research.   Bandura writes (1986): "Learning cognitive skills can be facilitated simply by having models verbalize their thought strategies aloud as they engage in problem-solving activities [p. 74]. . . . Learning cognitive strategies that are not directly observable can be greatly facilitated by cognitive modeling [p. 89]. . . . Of particular interest . . . is evidence that modeling improves conceptual functioning, even in children who are lacking such cognitive skills [p. 102]. . . . Children and adults who suffer deficiencies in problem solving learn effective strategies by observing how successful models go about gaining information for evaluating alternatives [p. 103]. . . ."

"Observers who code modeled activities into either words, concise labels or vivid imagery learn and retain behavior better than those who simply observe . . ." (Bandura 1987, p. 720).

Teacher Self-Talk. "I will attempt to model my own mental processes for you whenever we encounter a new and different kind of problem by 'thinking aloud' etc. I want you to watch what I do and listen to what I say, because I am attempting to share my thinking with you."

Student Self-Talk. "I should watch and listen for good thinking."

Strategies

TEACHER MODELING   At every opportunity, especially when introducing new ways of thinking (e.g., problem solving, classifying) we should show students how we employ the process or skill using the precise vocabulary of the processes we are modeling (e.g., "generating alternatives, comparing, evaluating"). This will not be easy if you have never done it before. But here's a way to begin:

Begin by observing and attempting to describe how you think through a difficult situation: "How did I approach it? How did I plan to take action? What helped/hindered my progress? How did I feel? Did I visualize? Reduce the problem? Relate it to others? What did I learn about my own processes?" Identify specific thought processes, for example, relating.

Next, I attempted to make sense of what I had done by analyzing and evaluating my thinking, using criteria such as effectiveness and openness; then I put them in an order.

Then I might share my thinking with a friend or with my class to learn more from their feedback.

This form of modeling—using one's personal life—I term *retrospective modeling*—it looks back to a pattern of thought experienced in the past.

Another form that I use is to think aloud through a situation or problem that I haven't seen before. This I call *real time modeling*. Here we think through a problematic situation that we haven't seen before, to give our students the experience of watching the thinking develop. Any problem within our own subject matter is useful for this, and I have seen experienced teachers share their thinking through very complex problems presented by their students, and, much to their credit, they say, "You know, this is giving me a lot of difficulty, but I'm sure I can figure it out."

Students are not given many experiences in observing our vulnerabilities when it comes to thinking through problematic situations. One English teacher, Doreen Guzo, presents her short stories to students and "thinks aloud" through some of her difficulties with such elements as plot and characterization, thus modeling the essence of the creative process. This is a most powerful strategy in our effort to create a community of inquirers.

Problem Posing.   In his book *Frames of Mind* Howard Gardner has developed a definition of intelligence that focuses upon problem solving: "enabling the individual to resolve genuine problems or difficulties that he or she encounters and, when appropriate, to create an effective product" (1985). This definition also includes the ability to find and create problems as well, "thereby laying the groundwork for the acquisition of new knowledge" (p. 60).

In presenting problem posing as an instructional process, I am focusing upon what we do to foster thinking. We present situations, conflicts, dilemmas, questions, problems that will cause students to initiate an inquiry process—that is, they begin to question and pursue meaning and/or solutions. I realize that this process is a twofold one: Usually teachers present the problems, but we are striving for students' being empowered to pose some of their own dilemmas and work toward solution. The research and strategies presented below will consequently deal with both.

Research. Most of the talk in the classroom is done by the teacher, and most of this talk seems to make few intellectual demands upon students. "Not even one percent [of teacher talk] required some kind of open response involving reasoning or perhaps an opinion from students" (Goodlad 1984). In other words, not many problems are posed that require reasoning from information.

Problems that are posed are framed primarily by the teacher or a textbook. Research on 500 college laboratory science manuals indicates that there were no exercises "where students were required to play any role in recognizing a problem or designing an experiment or methods and materials needed to investigate a problem" (Hegarty-Hazel 1987 p. 300).

". . . instruction which has as its aim the development of thinking should allow students opportunities to generate and test hypotheses within the context of the discipline being taught. Simply providing students with ready-made hypotheses and cookbook recipes for their verification is not sufficient" (Lawson, Karplus & Adi 1978, p. 471).

The "predominant use of higher level questions during instruction has a positive effect on student achievement" (Redfield & Rousseau 1981, p. 244).

Reasons of equity may be among the most important ones for challenging students with problems to solve. Fromberg (1989) reports that in some schools the press is for children to respond behavioristically to academic workbook type problems stressing rote learning. Often the students who receive this approach come from "low-income and culturally varied groups" (p. 395). On the other hand, "more successful children are more often engaged in creative tasks and are asked to respond to questions that call for analysis, evaluation, and synthesis." Fromberg's major interest is in the kindergarten curriculum, but her observations and resulting call for greater intellectual equity resonate throughout the curriculum from kindergarten to high school and college.

Teacher Self-Talk. "Instead of giving you [the students] questions that can be answered 'yes or no,' I'm going to give you situations that have some kind of conflict or dilemma within them so we can all think productively."

Student Self-Talk. "I expect to be challenged with situations where I have to use my head, and not just fill out Scantron-sheet kinds of multiple choice answers."

Strategies. We will spend a lot of time in Chapter 7 reflecting on the process of posing dilemmas or conflicts for students. Here I will present a few suggestions for a problem-posing approach to instruction.

TEACHER GENERATED PROBLEMS You might begin with "content free" problems such as, "You left your key inside the house and are locked out" to see how well students can identify the problem and generate alternatives. You can move to problems in your school and to ones students identify to give them the same kind of practice. We began this way both in Mary Mulcahy's first and second grade as well as in Rosemarie Liebmann's high school classrooms. The purpose here is to give students practice in identifying and responding to these questions: What is the problem? How can you/we solve it?

The next step is to move to problematic situations within your content area and to respond to questions like these:

How many different solutions/responses can you think of?
What would happen if we used this solution? What would be the consequences of each?
How are they similar and/or different?
Which would you choose? Why?
Can you generalize from this example about solving problems like these?
What have you observed about your own thinking by using this process?

This process can be used in any subject at any grade level; it only depends upon our (or students') ability to identify problematic situations, conflicts, or uncertainties.

Another way of presenting students with dilemmas is to confront them with constraints in their search for alternatives. Sigel (1985) uses what he calls a "distancing strategy" to help students think through a complex situation. For example, in speaking with a young child, he would ask, "How did you get to your grandparents' house yesterday?" The child would respond, "In Daddy's car." "How else might you have gone?" Sigel would then ask in an attempt to help the child move away from the immediate and concrete to think productively of alternatives. We can use this strategy of searching for alternatives whenever there are different ways of solving a problem, varied interpretations for a passage, different means of testing a hypothesis, multiple causes for an event, etc. This search for alternatives is one way of helping students recognize and deal with those "discrepancies" that often stimulate thinking. In asking the child to consider alternatives, the teacher or parent is "creating a discrepancy between what was (the ride in the car) and *what might be* or *might have been*" (Sigel 1979, p. 175). In this example, we place the responsibility for generating a solution upon the child, and "it is this type of responsibility, in the context of problem solving, that enhances cognitive growth" (Sigel).

Another strategy is to use a hierarchy of questions such as that published by the Illinois Renewal Institute. (See Figure 5.3.) We can ask questions that proceed up the scale from input, through process, to output in order to foster more complex mental operations. For example, you might ask "who was Columbus?", then proceed to the analyzing level with "How would you compare Columbus with present day astronauts?" Finish with the more complex issue, "Suppose there were no explorers in the twenty-first century, what would be the consequences?"

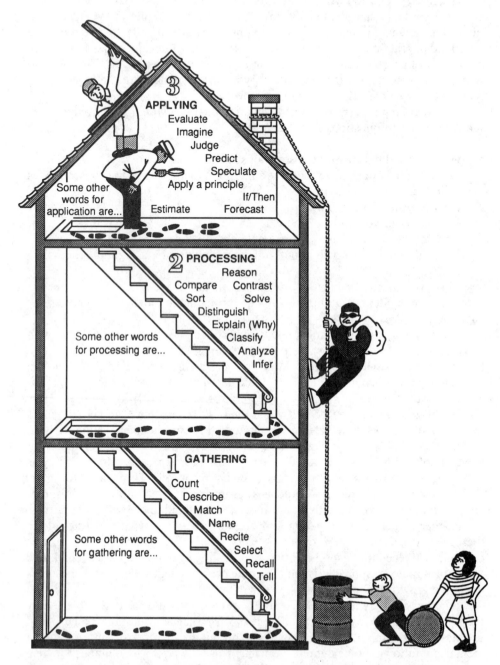

Figure 5.3. Three-Story Intellect. *Illinois Renewal Institute/Skylight Publishing Inc., 1990.*

A more challenging way is to present students with a dilemma that starts with a "What if" or "Imagine" question. In other words, start at a more difficult level to engage students' interest and then gather the required information as you work through the problem. For example: "What if the ozone layer continued to deplete? If the globe continued to warm?" This problem requires a lot of research and acquisition of information, as well as application of principles and comparison of data to arrive at a reasonable set of conclusions.

All of these operations invite the search for alternatives, overcoming obstacles, selecting from options, using criteria; acting, and evaluating.

Thus, this taxonomy need not be followed in a lockstep fashion. As I suggest later (Chapter 13), it is an excellent practice to observe and monitor the kind of questions we ask in the classroom. We know from many years of classroom observations that our questions are usually toward the lower levels of this taxonomy, and many of us have set goals to work toward more complex challenges.

STUDENT GENERATED QUESTIONS Isidor Rabi became a physicist because his mother always asked him, "Izzy, did you ask a good question today?" We need to spend a lot more time with students posing their own questions and not merely responding to ours. There are many ways to begin this process:

While inquiring about dilemmas and problems suggested above, provide students with opportunities to pose their own questions: What puzzles you now? What are you curious about? What do you wonder? This can be done by having students write down their own questions during class or for homework and then grouping students heterogeneously, challenging them to answer each others' questions. Those questions that students cannot answer can then go to the teachers. This is a good opportunity for more cooperative thinking and learning.

Another strategy is to challenge students to pose their own questions as they read material and to come to class prepared to put them up for discussion. Usually my students pose two kinds of question: ones reflecting their lack of understanding of a concept ("I'm not sure what he means by . . .") and ones that are speculative ("I was wondering what would happen if . . ."). Both kinds help me create a discussion about the major ideas within the chapter we are reading. Again, I group students to answer their own questions cooperatively, and our general large group discussion alternately focuses upon questions that clarify difficult concepts and those that speculate, wonder, or otherwise go beyond the text (Level 3 in Figure 5.3).

One of the best strategies I know of now for helping students pose their own problems comes from my friend Doreen Guzo, a high school English teacher. She has students write a process or Thinking Journal while they are reading a novel. Students respond to various stems like "This reminds me of . . ." "I wonder why . . ." and "This seems important because . . ." In Chapter 11 I share several excerpts from her students' journals and discuss how they reflect their thinking. These process journals are very valuable resources, which help students communicate their understanding and lack thereof very directly to us. We can ask students to share their puzzlements in dyads, small groups, or with the large group, and in time we will have the environment described above: "We are like a family."

Finally, some teachers have taken the questions in Figure 5.3 and taught students the differences between the several levels of questions and used this knowledge to help them pose better questions about their reading and problem solving. For example, Jo McCauley of Jamestown, Pennsylvania, has developed a long-range strategy for elementary students to improve their reading skills through generating three different levels of questions: literal, inferential, and problem-oriented. Students might examine photographs and pose questions about them. "The children analyze the questions generated and evaluate them using the criteria given. . . . The questions are then analyzed to determine what key words may be clues to literal questions" (1988). This process is repeated for inferential and problem-solving questions, and then Jo moves on to helping students pose questions about complex sentences such as "Three young boys with guns over their shoulders walked quietly into the woods following the barking dog." Obviously, student-generated questions can spark much productive discussion.

Silence.   Once someone, presumably the teacher, has posed a question, how long does he/she wait before rephrasing the question or calling upon someone else? In other words, how long does the potential respondent have to think about his/ her response?

Research.   The average wait time for teachers is approximately two to three sec-onds—that is, from the end of the teacher's question to a response from a student, or from the end of the student's response to the teacher's response. When we increase the wait time from two to three seconds to, say, more than five, we observe these positive results:

1.   The length of student responses improves between 300 and 700 percent.
2.   The incidence of speculative reasoning increases.
3.   Students' responses reflect more inferential thinking, and more infer-ences are supported by evidence.
4.   The number of student questions increases.
5.   Failures to respond decrease.
6.   Disciplinary moves decrease.
7.   Student self-confidence improves. (Rowe 1987)

Teacher Self-Talk.   "I will wait for you to answer. Please don't expect me to move along quickly just to get any answer. I am very interested in what your thinking is, whether or not you know the answer." (To self: As I wait upon students' answers/responses, am I really ready for anything they might say? Am I ready to follow up by probing their thinking? Will I be genuinely interested in how they are processing the information, what it means to them, etc.?)

Student Self-Talk.   As I wait I should be thinking of the following: "What is the question being asked? What do I know about it? How would I approach answering it?" (When someone else answers the question) Would I have answered the same way? Why? What might I have done differently? Why? Do I want to ask any clarifying questions?

Strategies

OBSERVE YOUR OWN SILENCE OR WAIT TIME DAILY   This kind of limited, specific objective is the best way to begin. By means of videotape, audiotape, or student/ faculty observers, begin to obtain an objective record of how long you wait between the end of one question and the beginning of another question or statement. Work consciously, by counting silently to yourself after a question: "One thousand one . . . one thousand two . . . one thousand three . . ." etc. You can devise a variety of strategies that help you become more conscious of this most important element in classroom interaction.

One mathematics teacher I worked with, Richard, was not aware of the short time he gave students to work out very complex second-year algebra problems until he and I sat in front of a video screen and actually measured his wait time. He was surprised that it was only between two and three seconds. Thereafter, he set his own professional development goal: to improve his wait time, and this he did by making several audiotapes of his teaching the same class.

RESTRAIN YOUR ANXIETY   How do we overcome our anxiety about the silences that we will encounter? I still, after years of realizing the importance of wait time, become anxious with graduate students when I pose a question, look around the room, see and hear no indications of responding. I must bite my tongue and tell myself, "You've just asked a very complex question! Wait. Give them time to think." Eventually, someone will break the silence.

Some suggestions that might work for you are the following:

Clueing students that you are interested in this specific behavior and giving them the reasons. Let them help you listen.

Developing a significant acronym as the teachers in River Edge, New Jersey did: TNT—Thinking Needs Time. They set this expectation for their elementary school students, and eventually students would say to them after receiving a thought question, "I'm still thinking. Remember, TNT!"

Two schools I know of have devoted entire school years to examining the meaning and function of wait time. In these schools, one of which was directed by Esther Fusco (Babylon, New York), devoted whole faculty meetings to this significant topic. The reason I mention this here is that when everybody is focusing on her/his wait time, it becomes much easier to share what occurs within the classroom. With such collegial support, teachers were able to probe the question Esther posed: "When we, the teachers, are waiting, what are the students supposed to be doing?" This question focuses upon the Student self-talk I mention above for "listening" and "silence."

TEACH THE MEANING OF WAIT TIME   Sylvia Mathis of Wasatch Elementary School in Salt Lake City, Utah, has taught many students in all grades the meaning and value of wait time. Here are some of their definitions:

Dane (Grade 3): "Wait time is better because the teacher waits and the kids get better ideas. Wait time is a good idea I think because it gives time to imagine."

Elizabeth (Grade 3): "I think wait time is fair because then more people have more [time] to think."

Annie (Grade 3): "Wait for someone to stop talking. Think of something wonderful. If you listen you can learn more. . . ."

Julia (Grade 5): "Wait time is to wait before you answer a question or to think before you do something to see if you should do it or not."

Sylvia has demonstrated that young students can become familiar with pedagogical practices that affect the quality of their thinking. The above comments were written to me in the form of letters that attempted to explain "anything that might be helping you become a good thinker." This was an excellent assessment instrument.

Quality Responding.   In this section I am concerned with how we respond to each other as human beings, as persons who recognize and value the other's worth and individuality. We invite students' thinking to the degree we respond with words, gestures, and tones that are encouraging.

Research

1. The tone of voice we use in responding to a student's question or answer communicates our interest in what that student has said. Over time these messages tell the students whether or not we are genuinely interested in hearing from them, in knowing what they have on their minds and in learning from them (Sigel, 1985).

2. There is an evident dearth of "process questions" in most classrooms K–12. We are seldom interested in the students' reasoning, focusing much more closely upon their attainment of the "correct" response.

3. Effective teachers spend more time working with individuals "especially attempting to elicit *improved responses*." (Emphasis added.) "There was much support for aspects of what Flanders has called indirect teaching, particularly praise (at least in public interactions) and use of student ideas. Again . . . this assumes a context of strong academic and demanding orientation" (Brophy & Evertson 1978, p. 117).

4. "Teachers were not responding to students in large part because students were not initiating anything. Or when a teacher sought and got a student's response, the teacher rarely responded in turn directly to that response with supportive language, corrective feedback, or some other meaningful acknowledgment. Teachers' responses . . . were more likely to be non-personal, such as 'all right'—a kind of automatic transition device in a presentation directed to the whole class" (Goodlad 1984, p. 229).

5. Teachers rarely, if ever, respond to the emotional content of a student's answer or comment (Aspy 1985).

Teacher Self-Talk. "Do I understand how the student arrived at his/her solution/ question/response? How can I ensure that all students understand what is being said? How can I learn more about what the students are saying, thinking and feeling?"

Student Self-Talk. "Do I know how I would respond to that question or statement? How would my response be different? Do I understand why the other person responded as she/he did? What can I do to find out how she/he arrived at that conclusion?"

Strategies. There are many ways for us to alter how we respond to students. We can observe our patterns of interaction informally and in the privacy of our own rooms. Here are several suggestions:

USE AUDIO- OR VIDEOTAPE   This can reveal significant patterns of interaction. For example, the last time I taped my own teaching, I learned that in responding to a question I began to associate freely, generating a host of ideas to which others responded. The result was that the young man who asked the question began to feel that his inquiry had been lost in the shuffle. I learned to be more direct in my responses.

INVITE A COLLEAGUE TO OBSERVE YOUR CLASS   The observer will be able to provide feedback on the kinds of questions you pose (see Figure 5.3) and the responses you use (see below).

There are many different ways of analyzing our responses to students' comments. One effective framework examines responses according to whether or not they facilitate further thinking or effectively prevent thinking from developing. Responses that might *impede further thinking* include

"Correct. Next question!"
"No. That's not what I was thinking of. Does anybody else know the answer?"
"O.K. But there's more to it than that. Anybody else?"

Responses that *invite thoughtfulness* include

Redirection: "Amy, what do you think of Terri's answer?" "Who can answer David's question?" "How many agree or disagree with Jennifer's reasoning?"
Eliciting feelings: "How did that make you feel?" "How do you feel about this?"
Elaboration: "Very interesting. Please tell me more about what you are thinking."
Clarification: "I'm not sure I understand. Can you clarify this idea?"
Probing for thought processes: "I see. Please tell us how you arrived at your answer." "How did you arrive at that question/statement/perspective? Share your thinking with us, please."
Extension: "How does your response compare with Sarah's?"

Rethink original situation after changing variables: "I see. Now what if we restated the situation in this fashion?" "What would happen if we changed this?"

Transfer to own experience outside school: "Now how does this relate to your own experience?"

Transfer within subject area: "I see. How does this relate to what we have studied so far?"

Search for good reasoning—e.g., use of evidence: "Fine. Now, what are your reasons for thinking in this way? What evidence leads you to this conclusion? What assumptions are you making here?"

Evaluation: "Which response do you think is best and why?"

Let us look at several of these in greater depth:

ELICITING FEELINGS Unless we elicit feelings, we may not help students identify and deal with initial anxieties as they confront difficult problems. Feelings of frustration and doubt too often cause us to say impulsively, "Oh, I'm no good at this!" and to give up. Eliciting feelings provides an opportunity to acknowledge our discomfort and then to move on to more rational approaches to problem solving. We don't do this often enough, because there have been too few models in our experience from whom to learn, and we get embarrassed by others' feelings. Here are a few more model responses:

"Tell us, if you wish, how you feel about this kind of situation." (Elicits initial feeling response to a problematic situation.)

"I can see why you're confused. Those directions are unclear to me, too" (Costa 1985, p. 134). (Communicates empathy with students' difficulties in completing a task or solving a problem.)

One of the best entrees to students' feeling is their writing. As we shall observe later in considering Metacognition (Chapter 11), students like Rich, upon encountering a difficult problem, will write in their Double Entry Journals, "This problem scared me while reading it."

This is a very significant observation and a gutsy admission to his teacher. Rich has realized that problematic situations can send slight tremors of terror coursing through our bodies—and here was an algebra problem that had done so. He acknowledged his fear and then noted, "It got better after I read it 6 or 7 times. I just took it step by step. . . ." The writing helped Rich to follow a step-by-step procedure in overcoming his anxiety.

Another way to commence this process of empathic responsiveness is to ask children and adolescents, when confronted with a complex problem, "How do you feel about doing this?" Then, as Costa suggests, admit that we are often confronted with similar feelings. Our admission shows students that they are not alone, that they perhaps have an ally in working through the situation.

Finally, the concept of dealing with feelings by discussing the emotions of characters in literature and history is familiar to most teachers. "How did Lady Macbeth feel when Macbeth told her about the prophecies of the three weird sisters? How would you feel in similar circumstances? Have you ever been in such a situation?''

"How do you imagine Columbus's crew felt after being on board the *Santa Maria* for three weeks—sailing into the unknown, possibly over the edge of a flat earth? How would you feel? Have you ever felt like that yourself?" Fifth graders recently empathized with these crewmen: "I'd be very uncomfortable, hungry, tired, bored. . . . I'd feel dirty without my pajamas."

Feelings are the first indication that we are in a problematic situation, and we need to recognize, accept, and deal with them.

EXPLORING FOR GOOD REASONS We know from recent research (National Assessment of Educational Progress 1986) that very few of our students are able to provide evidence for their points of view (p. 9). Providing evidence suggests that one has a better reason for making a decision or judgment than someone who says something "just because that's the way I feel and my opinion is as good as anybody else's." Behaving intelligently means, in part, that we can provide reasons that rely upon evidence, experience, appropriate criteria, and so forth. For example:

TEACHER: Who do you think will win the next election?

STUDENT: The Republicans.

TEACHER: I see. Why do you think that?

STUDENT: Well, they always focus upon what's good for business, and the economy seems to be steaming right along, so I think more voters will return them to office.

TEACHER: I see. Can you share with us your evidence for this general statement? What assumptions are you making about political parties, the economy?

Here the student has given us reasons that can be debated. We can also tease out his criteria for making judgments.

ELABORATING UPON RESPONSES Very often students provide us with short, one-word, sometimes superficial responses. By asking for elaboration ("Please tell me more") we are placing a demand upon them to become more specific, to provide us with more of the thinking that led to the response and, perhaps, to provide enough detail so we and others in the class can decide whether or not we agree or disagree. For example,

TEACHER: Which play did you enjoy more, *Hamlet* or *Macbeth?*

STUDENT: *Macbeth.*

TEACHER: Can you tell us why?

STUDENT: Because of the murder.

TEACHER: Please tell us more about this reason.

STUDENT: I don't know. I just liked that part.

We are not always going to be successful in asking for elaboration upon her or his choices or reasons. Many students are not used to exploring their own thinking and some will probably feel uncomfortable doing so initially.

SEARCHING FOR CLARIFICATION   Very often responses we hear do not initially make sense to us, perhaps because we expect a different answer or because we find it difficult to follow a student's line of reasoning. For example:

TEACHER: Stephen, I don't think I understand what you mean by *weird*.
STUDENT: Well, you know, *weird, crazy,* or uhmm . . . *imaginative*.
TEACHER: What does the word *imaginative* suggest to you?
STUDENT: Oh . . . *unreal,* you know, *fantastic*.

EXTENSION OF MEANING   Sometimes we want a student to extend his/her thinking to relate it to another's way of approaching the subject. For example:

TEACHER: "Sarah, how does your analysis of this chemical reaction compare with Bill's?"
STUDENT: I think it's better.
TEACHER: I see. Why?
STUDENT: Bill has neglected to take into account the characteristics of one of the reactants, nitrogen, and because of this omission he has miscalculated. . . .
TEACHER: Bill, do you agree?

TRANSFERRING THINKING PROCESSES OR CONCEPTUAL UNDERSTANDING   Very often we will want to break down some of the barriers between school and life beyond classroom walls. We want students to apply what they have learned in class to their lives at home or work or at play. We call this transfer. We know (Perkins & Salomon 1988) that transfer does not happen automatically, if at all. We can help students transfer their knowledge of concepts and skills close by, into the subjects they are studying by asking, "Where else have we used the idea of reciprocity?"

We can work toward expanding our use of concepts into other subject areas by asking, "Now, how can we apply these rules of equivalence to any other subject?"

We can help students build bridges from the classroom into the world beyond by asking, "Who can find examples of how builders use a knowledge of geometry in their home construction?"

And, perhaps even more importantly, we can help students bridge the yawning chasms between school and their personal lives by asking, "Brendon, how do you analyze problem situations that you encounter with your friends, parents, relatives, etc.?"

SEEKING METACOGNITIVE AWARENESS   Asking students to think about their own thinking ("Tell me how you arrived at that. . . . How did you solve/resolve that problem?") is part of a process of raising their consciousness and therefore improving their control over how they approach tasks. For example:

TEACHER: Who has an answer?
STUDENT: Twenty minutes.

TEACHER: Twenty minutes. Please tell us how you went about figuring this problem out.

STUDENT: Well, first I remembered doing a similar problem yesterday, so I knew I could solve it. [Related to prior learning.] Then I saw it as a time-distance problem [classification], so I looked for the key elements and first solved for time to get ready [reduced problem to several parts], and then solved for the final time and then I checked it backward [evaluated work].

TEACHER: That's an intriguing way of approaching it. Did anybody else proceed a little differently?

In her final comment the teacher is aware that this student's process achieved success, but another student might very well have analyzed the situation a little differently, and we can all learn from another approach.

One final note: Many students will have difficulty elaborating on their thinking or sharing their thought processes. We must be patient; we must also model our own thinking very extensively to show students how we share feelings or reflect.

Peer Interaction.   Most of the "responding" that occurs in classrooms does so between one student and the teacher. But if we give explicit instructions to students and provide opportunities for them to speak directly to one another, a practice called peer interaction, it will benefit their own learning and create an atmosphere of healthy inquiry. To use a basketball metaphor: We want to encourage all players to pass the ball around among themselves, not just toss it back to the coach/teacher. Such practices are the foundation for openness to the ideas and feelings of others as well as our intellectual growth.

Research

1. Students are rarely, if ever, encouraged to respond to the comments of their classmates.
2. In a study conducted in college classrooms, it was determined that if there were more student-to-student interaction and more use of student ideas, there would be an improvement in critical thinking (Smith 1977).
3. Controversy within the classroom when experienced among peers can result in "cognitive and moral development, the ability to think logically, and the reduction of egocentric reasoning." When students are challenged again and again through disagreements and arguments and are forced to "take cognizance of the perspective of others," they encounter the dissonance or discrepancy with their own viewpoints that can foster inquiry into other ways of thinking. These inquiries can result in high quality problem-solving and decision making (Johnson & Johnson 1979).
4. "Interpersonal interaction increases the number of ideas, the quality of such ideas, feelings of stimulation and enjoyment and originality of expression in creative problem solving" (Johnson & Johnson 1979).

Teacher Self-Talk. "How would you respond to Laura's comment? Clarify it? Expand upon it? Relate it to your own experience? How would any of you respond to Laura's thinking?"

Student Self-Talk. "What do I think of Laura's response? How would I respond similarly (for different reasons) or differently? and why? Do I agree/disagree and why? What can I add? What isn't clear to me about the topic? What questions do I have about what she is saying?"

Strategies. I find that peer interaction within the classroom is the element that makes teaching most exciting for me. When students spontaneously listen to and respond directly to one another's comments and arguments, I can assume several different roles: observer, learner, facilitator, monitor of progress, and devil's advocate. All of these roles are fun to play, and perhaps the most enjoyable is helping student reflect on their own thinking by asking, "What have you observed about your own thinking in this discussion?" Very often students note that they approach problems from very different perspectives. "Why is this important?" I ask, and they respond, "Because we can learn from each other. Perhaps there will be a problem in the future we can work through using someone else's ideas or strategies." This is one of the most beneficial aspects of our working hard to get students to listen to and respond to each other using strategies such as these:

SET HIGH EXPECTATIONS Tell students you expect them to listen to their classmates and respond to them as well as to you. Barbara was amazed one day in her high school English class to observe that students had actually listened to each other and commented upon their responses. "Why do you think this happened?" I asked. After some thought, she said, "Well, for the first time I told them right at the beginning that I wanted them to listen to each other and think about what the other person had said before they answer." It worked! All Barbara did was to communicate her expectations clearly, which she admitted she had not done up to that point.

USE QUESTIONING EFFECTIVELY Use redirect questions: "Who agrees or disagrees?" In her fourth grade classroom Carol Cutrupi always encouraged students to listen and respond to their classmates in a discussion in this manner: "I agree/ disagree with your statement, Jessica, because. . . ." She always told students not to raise their hands, because this fostered students' merely listening to their own ways of answering and not to their classmates. It worked very well. Try the no-hands-raised strategy.

USE COOPERATIVE LEARNING STRATEGIES Previously I have suggested several cooperative learning strategies you can easily use to encourage student cooperation. Obviously, they also nurture student interdependence, listening, and perspective taking. Strategies that will work very effectively include paired problem solving, homework and worksheet checkers, concept clarifiers (where pairs of students work to come to common understanding of a concept, e.g., mass), small-group problem solving, and jigsaw (Johnson, Johnson & Holubec 1987). In each case students are expected to work toward common understandings and be able to explain how others arrived at answers or perspectives. Very important questions about the meanings of concepts and ideas often result from such sharing— questions that sometimes students can answer and at other times require the teacher's response.

Barbara used small groups for homework checking and discussion very effectively. The assignment was to generate several alternatives open to Arthur Dimmesdale and to give a rationale for each (*The Scarlet Letter*). In their groups students were to analyze each, and, using a set of criteria, to determine the one they thought the best, giving their reasons why. It was during this sharing that students were listening to and responding to each other's ideas—thinking about their agreement/disagreement and offering critiques and evaluations.

Peer interaction is one of the most electrifying and stimulating processes when it occurs in our classrooms. It is worth all the effort we make to bring about this fundamental change. Peer interaction is one of the mechanisms that fosters the discrepancies and incongruities that stimulate inquiry. It is the means whereby we encounter new ideas and ways of seeing the world that foster our intellectual growth.

CONCLUSION

In this chapter I have attempted to outline several characteristics of the environment that invite students to think, take risks, and ask good questions. I hope that, by presenting some significant research findings together with practical, doable suggestions, we will be empowered to look at our own classrooms and ask, What patterns do I see? and, Do these help or hinder students' and adults' thinking? We might also attempt to determine the reasons why such patterns exist and if these reasons promote or constrain the development of thinking. Finally, we ask ourselves, What are my alternatives and which will I attempt first? Following such a process, we become models of good thinking, inquirers about what exists, and experimenters with a wide range of possible alternatives.

REFERENCES

Ashton, Pat, and Rodman Webb. 1986. *Making A Difference—Teachers' Sense of Efficacy and Student Achievement.* White Plains, NY: Longman.

Aspy, David. 1985. Personal communication.

Bandura, A. 1986. *Social Foundations of Thought and Action, A Cognitive Theory.* Englewood Cliffs, NJ: Prentice-Hall.

Bandura, A. 1987. In McLeod, G. R. "Microteaching: Modelling." In *International Encyclopedia of Teaching and Teacher Education,* ed. M. Dunkin. New York: Pergamon Press.

Baron, Jon, and Alan Glatthorn. 1985. "The Good Thinker." In *Developing Minds,* ed. A. Costa. Alexandria, VA: Association for Supervision and Curriculum Development.

Boyatsis, Richard. 1982. *The Competent Manager: A Model of Effective Performance.* New York: Wiley.

Brophy, Jere, and Carolyn Evertson. 1978. *The Texas Junior High School Study: Final Report of Process-Outcome Relationships.* Vol. 1. Austin, TX: University of Texas ED 173 744.

Costa, Arthur. 1985. "Teaching for, of, and about Thinking." In *Developing Minds,* ed. A. Costa. Alexandria, VA: Association for Supervision and Curriculum Development.

Daniels, C. W. 1990. In *Cooperation in the Mathematics Classroom,* ed. N. Davidson. Reading, MA: Addison-Wesley.

de Charmes, Richard. 1968. *Personal Causation, The Internal Affective Determinants of Behavior.* New York: Academic Press.

Dillon, J. T. 1988. *Questioning and Teaching: A Manual of Practice.* New York: Teachers College Press.

Fromberg, Doris. 1989. "Kindergarten: Current Circumstances Affecting Curriculum." *Teachers College Record* 90 (Spring), 3:392–403.

Gardner, Howard. 1985. *Frames of Mind. The Theory of Multiple Intelligences.* New York: Basic Books.

Good, Thomas, and Jere Brophy. 1984. *Looking in Classrooms.* 3d ed. New York: Harper & Row.

Goodlad, John. 1984. *A Place Called School.* New York: McGraw Hill.

Hegerty-Hazel, E. 1987. "Science Laboratory Teaching." In *The International Encyclopedia of Teaching and Teacher Education,* ed. M. Dunkin. Elmsford, NY: Pergamon Press.

Hoff, Ron. 1988. *"I Can See You Naked." A Fearless Guide to Making Great Presentations.* Kansas City: Andrews and McMeel.

Johnson, Roger, and David Johnson. 1979. "Conflict in the Classroom." *Review of Educational Research* 49, 1, 59–70.

Johnson, Roger, David Johnson, and Edythe Holubec. 1986. *Circles of Learning: Cooperation in the Classroom.* Edina, MN: Interaction Book Co.

———. 1987. *Structuring Cooperative Learning: Lesson Plans for Teachers.* Edina, MN: Interaction Book Co.

———. 1988. *Cooperation in the Classroom.* Edina, MN: Interaction Book Co.

Kohn, Alfie. 1986. *No Contest—The Case Against Competition.* Boston: Houghton Mifflin.

Langer, Ellen. 1989. *Mindfulness.* Reading, MA: Addison-Wesley.

Lawson, Anton, Robert Karplus, and H. Adi. 1978. "Acquisition of Propositional Logic and Formal Operational Schemata During the Secondary School Years." *Journal of Research in Science Teaching* 15 (November):465–478.

Mahn, Karen. 1989. "Mr. Detective, Can You Help Solve This Problem?" Unpublished manuscript. Montclair State College.

McCauley, Jo. 1988. "Questioning Techniques in the Elementary Classroom." *Cogitare* 2, pp. 3–4.

McLaughlin, Milbrey, and David Marsh. 1978. "Staff Development and School Change." *Teachers College Record* 80, 1:69–94.

National Assessment of Educational Progress. 1981. *Reading, Thinking and Writing.* Princeton, NJ: Educational Testing Service.

———. 1986. *The Writing Report Card.* Princeton, NJ: Educational Testing Service.

Perkins, David, and Gavriel Salomon. 1988. "Teaching for Transfer." *Educational Leadership* 46, 1:21–31.

Peters, Tom, and Robert Waterman. 1982. *In Search of Excellence.* New York: Warner Books.

Peters, Tom. 1987. *Thriving on Chaos, A Revolutionary Agenda for Today's Manager.* New York: Alfred A. Knopf.

Pressley, Michael, et al. April 1987. "What Is Good Strategy Use and Why Is It Hard to Teach? An Optimistic Appraisal of the Challenges Associated with Strategy Instruction." Paper presented at the annual meeting of the American Educational Research Association. Washington, D.C.

Redfield, D., and E. Rousseau. 1981. "A Meta-Analysis of Experimental Research on Teacher Questioning Behavior." *Review of Educational Research* 51 (Summer): 237–245.

Rowe, Mary Budd. 1987. "Wait Time—Slowing Down May Be a Way of Speeding Up." *American Educator* II (Spring), 1.

Sigel, Irving. 1979. "An Inquiry into Inquiry: Question Asking as an Instructional Model." In *Current Topics in Early Childhood Education,* Vol. II, ed. L. Katz. Norwood, NJ: Abex.

———. 1985. Personal communication.

Smith, D. 1977. "Classroom Interaction and Critical Thinking." *Journal of Educational Psychology* 69:180–190.

Sternberg, Robert. 1985. *Beyond I.Q.: A Triarchic Theory of Human Intelligence.* Cambridge: Cambridge University Press.

Thomas, J. 1980. "Agency and Achievement: Self-Management and Self-Regard." *Review of Educational Research* 50, 2:213–241.

Waterman, Robert. 1987. *The Renewal Factor, How the Best Get and Keep the Competitive Edge.* Toronto: Bantam Books.

Weinstein, C. S. 1987. "Seating Patterns." In *The International Encyclopedia of Teaching and Teacher Education,* ed. M. Dunkin. New York: Pergamon Press.

CHAPTER 6

Modeling, Inquiry, and Experimentation

OVERVIEW

There are three questions we should ask ourselves as we work with the environment that invites thoughtfulness: What am I learning about my own thinking? What am I learning about my students' thinking? and What are my students and I learning about the change process in designing this environment? Posing these questions for ourselves challenges us to confront and alter ineffective patterns of student and teacher behavior.

What would a school be like where one of the primary responsibilities of students was to learn to ask questions? There are not many models we can observe to answer that question, but at least there is one: Hampshire College. Established only two decades ago, Hampshire has been through some rough times, yet it survives.

"I've learned a lot here," one student recently observed, "[such as] how to ask questions. . . . You learn you should say what you want to say." Another noted that she had taken a course at a nearby university and "nobody asked questions" (Brown 1990, p. 58). "If the question mark had not existed, Hampshire would have invented it. The heart of the curriculum was asking questions: students learned 'modes of inquiry.' The new philosophy was summed up in the motto *Non Satis Scire*, To Know Is Not Enough" (p. 46).

The degree to which Hampshire has succeeded is not my interest here. What I appreciate is the fact that some people think what is important is teaching students—not just the body of knowledge within a subject, but the ways of thinking and inquiring within it. This may be more suitable for higher education, but I submit that we can and should adopt the underlying Hampshire philosophy: that inquiry is one of our most significant endeavors.

In the spirit of inquiry there are three questions that I think each of us needs to reflect on continually within the categories of modeling, inquiry, and experimentation:

Modeling: What am I learning about my own thinking?
Inquiry: What am I learning about my students' thinking?
Experimentation: What are we, collaboratively, learning about how to construct a thoughtful, invitational environment?

These questions are ones that guide the thinking of the reflective practitioner (Schon 1987) in her/his classroom. These questions are, for me at least, ones that enhance my teaching by presenting to me a challenge that changes with every classroom, every new group of students, and every new problem. I know the "material to be covered," but I seldom know in advance how my students will respond, how their thinking and feeling will wrap themselves around the ideas to draw conclusions and create their own meanings.

MODELING

I spent some time in the previous chapter with modeling and so will not cross over that territory in great detail. Let me just mention a few items.

What I wish to convey to students is an inquiring disposition or habit of mind about my own thinking. It is important for me to present my thinking, not as something that has reached a terminal point, but as a process I am continually attempting to refine. Once again I suggest a personal life strategy for its capacity to communicate meaningfully.

For example, I recently took my car in for a change of oil. I was pressed for time and for that reason did not step back and ask myself if there was anything else I should have taken care of while I was at the garage. Well, after the job was performed, I recalled that the last time the oil was changed, the mechanic used the wrong kind of washer, and all the oil subsequently leaked out within a few days. Following that incident I went to the manufacturer and purchased several washers to make sure it never occurred again. Unfortunately, this knowledge remained unused when it was most needed. Consequently, I spent a few minutes on hands and knees examining the spot beneath the car where the oil would leak if it were going to, and it didn't. I learned to be a little more circumspect in seemingly routine operations by asking, "Are there any other factors I need to consider here?"

In presenting this example to adults, I am attempting to model several process concerns:

That examples from our everyday lives should be brought into the classroom, because they tell students that the thinking that occurs outside school is important. This message is intended to show students that what they do outside school is think, and that this thinking can be helpful in mastering school subjects.

That my thinking is just like theirs: There are times like the above when I wished I had related one experience to another and thereby saved myself some discomfort. I wish I had been more deliberate.

That I am always striving to improve by becoming more conscious of the processes I do and do not use. As Costa and Lowery (1989) note, we should use the language of thoughtfulness, and here I referred to relating, being deliberate and not impulsive.

Of course, on other occasions I share with participants thought episodes that are different in that they model a better use of some of the problem-solving processes. For example, in checking into a hotel in Atlantic City, my wife and I encountered a darkened room. The young woman attendant said, "The light's probably burned out. I'll call Maintenance." My wife asked how long that would take and was told, "About half an hour." I didn't want us to wait that long in the dark, so I went over to the lamp by the window and did the following:

Reached down through the lampshade far enough to see if there was a bulb. There was, and it was screwed in tight.

Next, I tried the lamp switch to no avail.

Then I got down on my hands and knees to find the cord. I found one and followed around to the socket. It was plugged in.

I thought there might be another one, perhaps for a different fixture in the room. Yes, there was one, and it wasn't plugged in. After plugging it in, I again turned on the switch, and the light came on.

POINT TO PONDER: How would you analyze and evaluate my thinking here?

Some have noticed a methodical process. Some of you saw exploration of options and persistence. Others say, "I would have stopped at the light switch the first time." Here you are comparing your own problem-solving processes and seeing that there are other ways of approaching complex, nonroutine situations. This is one of the major objectives of this kind of openness about our thinking: that we encourage an open sharing of approaches, because we all learn from each other. This is why small-group problem solving is so important: We can learn from others' ways of thinking (Forman & Kraker 1985).

Modeling, then, can be a first step in the inquiry process, because it shows our willingness to share our thinking with students. It was said of Mark Van Doren that "his unique genius as a teacher was to speculate publicly; in opening the play of his mind to students, he gave each student a self-assigned role in resolving these questions his teaching dramatized" (Sarason 1982).

INQUIRY

The spirit of inquiry, for me, is generated from many different sources. Here are a couple that have crossed my mind most recently.

Walt Whitman in *Leaves of Grass* writes that "Man is a summons and a challenge." What does this suggest? Well, for me it suggests that each of us as adults has a calling to work, to aspire to greatness, to compose her or his own story on the journey of life. We may, for example, be a summons to pose and resolve great questions: What shall we make of life? What shall we contribute to the world? What can we contribute with the stories of our lives?

Accepting this, if you can, as an introductory premise, then what are children? Children come to us in schools with a billion or more unposed questions—or at least the potential for posing as many questions of us and the world as there were neurons and synaptic connections within their brains—just about as many potential questions within them for the rest of their lives as there are stars not only in the Milky Way but in all the galaxies within the universe. These questions will ultimately form their challenge to us and the rest of the world. This is the challenge of Izzy's mother when she asked, "Did you ask a good question today?"

Sometimes classrooms are wholly unresponsive to this spirit, for many reasons: accountability to state and local assessments, covering content, and you-know-many-more.

Here I should like to focus upon us as teachers. What are the questions with which we enter the classroom? For me, these questions center upon how my students are thinking. How did they arrive at the conclusions they offer in class? What led them to ask the questions they did? How are they interpreting the "stuff" of the content that I have presented?

These are questions I enter classrooms with—without them my classroom life would be exceedingly boring, because I've read most of the material they are being asked to read and think about. I want to know how they are thinking about it. I want to know how their minds and feelings are wrapping themselves around the subject and what they end up with: How do you think about this stuff? What sense are you making of it? What can I learn about your ways of approaching the subject matter?

Sour Grapes

When I was asked to teach problem solving in the first grade, I selected a fable, "The Fox and the Grapes." I wanted students to generate alternatives for the fox's action, but I had to work at identifying my line of inquiry. I decided that I wanted to know what kinds of solutions students generated and how they arrived at them.

Similarly, when I was asked to do a similar thing in the third grade, my inquiry focused upon how well students had learned a problem-solving process taught them by their teacher. In a way, my experience with them was a midcourse evaluation.

When I enter a middle or high-school classroom to work with specific intellectual processes, such as identifying reliable sources, I usually adopt an inquiry stance: "What do students already know about these processes? How have they learned to figure out about sources, evidence, assumptions, and so forth?"

Whenever we enter a classroom we can pose this question: "What am I going to learn about my students' thinking? About their understanding of complex material?"

Then, of course, we take the evidence collected and act upon it; we may engage in direct teaching of a process or reteaching of a concept.

And Cowboys Came Later

Another example illustrates how the spirit of inquiry fosters the invitational environment. A kindergarten teacher was introducing a unit on holidays, and she proceeded in this fashion:

> "Now, who was at the first Thanksgiving dinner?"
>
> "Me," one student responded.
>
> "Oh, that's good, Johnny, you raised your hand. Now, who was at the first Thanksgiving dinner?"
>
> "Me," Johnny said again.
>
> "Give him time, he just wants to think," the teacher said about another student.
>
> "The Pilgrims."
>
> "Yes, the Pilgrims," the teacher responded. "And who else?"
>
> "Indians," replied another student.
>
> "Very good. Now we're going to—" She was abruptly interrupted from the back of the room.
>
> "And cowboys came later."
>
> "Right." (White 1983)

POINT TO PONDER: When I share this with teachers, I ask the following question: "Now, what would you want to know about this little episode?"

Here's what others in your situation have responded:

"I wonder why the first student said, 'Me.' " (What are your hypotheses?)

"Well, he or she could have meant that they attended their own first Thanksgiving Dinner . . . or, I guess, they could have meant that they think they were at the first-ever Thanksgiving Dinner, but that doesn't sound too logical."

"It might just be, however, that this child is sending a signal to be called upon: 'Me! Me! Over here, teacher!' "

"You know, another statement that I like is when she says 'Give him time, he just wants to think.' "

"But that's the point—they aren't thinking!" (How do you know?)

"Look at the last statement: 'And cowboys came later.' " She doesn't do anything with that." (What would you do with it?)

"Why, you could ask: 'Yes, and what made you think of that, Johnny?' "

"Or just say: 'Good! Please tell me what you know about the cowboys coming later.' " (Why do you think she/he said that?)

"Maybe the child associates cowboys with Indians—you know, like on television. . . ."

"Or perhaps they're thinking about U.S. history, when the cowboys appeared during the nineteenth century out west."

"Yes, but I don't think little children think like that."

"Another possibility is that the child meant something like: 'The cowboys came later—for dessert!' "

"Or they might have meant that the Dallas Cowboys came later on TV to play the Washington Redskins."

All these are possibilities suggested by people like yourself. And the point of presenting them is this: If we do not listen carefully to what children and adolescents are saying, we will miss many opportunities to learn about how they think: where their ideas come from, how they draw their conclusions, upon what evidence it's based, using which assumptions and rules for processing information.

We are (or should be) just as interested in the character of the ideas students generate as we are in the nature of their thinking processes. Here "cowboys" represents something of importance for the child, and it should be of interest to us because of its relation to Thanksgiving and to her developmental level.

Here are two suggestions that build upon Chapter 5's emphasis upon quality responding:

> Always be alert for the unusual and unique in our students' thinking. It may not blossom as fully grown as the unexpected "cowboys came later." We may have to dig a little by asking, "How did you arrive at that question/answer? What made you think of that idea?"
>
> How we respond may vary from "What do you think?" to "Does anybody else have an idea about Judy's question?" to "Let's think about this together [or in small groups for a few minutes]."

Many years ago I observed one of the best examples of following students' inquiry with a good follow-up question: Cliff was teaching a seventh grade science class about the origin of galaxies. Students were classifying pictures of galaxies by size, shape, luminosity, etc. Then one student, Pam, raised her hand to ask, "Does anybody really know how old the galaxies are?" Cliff paused a moment, as if wondering what to do with the question, but then he turned the query back to his students: "All right. Pam's question: 'Does anybody *really* know how old the galaxies are?' " There followed for the next ten minutes a very intense period of hypothesizing by several students: "The brighter they are the older. . . . The darker, the older . . . . The more spread out the older [because of the effect of the Big Bang] . . . ."

I have shown the videotape of this episode over and over again for a variety of reasons: It shows good teacher inquiry strategies (turning the question back to the students); it shows the different developmental capabilities of seventh graders—some of them could think about abstractions like origins, while others merely sat there seeming to be a little bored, perhaps because they could not visualize the abstract possibilities of origins. It also is a wonderful example of an instructional strategy: After the brief discussion Cliff observed, "This has been just like a meeting of astronomers. Each speculates just as you have done, and what you have to do now is to gather more evidence." He allowed his students to model scientific inquiry for the whole class.

Both of these examples (of "cowboys" and "galaxies") illustrate what we can discover or miss discovering about our students' thinking. We can be enriched by spending a little time exploring for deeper meanings, but too often miss the joy of discovering how different people think, ponder, and wonder about the mysteries of life.

Let me conclude with a few words from the Czech author, Milan Kundera, from his novel, *The Book of Laughter and Forgetting* (1980):

> The stupidity of people comes from having an answer for everything. The wisdom of the novel comes from having a question for everything. When Don Quixote went out into the world, that world turned into a mystery before his eyes. . . . The novelist teaches the reader to comprehend the world as a question. . . . The totalitarian world, whether founded on Marx, Islam or anything else, is a world of answers rather than questions. (p. 237)

Too often our classrooms are worlds of answers and not questions. Inquiry in the classroom comes in the form of wanting to find out what questions students are posing and resolving for themselves and for us. Inquiry demands of you and me a disposition toward finding out—being curious about our students' thinking by posing such questions as "How did you arrive at that answer? What made you pose that question? What brought you to that conclusion?"

We need, whenever possible, to enter our classrooms not only with an open mind, but with one that possesses Kundera's spirit of inquiry.

EXPERIMENTATION

"What can we—teachers and students together—learn about the process of change that will affect the teaching of thinking in the classroom?" This question comes to mind from studying the work of Seymour Sarason, especially his book *The Culture of the School and the Problem of Change* (1982). One of Sarason's major interests here is to challenge us to reflect on what he calls the classroom "regularities" or patterns of interaction with which we live. For example, here are several noticeable patterns that seem to characterize life in classrooms:

Teachers ask most of the questions.
Students pose few complex problems on their own.
Teachers speak, and students are spoken to.
Students sit at desks in rows facing the teacher, not each other.
Most learning comes from print-oriented media.

Most of the time every student is working on the same content.

Students make very few decisions about their own learning.

Teachers always evaluate students.

Students generally have very little to say about the establishment of classroom routines and the governance of the classroom.

Supervisors very seldom visit classrooms.

Teachers very seldom interact with each other during the school day about instructional problems affecting them.

POINT TO PONDER: What patterns do you notice in your classroom?

The questions Sarason poses—"Why do such patterns exist?" and "What alternatives exist to these patterns?"—subsequent to making such a list are very significant. They engage us in problem posing and resolving; they help us reflect on our own experience to identify those ways of interacting and being in the classroom that might or might not help attain our goal: fostering critical, creative, and reflective thinking. I have used these questions with teachers to encourage them to reenter their classroom to search out those patterns that might be inimical to thinking.

Many teachers have been able to reflect on their experience and to effect changes that are worth our noting. One of the themes or issues introduced in Chapters 3 and 5—sharing some control of decision making with our students—is evident in the following episodes. As we shall see, when we experiment with "traditional" patterns of organization within our classrooms in order to challenge students to think, we very often end up opening the control systems to be more responsive to students' needs.

First Grade

Diane went into her first grade classroom and noted that the end of her day was extremely hectic. Students during the last forty-five minutes were always tugging at her with questions about unfinished business, about what to do next, about myriad chores and academic tasks. She didn't like this state of affairs at all.

What seems to be the problem? she asked herself. Perhaps the schedule is awry. Maybe my kids are not working at their comfortable potential.

What to do?

Diane decided to engage her students in facing this problem and seeking alternatives themselves. She realized that, in allowing her boys and girls to confront this situation with her, she was taking a risk: Her students might decide to do something she didn't want them to do. Diane also realized she had a vested interest in teaching Math after lunch and Language Arts first thing in the morning. She had her heart set on these patterns (what Sarason would call "programmatic regularities"). Why was she so intent upon her agenda? Here are a few hypotheses:

Diane's diagnosis of students' learning styles suggested that this was the best way to teach these two subjects.

She might think that a subject like Math is best undertaken after lunch because of students' attention spans.

Or her decision might be entirely arbitrary.

We could go on. The point is that Diane was challenging her own thinking—her own conclusions. The decision to share control with students regardless of their age is one of the most monumental ones a teacher of any subject can make, because it involves questioning many underlying patterns and the assumptions that support them. It is at times a little frightening, and we will undoubtedly encounter some anxiety in the process.

Well, what do you suppose happened when Diane and her first graders sat down on the carpet to engage in problem solving one fine afternoon early in spring?

Many of you probably figured out what Diane encountered: Her first graders were quite adamant about one change. They wanted to do Math right off the bat at 9 A.M. and Language Arts/Reading after lunch. Her most cherished classroom regularity or pattern had been challenged. What was she to do? The only honest thing she could at this point.

"O.K., children, we'll try it!" she said with a resolute smile, hoping that it would work.

And it did! She reported that her first graders seemed to enjoy Math a whole lot more when they did it in the morning. Why? Perhaps because they had had a stake in the decision-making process—they didn't want to let themselves down. It may occur to you as it does to me that there is another connection—that between thinking and feeling. Perhaps Diane's students improved because they felt better about mathematics: They had made a decision about their own future. Diane also reported that their performance seemed to improve with this change as well. And, finally, the problem of the afternoon was solved.

What did Diane and her students learn from this experience? That they could work together to confront sticky problems within the classroom. I think Diane learned that she could entrust her students with shared control of classroom routines. This was a tentative first step—one that we must all make if we are to explore the possibilities of inviting students to think productively about their responsibilities within the classroom.

And Diane's experiment is nothing novel: John Dewey advocated seeing the classroom as a learning community where students encounter problems of the "everyday world," and early child-centered educators, such as Caroline Pratt in The Play School (circa 1910), involved students in problem solving related to curriculum at a very tender age. But the point is this: Each of us must relearn for ourselves all the lessons that the Deweys and the Pratts have taught. We must be our own experimenters.

Second Grade

Mary Ann went back to her second grade classroom, examined the routines, and discovered that the arrangement of desks was very inefficient. She had a lot of difficulty getting around, and students could not interact with each other at ease.

She too posed the problems to the students:

"Children, does the way the seats in our room are arranged seem to help us or get in our way as we learn?"

"It's too hard."

"How?" Mary Ann asked.

"We can't get to your desk when we want to. . . . I can't work with my friends either."

"So, what shall we do about it?"

"We could make a new plan."

So they did. In fact, Mary Ann asked each child to make a new plan, and consequently she collected twenty-two different drawings of how best to arrange the seats: from horseshoes to circles to clusters of small circles and so forth. She also turned the problem into a math lesson.

The result was that the students decided upon one plan of action, one that, surprisingly, included using the teacher's desk as a resource center for most of the class time. Thus, Mary Ann embarked upon a course that ultimately resulted in her losing some of her territory. This she had hardly planned in advance, because she too was rather tentative about this kind of challenge.

What did she learn? Mary Ann learned something about her students primarily. She asked her students: "What did you learn from this experience?"

"We learned we could trust you!" came their reply.

Somewhat taken aback, she said, "What do you mean by that?"

"Well," they offered with much conviction and enthusiasm, "some teachers ask you to do things like this—you know, give them ideas about things and stuff like that—and then they don't use them. But you like our ideas and let us use them in the class."

Mary Ann learned that students' feelings are very important. If we are willing to take students' feelings into account as Mary Ann has done, chances are we will create an environment that is open and trusting. Without trust how can one engage in the sharing of ideas and feelings?

Ninth Grade

Rosemarie's ninth graders, not too unlike many other ninth graders, were seldom ecstatic about algebra or college preparatory math. She often struggled not only with their lack of comprehension, but, more significantly, with the underlying attitudes: "This is boring. . . . It's too difficult for me, I just can't do math problems anyway. . . ."

What to do?

After attending a conference on Thinking Skills where she participated in paired problem solving under the direction of one of its co-proponents, Jack Lockhead, Rosemarie decided to experiment with it in her classroom. It wasn't a blazing success at first: Students seemed to play out the roles of problem solver and active listener best when she was around. This, of course, was frustrating, because adults can do it, so why can't ninth graders?

Well, she compromised and used the whole class as those who think aloud through the problem, while she played to role of listener in the Whimbey-Lockhead model (Whimbey & Lockhead 1982). The essence of this strategy is to empower students with strategies that will help them approach math problems with some confidence—it is no longer a matter of memorizing specific algorithms.

How did the students respond?

> Students' on-task behavior was notably increased. The group work made the students more aware of the commonality of feelings regarding problem solving; such as, frustration, the fear of being judged, discouragement, and anxiety. The students tended to band together and work as a team, interjecting their own ideas and thoughts. Passive learners became more involved and *there seemed to be an increase in their natural curiosity.* [Emphasis added.] In particular, the students posed many more "what if" questions. The verbal feedback not only helped the students grow and experiment with ideas but also provided me with valuable insights into learning deficiencies. (Liebmann 1986)

Here's what some of her students noted at the end of the semester:

> The past couple of weeks have built up my confidence in myself because I've learned that if you really think, you'll surprise yourself when you find the answer.

> I've learned that I've been leaning on my teachers too much and so I could never solve the problems when they appeared on a test.

> I no longer feel that problem solving is a mystery only understood by teachers. While I am still not very good at it, I at least feel there are some tools I can fall back on that will help me out.

So what did Rosemarie learn from all this? One of the things she learned, I think, was that if we want students to engage in complex thinking that involves risk of being wrong, trying out new hypotheses and thinking aloud, we must be willing to experiment with varieties of teaching strategies, such as small-group problem solving. In the beginning she had little confidence that it would work all that well.

Her students at the end of the semester gave Rosemarie one of the highest compliments by saying, "This class is more like a family than a classroom."

This experiment involved both the nature of the learning environment and the nature of complex thinking itself: students' pursuing their own curiosities, posing "What if" questions (the essence of mathematical thinking according to Marshall Gordon 1978), and offering varieties of hypothetical solutions and strategies for improved solution attainment. The quality of mathematical thinking, after all, was the primary objective.

CONCLUSION

These are teachers I have had the pleasure of working with over the past couple of years. For me, they represent the best within our profession today. Why? Because they are risk takers, who are undertaking to modify the traditional classroom setting in ways that are definitely more conducive to fostering thoughtfulness.

These teachers, for me, exemplify the truth of philosopher William Barrett's claim (1979, p. 194) that "Possibility penetrates the actual and makes it what it is. . . . We are what we are through the horizons that lie open to us."

These are teachers who are searching for the horizons that lie open to them and seizing opportunities to set out for them, to explore and conquer new lands. These are teachers who live life as Huck Finn decided he had to after exploring the eddies and banks of the Mississippi with Jim. It's time, he said, "to light out for the territory," before Aunt Sally can adopt and "sivilize" us.

Schools have a way of adopting and coopting our best resolve: to play the role of Huck Finn and be one of those who are constantly pushing back the horizons of the known world to discover new truths about themselves (What am I learning about my own thinking?), about their students (What am I learning about their thinking?), and about life in the classroom (What are we together learning about the change process that affects thinking?).

What are we waiting for? The new territory awaits our reconnoitering.

REFERENCES

Barrett, William. 1979. *The Illusion of Technique*. New York: Anchor Press/Doubleday.

Beyer, Barry. 1988. *Developing a Thinking Skills Program*. Boston: Allyn & Bacon.

Brown, Chip. 1990. "What's New at Frisbee U.?" *The New York Times Magazine*. 10 June, p. 46.

Bruner, Jerome. 1960. *The Process of Education*. New York: Vintage Books.

Costa, A., and L. Lowery. 1989. *Techniques for Teaching Thinking*. Pacific Grove, CA: Midwest Publications.

Forman, Ellice, and Myra Kraker. 1985. "The Social Origins of Logic: The Contributions of Piaget and Vygotsky." In *Peer Conflict and Psychological Growth. New Directions for Child Development*. ed. M. W. Berkowitz. No. 29:23–29. San Francisco: Jossey-Bass.

Gordon, Marshall. 1978. "Conflict and Liberation: Personal Aspects of the Mathematics Experience." *Curriculum Inquiry* 8:251–271.

Kundera, Milan. 1980. *The Book of Laughter and Forgetting*. New York: Penguin Books.

Liebmann, Rosemarie. 1986. "Enhancing Students' Problem Solving Abilities." Unpublished manuscript. Montclair State College.

Sarason, Seymour. 1982. *The Culture of the School and the Problem of Change*. Boston: Allyn & Bacon.

Schon, Donald. 1987. *Educating the Reflective Practitioner*. San Francisco: Jossey-Bass.

Whimbey, Arthur, and Jack Lockhead. 1982. *Problem Solving and Comprehension*. 3d. ed. Philadelphia: Franklin Institute.

White, Jane. 1983. "Politeness Strategies and Power: The Control of Knowledge and People through 'Niceness.'" Paper presented at the annual meeting of the American Educational Research Association, Montreal.

Whitman, Walt. 1962. *Leaves of Grass*. Comprehensive Reader's Edition. New York: University Press.

CHAPTER 7

Doubt, Uncertainty, and Difficulty: Instructional Planning for Problem Solving and Inquiry

OVERVIEW

Why would you spend hours discussing revolutions, changes in systems, or how to generate alternative solutions? Perhaps because these concepts and skills are robust with meaningfulness. How would you fashion a lesson and/or unit that focused upon these or similar ideas or principles? And how do we incorporate the concepts of students' problem posing, metacognition, and transfer into such instructional plans? This chapter provides some ways of thinking about these questions.

I was once asked by teachers to demonstrate problem solving in a first grade classroom. Having spent only one year as a first grader, I felt the need to call upon one of my graduate students, a teacher of first grade, for her assistance. Diane said, "Why don't you tell them one of Aesop's Fables? I just finished doing that with my first graders."

So I selected "The Fox and the Grapes" and told it to the children. My strategy was to tell the story of the hungry fox wandering down the lane until he spied the grapes hanging from a vine over his head. He leaped up, attempting to pull some grapes down, but failed. Here I stopped the story and asked the children, "What would you do to get the grapes, if you were the fox?"

They responded: "Climb the tree!" "Get a long stick." "Find some rocks to climb on top of." "Shake the tree hard." "Call other animals to help me."

I accepted all their answers, listed them on the board with the child's name beside them, and then asked them to decide which solution was best and why. As I recall they said that using a stick was probably the easiest to do, since other animals and rocks might not be around. Finally, I asked them, "How did you come up with all these answers?"

One girl, Betsy, said, "I remembered what we did at home [in a similar situation]." So Betsy was using her background knowledge, and her comment convinced me that some youngsters, even first graders, could reflect on their own thinking processes. This experience suggested to all of us that we could, indeed, present students with problems to solve and challenge them to become more aware of the kinds of intellectual processes they used: for example, background knowledge.

Now, what does this episode illustrate? For me, it suggests that problems that will engage students in the kinds of thinking processes we deem appropriate can, indeed, be located within the existing school curriculum. I disagree with those persons who say problem solving is a more complex skill and should be relegated to the upper grades. Young children solve problems all the time. Piaget's research on object permanence shows that at eighteen months babies begin to inquire about the object that, once in front of them, is placed behind Mommy's back or under the rug. Kids are finding solutions to problems all the time, at home and in school—as well as causing a few themselves.

By what kinds of processes can we locate, disclose, or formulate what we might call "the problematic"? We found out in Chapter 2 that thinking often originates with some dilemma, conflict, "discrepant experience" (Sigel), or controversy. Therefore, it makes sense to begin looking at our curriculum—the written document, the textbook, or the successive activities we engage in daily—to disclose the problematic situations that foster thoughtfulness. I call this process one of "disclosure" of that which is already there, rather than "infusion." The latter suggests that we are taking skills that lie outside the subject (such as relating problematic situations to one another) and injecting them where they haven't been. "Infusing" our lives with enthusiasm where it has been absent comes to mind. I prefer disclosure as a model, because it suggests that these intellectual processes are what good historians, biologists, or poets already engage in. What we need to know then is what good historians or biologists do when inquiring into their subjects.

As we think of this disclosure model it seems to me that we might consider these questions:

Within our content, or within a unit of instruction (say on the pioneers) what is worth thinking about over an extended period of time? In other words, what are those concepts, ideas, principles, and/or skills that are worth remembering, understanding thoroughly, and transferring to other areas?

How do we frame these concepts, for example, within the structure of a problem, conflict, or dilemma? How do we approach those subjects within the humanities, sciences, and mathematics to identify or disclose "the problematic"?

What kinds of planning frameworks might be helpful for structuring our inquiry on Monday and useful in guiding instruction for the next several weeks? A modified version of the Tyler (1949) framework will be used here to help us plan lessons and units that foster intellectual development.

Let us take up these questions one at a time.

IDEAS WORTH THINKING ABOUT

The perennial curricular question is, "What is worth knowing?" We want to know what is worth thinking about. Thus, our first principle of instructional design is to focus upon *significant* concepts, ideas, and skills. This is the "stuff" worth thinking about and, perhaps more importantly, worth transferring into related and novel contexts.

One way to proceed is to identify ideas within the subject matter that are worth thinking about over an extended period of time. Very often we find these concepts highlighted nicely in the textbook as chapter titles or subtitles. I sat in on a high school English class not long ago where the teacher was having students in small groups identify what they thought would be on the forthcoming test. In other words they had to answer the question "What is worth thinking about?" I asked one group how they knew something in the text was important. "By what's highlighted in different colors or at the head of the chapter."

Principles of Lesson Design

Lessons to Foster Thoughtful Engagement With Concepts and Skills Should
Focus upon significant concepts, ideas, and/or skills determined by reasoned criteria.
Be problem oriented, asking "what is the problem, dilemma, question to resolve?"
Be structured to include initial, core, and culminating activities.
Provide opportunities to practice and/or use concepts and skills in varied and reflective fashions.
Allow participants to learn details of specific thought processes.
Provide for metacognitive awareness of thinking/feeling processes.
Encourage transfer of significant concepts and skills within the subject, to other subjects and to students' personal lives.
Evaluate students' progress toward creating meaning and developing skills.

But of more value is to be able to distinguish for ourselves, students and teachers alike, what is important from the relatively less important. Sternberg (1985) would call this skill "selective encoding"—deciding upon what is important. Repeatedly, within staff development meetings with teachers and administrators, we discover that this process is key to many other mental operations, like finding the main idea and analyzing virtually any kind of problem. Nevertheless, it is not always easy for us to make these decisions.

Let me offer a set of criteria that help us determine which concepts are worth thinking productively about: robustness within the subject; societal significance; importance to the students' needs/interests/aspirations. We shall see that these criteria focus clearly upon making the stuff of the curriculum more meaningful within the subject and to us.

Robustness within the Subject Matter

Robust means "strong, healthy, powerful, full bodied." I use this word here to suggest criteria that empower us to use and understand ideas and concepts within the subject matter and to transfer them into other subjects as well as into our personal lives. In these ways the stuff becomes meaningful.

Historical Significance. Phlogiston and the Geocentric Theory of the solar system are concepts no longer accepted, yet current understanding is enhanced when we know what others thought before us. Being able to place ideas within a historical context enhances their meaningfulness.

Analytic Significance. Principles of force and motion are necessary in order to understand complex physics problems. Here we are concerned with concepts that are closely related to other key concepts, and a lack of understanding of them would impair understanding.

Logical Sequential Significance. In order to understand what a main idea is, we need first to know something about subject and verb as well as the difference between the concepts of "general" and "specific." To understand Hitler's rise to power, we first need to know the provisions of the Treaty of Versailles.

Integrative Significance. Understanding balance of forces in science helps us with equivalence in mathematical formulas, with international relations in history, and in aesthetic appreciation of the Sistine ceiling and the Parthenon. "Robust" concepts such as control, choice, and systems are transferable into other subjects as well as into our personal lives.

The final criterion, integrative significance, might be the most robust of the four because of its potential for transferring ideas and concepts to other subject matters. Why is this important? Because the more connections and relationships we can formulate around the notions of control, choice, systems, force, and equivalence, for example, the more we will understand them, the more meaningful they will be. The better we understand them, the more likely we are to be able to use them in unstructured situations or novel problems.

Societal Significance

There are other reasons for spending time on specific concepts. A concept or idea may have social significance at that moment or in the future. Our curricula are now full of courses dealing with health, family life and computer education because of responses to demands by society.

What criteria seem important here?

Transmission and Rethinking Cultural Values. We teach punctuality, responsibility, respect for each other, and obedience (among others) because they help maintain society on an even keel. We also want to ensure that our young encounter the best and most enriching ideas created by human beings—the life of Socrates, the Sistine ceiling, and the Bill of Rights, for example. These are the treasures of our culture, and without engaging them, rethinking them, and arriving at our own conclusions we not only lose continuity with the past, but we also deprive ourselves of solutions to the world's problems that may have already been conceived.

Transformation of Society. We might elect to teach problem solving within a social context because we want students to become, in the words of one of my college colleagues, "movers and shakers." We might want our students to respond with a hearty "Yes!" to George S. Counts's question of the early 1930s: "Dare the schools create a new social order?" in order to ensure an equitable distribution of goods and services.

Health/Safety and Welfare. We stress various precautionary measures within our curricula in order to protect society from social and communicable diseases. We spend time in science curricula teaching about environmental pollution in order to protect the balance of future ecosystems. We devote many resources to ensure that students can grow up in a drug-free environment and that their family lives are free of undue stress.

There are other criteria, but you get the idea that there are times when we will choose a concept or principle because we want students to be aware of how they affect or translate into social and/or environmental situations.

Student Needs/Interests/Growth

And there are reasons derived from the nature of our student body:

Need/Practicality. We will teach decision making, because we are convinced that students will need such a skill in order to succeed and compete in the twenty-first century. Their practical application is evident.

Meaningfulness and Interest. We will focus upon a unit on the ocean and its beaches because first graders are interested in the topic. Similarly, we might teach *Catcher in the Rye* because the novel is often personally meaningful to students of the same age. Personal meaningfulness results when we can relate subjects to our lives, our experiences, aspirations, emotional needs, and developmental strivings.

Human Growth and Development. We will spend time helping students become more empathic with characters in literature and be able to take another's perspective because these foster their intellectual and emotional growth.

Potential for Continuity and Transfer

The potential for becoming an "integrative thread" woven spirally up through the curricular years and horizontally throughout one year's studies may be one of the most robust of criteria when considered with the previous three. Perkins (1989) identifies other criteria for integrative threads: broad applicability, pervasiveness, disclosure of patterns, illuminating contrasts, and those that are just plain fascinating to think about. For example, spending time working in early years with the notions of systems as groups of interacting parts (in numbers, alphabets, and families) and of personal control (in goal setting and problem solving) will have tremendous potential if continued upward through students' schooling. But we must take the time to see how they transfer into other subjects we are studying.

POINT TO PONDER: What are you teaching right now that is worth spending a lot of time on, and what criteria can you use to justify these decisions?

Do you have other criteria you think are just as or more important than the above? What are they?

In sum, these criteria can provide an answer to the significant question "Why am I teaching this?" If we spend some time focusing upon this question in our planning, we will invoke these and similar criteria, and our instruction will become more purposeful.

DISCLOSING "THE PROBLEMATIC"

Now comes the more difficult part—finding the problem, dilemma, or discrepancy within the subject matter we teach. I say this is more difficult because in working with teachers K–12 and with college professors I find that for a variety of reasons we tend to see our subject areas sort of as a Rolodex card file, with so many facts that "they must understand" before they can do any thinking. I once worked with a history teacher whose supervisor said, "In U.S. History I, they have to get the facts; they can think about them the following year in U.S. II."

Other reasons why we perceive our subjects in this fashion include the following:

This is how we were taught for many years.
Our assessment instruments are often geared toward retrieval of information, not use of it to solve problems.
Presenting facts seems to be in accordance with our role perception of what a teacher does: Stand in front of room and say, "Now listen to what I have to say. It will be on the test next week."
This information dispenser role helps us maintain good order and discipline within the classroom.

Another set of prevailing reasons for this top-down model used to be that schools and society in general did not provide us with cooperative, problem-oriented models. This is no longer true. Research and studies on school change (Lieberman & Miller 1990) and those on life in corporations (Peters 1987; Waterman 1987) indicate that we are swiftly developing models that place more control within the hands of teachers and employees who now participate in making decisions that directly affect their lives in the organization.

With these kinds of change underway, it becomes increasingly more likely that in our instructional and curricular planning, we will be engaged in identifying the problematic.

What I would like to share with you now are new sets of lenses with which to examine our "traditional" subject matter—lenses that may help disclose content appropriate for extended thoughtfulness.

The Humanities

We can think of the humanities as those studies that help us reflect on the essential nature of human beings. History, anthropology, philosophy, art, literature, and psychology provide us with ways of knowing what it means to be human. Essential to all of them are you and me, our hopes, fears, needs, wishes, problems, decisions, and the products of our imaginations: works of art, philosophies, theories, and legends. Unfortunately, schooling focuses mostly upon the products of other peoples' thoughts and feelings, instead of engaging students productively in re-thinking and feeling the situations presented with the humanities.

So when we examine these subjects, we readily have access to problems and dilemmas if we look for occasions where persons have done or experienced the following:

> Made a decision about which there were differing points of view, options from which to select, and possible consequences to project. (Truman's decision to drop the atomic bomb.)
>
> Confronted conflicting points of view, philosophies, values, needs, and goals. (Hester Prynne in *The Scarlet Letter;* abortion.)
>
> Attempted to reach a goal and encountered problems with strategies, resources, support, etc. (Captain Ahab in *Moby Dick.*)
>
> Confronted problems for which the possible solutions were not immediately evident. (Presidents Carter and Bush attempting to rescue hostages; solving the drug problem.)
>
> Attempted to find ways to make some phenomena meaningful, to clarify our role within a certain context. (Leonardo's "Last Supper"; King Lear's raging against the gods.)

Let me illustrate what various persons have done with these different sets of lenses as they examined their curricular content.

> Carol presents her fourth-grade students with this dilemma from her health curriculum: "A boy with red hair comes to school and kids call him 'Carrot Top.' He doesn't like this name. What would you do if you were in his situation?"
>
> Ken confronts his eighth-grade students with this situation: From now on all girls will get an A grade this semester because they have been better behaved than the boys (Schopp 1982). (An introduction to a unit on revolution.)

Richie says to his eleventh graders, "You are Thomas Jefferson. Would you have made the Louisiana Purchase? Why or why not?"

Cathy presents her college students in Introductory Ethics with this situation: You are selecting members for a board of education. Among the candidates are Adolf Eichmann, Socrates, a Mrs. Wong from China who had practiced infanticide, Mrs. Petit, an active member of a swingers club, and a transvestite in drag. Whom would you choose and why?

In History Joe asks his college students: "The textbook says, 'The threat of violence is a criminal act.' In view of this, should we consider any national leader who rattles his nuclear weapons a criminal?"

Remember the dictionary definition of a problem: "Any question or matter involving doubt, uncertainty, or difficulty" (Random House Dictionary 1967). In these situations the doubt comes about from having to decide what to do or believe; in the process we confront our sense of right and wrong, plus a whole set of values having to do with human conduct and economic feasibility. We can generate a set of options after analyzing the situation, comparing them with others we have encountered, breaking them into smaller parts, visualizing, and selecting a problem-solving strategy.

In all these problematic situations we will encounter "violated expectations" (Sigel), but we can also see the truth of Shrag's (1988) observation that thoughtful behavior is akin to embarking upon an expedition, requiring much deliberation and planning.

Two additional ways of creating "doubt, uncertainty, and difficulty" for students in humanities illustrate different instructional practices:

Identify expectations, values, perceptions held by students related to the subject and create a situation that challenges students to reconsider them. Mauri Sachs of Montclair State College described Middle Eastern culture patterns that call for "tipping" customs officials in order to bring her washing machine into Turkey, and one of her anthropology students immediately challenged her, "Isn't that immoral?" There ensued a most interesting discussion of the relationship between two different cultural ways of doing business. Students confronted the reality that, in this country, we often tip people in order to get a table at a restaurant, to gain favor with an automobile mechanic, and to make sure you get good service from your doorman. What Mauri did was recognize the "discrepancy" in her students' thinking as the question was asked, and then she opened the class for an exchange of points of view on this matter. We want to be alert for how the knowledge presented and discussed in class might be causing some students to rethink their own perspectives, values, and beliefs. She might have begun her class with this question: "Is it appropriate for one country to require 'tipping' for a person to bring a washing machine into the country?" In this way she could have created a situation where such discrepancies and difficulties would most likely surface.

Create a situation where students must search for solution to a human dilemma: "If you were Macbeth, how would you handle Lady Macbeth? If
you were Columbus, what would you do with near mutinous crew members
on your first voyage?" Here the operating mechanism is "What if?" that
asks the students to project themselves imaginatively into the psyche of
the Thane of Cawdor. We noted earlier (Chapter 1) that there is evidence
that students have difficulty with this kind of projection. This experience
requires that we use our ability to be empathic, and empathy is a process
fundamental to thoughtfulness within the social sciences (Newmann, in
press) as well as literature and the other arts.

In both of these, as in the dilemma of *Franklin in the Dark,* we confront
students with a difficulty that calls upon them to analyze the situation and then
generate options or possibilities. And, again, it seems as if thinking is significantly
involved with being able to produce such possibilities within situations that are,
as Resnick noted (1987), complex, ambiguous, and not given to rules that are
simple to follow.

The human condition daily presents us with opportunities that are fraught
with uncertainty. All we have to do is to be able to perceive them between the
lines of the textbooks that, if read uncritically, present us with a fixed, unchanging,
monodimensional view of the world, its history, and prospects for the future.

Science and Mathematics

In the sciences and mathematics we can find "doubt, uncertainty, and difficulty"
in places like the following:

Observing phenomena that seem to contradict our expectations, our traditional ways of viewing the world, or the evidence from our senses. (Pen-
guins' ability to withstand cold; humans' ability to withstand heat.)
Experiments that cause us to reconsider previously acquired knowledge, to
examine it from a different perspective, etc. (The nature of genes.)
Any nonroutine problem (mathematical or scientific) for which the students
do not have a mechanical or automatic way of responding. (Figuring out
ecological difficulties or redesigning the sailboat for greater efficiency.)
Goals that students set for themselves and for which they must design strategies. (Improve problem solving; acquire computer skills.)

How do we translate these guidelines into classroom life?

Seeming Contradictions.   We have probably all heard of the by now classic science
experiment with the bimetallic strip. Over a Bunsen burner you place a tool with
two metal strips, one on either side. (It looks like a file.) As you hold it over the
flame on one side, the whole structure begins to turn upward. If you turn it over,
the flame causes the structure to bend downward. Why does this happen? Richard
Suchman presents this problem as a means of improving students' inquiry processes. Once students have encountered the seeming contradiction, they proceed

to ask the teacher questions he or she can answer with a yes/no answer. The point of this activity is for students to form hypotheses about the causes of the phenomenon and to test them out by posing these questions. This is also an excellent activity to conduct using other dilemmas; it really helps focus our attention upon listening to each other and building upon each others' thinking (Joyce & Weil 1980).

Other such contradictory phenomena that will create the "discrepant experience" might be the following: Fill a glass of water to the brim and notice that it peaks over the rim. Why? Aromas released from the front of the room transport themselves to the back. How does that happen? Examine rock specimens from around the school to figure out how they were formed. What hypotheses can we generate on the basis of visible evidence?

The fact that the sun rises in the east and sets in the west appears to contradict the Copernican view of the solar system and "prove" the Ptolemaic view. Stephen Kowalski, a professor at Montclair, decided to play the role of Ptolemy in his general science courses and challenge his students "to prove" to him the correctness of the Copernican system. Students marshaled evidence about the seasons, for example, to "prove" their point, not always successfully.

Nonroutine Challenges—Science.   Another source of dilemmas is knowing what scientists in the past have puzzled over. For example, what would happen if we rode along a ray of light at 186,000 mph? (Barell 1980.) What would we observe? Why? How do these observations affect our understanding of Newtonian physics?

Jack Isidor is a professor of chemistry at Montclair. He says he always starts with an experiment in the laboratory, because he wants students to experience the data firsthand. Then the results challenge students to commence the inquiry process: "What does this make you think of? To what other results can you relate it? What can we assume? Infer? Predict?"

For example he demonstrated such a phenomenon during a panel on inquiry in the disciplines: He set on the table a standard chemistry beaker containing a clear liquid. He shook it vigorously and rather quickly the clear liquid turned sky blue. He set it down and left us to propose questions: "Was it because of the liquid? Would it be different in a different environment? What kind of liquid was in the beaker? Does it matter how hard you shook it? Would the same thing happen if you had not had a stopper on the top of the beaker?" As you can see, these questions attempt to identify the variables in this experiment. Dr. Isidor's observation is that students have some difficulty posing questions like these. They cannot easily locate the significant elements within such an experiment. (Perhaps they cannot ask the appropriate questions because they have not had enough chemistry, some would say. But the adults in the audience on that occasion seemed to demonstrate that you could ask reasonable questions even if you were not a chemistry major or a chemist.)

In too many science classes, the lab provides little or no experience in students' identifying their own problems, generating hypotheses, and figuring out experimental ways of investigating the causal factors involved. Most labs seem like exercises in getting the answers in the book, and consequently students learn little about proposing hypotheses and figuring out how to prove or disprove them.

Nonroutine Challenges—Mathematics.   In mathematics it all seems so easy. Myriad problems are presented within the textbook, and all we have to do is say, "Do all the even-numbered ones in your book." What's wrong with that? Unless we begin to look at math problems from a slightly different perspective, they will continue to bore students as they did me so many years ago. We need to help students learn how to approach complex situations, to become more metacognitive.

We can help students pay more attention to their processes of planning, monitoring, and evaluating. "What is the problem and what do I have to do?" Challenge students to stop, think, and plan a course of action. This is nothing unusual for readers of Polya's book *How to Solve It* (1957). It is here that we help students find those processes translatable into other disciplines, so they can say, "What I'm doing in algebra is similar to problem-solving approaches we are using with *The Great Gatsby* in English."

In elementary school Lois Granito has developed ways of helping students analyze word problems so they understand the concepts and do not just jump to adding or subtracting because of the words "more" or "less."

In college Evan Maletsky presents his students with a problem from the text but says, "Now, think along with me as I try out different possible strategies," some of which, he says openly, may be wrong. The point Evan is making is that it is important to "think through your problem solving," and to make public your approaches to the problem:

> Ask them [the students] where they came up with the plan of attack they used. If a mistake is made, challenge other students to find it. Don't erase incorrect solutions from the board; make these errors work for you by building on them. One useful strategy for this situation in the mathematics class is to ask how the problem might be restated so that the incorrect solution given would indeed be correct. Get the most you can out of the problems discussed. Make frequent use of the words "suppose" and "What if?" Once a student explains a particular solution, modify the problem and ask how the changes would affect the solution. . . . (Barell 1988)

What do these examples have to do with selecting what is conducive to "doubt, uncertainty, and difficulty?" For one thing, we do not generally have to look very far in math for "the problematic." Secondly, even though the problems are ready to hand, our focus should be upon making some of our students' thinking processes visible through their speaking and writing: "What is my problem, and how will I go about solving it?" Maletsky provides us with ways of extending the problems presented in the text by using student errors and modifying that which creates the difficulty with the "Let's suppose" or "What if" questions that rearrange the variables within the situation.

By emphasizing these questions we help students deal with the problematic in ways that research says is very productive (Sternberg 1985). Now, let us summarize what we have done so far:

Identify several criteria by which the problematic is recognized within the subject—that is, ways of identifying what was worth remembering and spending time thinking about. For example, we should spend a lot of time on how to get the main idea and showing students how to identify the important content clues, how to relate them, and how to draw conclusions, because this process is so important in all complex thinking. Similarly, we should spend a lot of time thinking about cooperation, interdependence, personal responsibility, because these concepts are important for personal growth and social stability. And finally, we should spend a lot of time thinking about the balance of forces, vectors, and motion, because these concepts help explain such phenomena as what makes a sailboat move through the water in a seemingly contradictory fashion. (What makes a sailboat get where it's going with the wind coming off the starboard bow is still not easy for me to comprehend.)

We have sought within the humanities and sciences a set of lenses with which to identify the problematic. Very often the "doubt, uncertainty, and difficulty" will come from encountering complex situations for which there is no clearly delineated pathway toward a solution; it will also come from encountering phenomena that create that "discrepancy" with our preconceptions, values, and ways of looking at the world.

Students' Problem Finding.   What we have presented so far relates to teachers' giving students problems to solve: The teacher identifies the problem and poses it for students. But what if we wish to encourage students to identify their own problems within the subject just as we asked them to identify their own questions (Chapter 5)? How do we go about doing this? Here are four suggestions:

As students read, challenge them to jot down in their journals problems and things that stimulate their curiosity. Use stems such as "What puzzles me" and "I wonder why" to foster their problem identification. (See Chapters 10 and 11.)

As students engage in any task (completing homework, a project, solving a textbook problem), teach them to become more aware of difficulties they run into and how they extricated themselves from these dilemmas. "What gave you problems in completing this assignment? [Identify.] How did you solve these problems? [Solve.] What did you learn by doing things this way? What might you have done differently? Why? [Reflect.]" These questions can become the focus of the Thinking Journals.

Help students identify problems faced by scholars in your subject area. What puzzles historians/physicists/poets, etc.? This is probably more appropriate for teachers' identification, but with a lot of practice and with certain kinds of students (more motivated) we can help them read their texts, newspapers, and journals with this question in mind: "What was the problem she/he was examining that enabled her/him to come up with this theory, principle, rule, theory, piece of artwork, etc.?" For example, when Michelangelo looked up on that empty Sistine ceiling, did he ask himself: "How can I, within the confines of this space, depict the glory of God and of His Creation?'' When Sir Isaac Newton sat under that apple tree and the apple fell close by, did he speculate, ''I wonder if the force pulling this apple toward earth is related to the force that maintains the orbit of the moon?'' Before placing the first words of *Macbeth* to parchment, did Shakespeare ponder thusly: ''What would happen if a king's loyal subject had ambition and a wife whose egomaniacal zeal for power ('screw your courage to the sticking place!') drove him relentlessly? How would each respond? What would their motives and consequences be?''

Armed with questions such as these, students can begin to think like the people whose laws, theorems, and works of art we study so diligently without ever wondering what brought them about. David Perkins's wonderful idea of *Knowledge as Design* (1986) will be helpful here.

It may be appropriate to teach students directly how to identify a problem. When do we know we have a problem?

POINT TO PONDER: Note when you know you have a problem.

Here are a few guidelines you might compare your responses with:

When there is a felt need, a discomfort about something. As noted earlier, it seems as if Emily's reflections began with an uncomfortable feeling about life in her classrooms.

When an expectation has been ''violated'' or unfulfilled: Teacher doesn't respond as you expect, or a parent does not provide you with something you want.

When you start out on a project like writing a book, you will realize that there will be challenges you haven't experienced before. This is the fun and the risk of it.

I recently asked a group of ninth graders, ''How do you know when you have a problem?'' This is the list they generated:

''When you want something to go another way—for example, to turn a D into a C.''

''Conflict in your life—when you want to make a team and haven't.''

''Someone tells you, for example, 'You're drinking too much. You're an alcoholic.' ''

''You see symptoms—illness or nausea.''

''When you feel guilty, like when you lied to someone.''

''When you're obsessed with something, like making a team, and your grades suffer.''

Students are very good at identifying their own problems, whether they are ones like these ninth graders' or others like Mary Mulcahy's first and second graders'. The latter's problems focused upon deflated kick balls, graffiti in the bathrooms, and flat tires on the way to Grandma's house.

Sternberg (1987) notes that few curricula give students practice in posing questions and problems of their own: "*We need to recognize the importance of problem posing and question asking in classrooms as well as on tests. . . . The time has come to measure and to teach not only how we answer questions, but also how we ask them.*" (Emphasis added.) We can do this by challenging students to identify problems within the subjects they study. The two unit plans presented below illustrate this inquiry approach.

LESSON STRUCTURE

Now that we have given some thought to the major stimulus for thought, let us attempt to create a meaningful structure for just such an experience.

Figure 7.1 provides the kind of framework that some might find meaningful.

Content

Content is the "stuff," the concepts, principles, or skills we think are worth spending time thinking about—for example, the process of generating solutions to problems as in "The Fox and the Grapes" fable. Here I wanted to introduce students to a process they would use for the rest of their lives. So it had lifelong value for applicability and transfer to novel situations. For another example I could focus upon the concepts of security and identity in *Franklin in the Dark*. The planning question is "What ideas/concepts/principles/processes are worth thinking about?"

A fallacy in much of what we call planning for thoughtfulness is to divorce thinking from content. As mentioned above, we are interested in the thought processes and feelings of those who are historians, biologists, poets, and mathematicians. We do not bring in the thinking processes from some separate domain and infuse them into the subject. They are there for us to disclose.

Objective

For an *objective* I could simply state: "Students should be able to generate at least two different solutions to the fox's dilemma." (If in the case of "The Fox and the Grapes" I wished to focus on the concept of "sour grapes," I would have specified an objective such as the following: "Students will try to figure out why the fox went away saying, 'Those grapes were probably no good anyway!' ") Here our emphasis is not on an intellectual process, but on extracting the meaning from the fable through concept recognition and development. Depending on developmental levels of students, we may become very specific and detailed about the elements of the thinking process. Here with first graders I wanted them to be able to state the problem and list several alternatives and then select the one they thought was the best. The planning question here is, What do I want students to

LESSON PLANNING FORMAT

Content: Concepts such as high expectations (Sour Grapes, etc.).
Generating alternative solutions to a problem.

Objectives: 1. Students should be able to generate several solutions to personal as well as literary problems.

2. Students will discuss, make meaningful, and relate story's concepts to own lives.

Strategy: 1. Initiating activity: "What can we do to solve a problem we have—for example, removing a wasp from our classroom?"

2. Core activity: Read "The Fox and the Grapes" up to the point where fox cannot reach the grapes. Then ask, "What would you do if you were in the fox's situation?" Generate alternatives and list on board with students' names."

3. Compare solutions: "Which is best and why?" Elicit criteria from students for choices made.

4. "Which would you select and why?"

5. Read remainder of the story (and, if desirable, discuss story's title and relate to own lives).

6. **Metacognition:** "How did we solve this problem?"

7. **Transfer:** "Where in your own lives do you use the same kind of steps?" Elicit solving problems with brothers and sisters, animals, etc.

Evaluation: There are many assessable understandings here:

1. Ability to understand the concept "sour grapes."

2. Ability to go beyond one solution.

3. Ability to compare and contrast (by identification of attributes and classification) different solutions and select "best."

4. Who participates and who does not?

5. What students learned: about foxes, themselves, their thinking, collaborative problem solving, etc.

Figure 7.1. Structuring to Encourage Thoughtfulness.

be able to do? Our instructional objective is stated in terms of student behavior—how we hope they will intellectually and emotionally engage content.

Failure to be specific here can lead to disorganized and less meaningful meanderings through any subject. At this point we need to make a significant decision: Do I want to introduce students to a new skill, such as problem identification or solution generation? Do I wish to introduce them to new concepts, such as identity (*Franklin in the Dark*)? Do I wish to develop and/or review the skills or concepts?

Strategy

Once we have these guideposts, we proceed to outline a *strategy*. A strategy is generally defined as a plan or an approach. (Some call it "method" or "procedure.") For example, one of the Allies' goals at the end of World War II was to capture Berlin, and their strategy involved the invasion of France by way of the Normandy beaches.

One important thing to remember about a strategy: A strategy suggests many possible ways for students to engage important concepts and ideas. There is seldom one way to get students involved. Think of a mountain peak: There are, even with Mount Everest, several ways of reaching the top.

A strategy can be conceptualized as containing these parts:

An *initiating activity*.

A *core experience* where we learn and practice skills and/or use our intellectual processes to think about ideas and concepts.

A *culminating activity* that provides opportunity to use skills and concepts in a productive fashion.

It might be helpful to think of these three elements as parts of what Costa (1989) calls the input-process-outcome model of intelligent behavior. It is also helpful to consider the "three-story intellect model" (Fogarty & Bellanca 1989) represented in Chapter 5; it suggests mental processes we can engage in at different stages: taking in information at the first story; using or processing it to make meaning at the second story; and applying or speculating at the third story.

We can start with an *initiating activity*. Our purposes at this point can be

To generate interest.

To relate content to prior knowledge.

To help students identify the discrepancy that generates thinking.

To bridge the gap between prior experience and new learning.

In the case of "The Fox and the Grapes," I "warmed up" my first graders by recalling an incident when a bee was in their classroom (it had been captured on a videotape we were making of their teacher). I asked them, "Do you remember when we made the videotape that we had a visitor?" (*"Yes!"*) "What was that visitor?" ("A bee!" "No, a wasp!" Here I got sidetracked by having them define the differences.) Here we were at Level 1: *Recall and Describe*. This was my way of linking what we were going to do with "The Fox and the Grapes" with their prior knowledge and experience.

Then I asked, "How would you get rid of the bee/wasp if you wanted to?" (Students generated a few solutions—Level 2: *Solve*.) Had I selected the "message" of the fable, I would have begun by asking, "Have you ever wanted something and not gotten it? How did you feel?"

Having given the students a taste of generating solutions, I then proceeded to the application or the *core activity*. The *core activity* is an experience either with practicing a new process or thinking productively about significant ideas.

For the *core activity* with "The Fox and the Grapes," I engaged the students in problem solving ("What would you do if you were the fox?") by listing their proposed solutions on the board alongside each person's name. This acknowledges the contribution of all members. I used a whole group strategy; with older students you might wish to use small groups or two-person problem-solving teams that report to the large group for evaluation.

Our sharing consisted of several steps within the decision-making framework: identifying pros and cons for each solution; comparing and contrasting; selecting the best solution; and, of course, determining why it was the best. Even with first graders, we could speak of criteria for "the best": easiest, least expensive, materials readily available, most familiarity with, etc. As you can see, I engaged these students in a lot of different thoughtful experiences and was not attempting to teach them how to perform a skill. Here I challenged them with Level 3: *Evaluating*.

A *culminating activity* helps us conclude the set of experiences, sometimes at a high point. This high point might be engaging students in using their skills or ideas to solve a new problem. In the case of "The Fox and the Grapes," I induced students to reflect on their own thinking. This is the *metacognitive* element of our intellectual framework.

After we had selected the best solution, I asked all the children, "Now, how did we go about solving this problem?" One girl, Betsy, said, "I remember what my mother did [in a similar circumstance]." A boy, David, said, "We made lists." So here we had students beginning to reflect on their own actions. Obviously, these are not adolescents, who are far more comfortable with thinking about the abstractions of their own thinking. It sets students on a course of generating their own rules for problem solving. (See Chapter 8.)

Now we come to *transfer*. Here we mean to suggest that it is very important to find ways of transferring the skills and concepts learned in one context to others, especially to life beyond the classroom. My first graders might have related this process to trying to figure out how to get what they want for their birthdays, how to settle disputes with their brothers and sisters, etc.

Evaluation

The final portion of the lesson can be *evaluation*. Here we determine if students have understood the idea of "sour grapes" and/or have developed or enriched their ability to generate alternatives. There are many ways of acquiring information to assess students' progress:

Use metacognitive and transfer questions.

Use application questions: "How can we create another instance of sour grapes to share with other first graders?"

Ask students to write stories (or design a project) illustrating the ideas.

Challenge students to create a model or metaphor: Here students relate what they have learned to their own experiences in ways that reflect their understanding (Barell 1980).

Ask students to self-evaluate: "Who can tell us what we have done so far? What have we learned? What do we need to improve on?"
Give standard written or oral tests.

This lesson format is designed to be flexible to meet a wide variety of needs at all instructional levels.

FROM LESSON TO UNIT PLAN: AN INQUIRY STRATEGY

A unit is a more complex curricular planning format than the lesson; it offers opportunities for a wide diversity of experiences as well as for more input from students. It seems logical to plan a longer time frame first and then divide it into smaller parts, like lessons. However, many find it easier to start out with a lesson format.

The major elements are the same as in the lesson. However, there are significant differences. The unit is longer than the lesson, of course, often several weeks in length. It is more complex, because it can encompass multiple concepts and intellectual processes, together with a broader spectrum of activities. It affords multiple opportunities for students with varying learning styles or propensities to participate and thus fosters meaning making, adventurous thinking, and the search for reasonableness. It can be used as a joint planning document for teachers and students, where both share control over establishing objectives and strategies.

Thus, the unit is an ideal vehicle for enhancing students' intellectual and emotional development, because it is a long-range, highly structured format that affords an enriching array of problematic situations to think about.

Planning the Unit

How do you go about planning a unit of instruction? Decide whether or not you wish to create a long-term and organizational framework to help you focus upon significant ideas, concepts, and skills within your subject. Decide the nature of the unit's focus: e.g., revolution, beaches, American short stories. You can expand the content from the lesson format or start with a question such as, What is the broad topic to be engaged?

Content: The Stuff to Think About.   One way to proceed from here is to identify the major concepts, ideas, principles, skills, and/or attitudes that will be the core of the unit's content. What is the stuff to think about? There are several ways to identify these concepts and skills. First ask yourself what it is you want students to spend time thinking about. Then make a graphic organizer (Figure 7.2), a spider map, a network tree (Jones, Pierce, & Hunter 1989). Start with your central concept (e.g., revolution) and spread out from there to all the related concepts and ideas. Then select those that are most significant according to your own criteria.

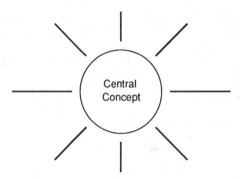

Figure 7.2

Thinking About the Stuff.   Once you have decided upon the conceptual core of the unit, you can ask yourself what intellectual processes you wish to stress in thinking productively (meaningfully, reasonably, and adventurously) about these ideas.

One way to start is to ask, "What do historians, physicists, poets do when they think about these ideas?" Here we try to disclose how the practitioner resolves issues within the subject.

If we pose this question, we can then isolate key processes: In what way can I use a problem-solving framework? (Chapter 8.) How can I encourage students to be adventurous in their thinking? (Chapter 9.) How are we going to stress reasonable solutions, interpretations, and perspectives? (Chapter 10.) How will I make it important for students to become more aware of their own thinking and in control of it? (Chapter 11.)

Using this kind of organizer with two teachers of eighth grade units, we identified these as central concepts:

Beth: Nature of a Good Town (part of a unit on adopting a town)
Connie: Vision of the American Dream in poetry (unit on American poetry)

Once we had our central concepts, we asked ourselves, "In what ways do we think about these concepts? What processes are going to be involved?" With Beth we realized that we wanted students to have criteria for a "good town" (e.g., students said, "Friendliness, recreational facilities, and schools"). Then we wanted them to draw reasonable conclusions, using reliable, objective, and accurate evidence (and counterevidence), about the towns they were corresponding with. With Connie we realized that students would be doing a lot of the same, in addition to comparing the American vision with present and past realities.

Designing a Strategy: Sharing Control with Students.   Next, design a strategy. Here is where we can experiment (Chapter 6) with sharing control with students to create the invitational environment (Chapter 5).

One way to do this is to generate a wide-ranging list of all the different kinds of activities you know will be important. List them and then arrange them in a

TABLE 7.1. Spectrum of Control

Teacher	Shared/Teacher & Student	Student
1. When must teacher make all decisions? When students are young, unable to accept responsibility, make decisions.	2. When can we share? When students can cooperate and accept responsibility.	3. When can students take more responsibility? After practice and experience, with greater maturity. When do students exercise control? When they listen, solve problems, and make content meaningful.

sequence that makes sense and that provides you with an *initial, core,* and *culminating activity.*

Another way to decide upon a strategy is to consider your major concepts and intellectual processes. If you want students to learn more about revolution or the beach on their own, then an inquiry strategy is most appropriate, two examples of which are given below. Or they can be divided into small or large groups and problem-solve together. In other words, you can derive the strategy from the major intellectual process: posing and resolving problems.

A third way is to perceive a strategy as a continuum from total teacher control over all instructional decisions through shared control over decisions to the seldom observed total student control. In Table 7.1 we pose this question: "When must the teacher be in control, and when can he or she share it with students?" As you can infer from the spectrum, we may begin the year in total control and gradually move toward more shared control. Shared control might begin in such domains as class rules, as when Carol Cutrupi asked her fourth graders, "What are rules? Why do we need them and what rules shall we make?" As students become better at group problem solving, we can gradually move toward sharing control over instructional decisions, as Rosemarie Liebmann did in high school. Once we have learned more about our students and observed how they accept responsibility, make decisions, and set goals for themselves, we can shift even further toward the spectrum's right.

Obviously, in longer units we can move back and forth along the spectrum, lecturing here, encouraging small groups there, and perhaps, when required, returning to direct instruction on key processes or points.

Considering the Spectrum of Control and deciding to share some control over time can be a momentous decision, for it communicates to students a willingness to work collaboratively, to learn from them, and to take a risk.

Once we make these decisions, we can select from a broad array of effective strategies, as shown in Table 7.2.

Once we have made some of these decisions, we can work with our three-tiered organizers: the *initiating, core,* and *culminating activities.* We shall see below how they worked with one specific unit.

TABLE 7.2. Effective Strategies

Teacher	Shared Teacher/Student	Student
Lecture	Group discussion	Self-directed independent
Direct instruction	Collaborative problem solving:	study/inquiry, group
Modeling	small/large groups	projects
Guiding practice	Role playing/simulation/jigsaw	
	teams/Independent practice	

Assessment of Outcomes.   Finally, we design experiences that will help assess what students have become better at doing: how they have grown, how our strategy may have affected them, and what suggestions they have for further inquiry and growth. For the lesson plan, we can use the kind of instrument mentioned in Chapter 4 and those on page 124. Very often the *culminating activity* is the means of assessment, where students demonstrate through various kinds of projects what they have learned by thinking so long and hard about the stuff of the unit.

Two Sample Unit Plans

Two unit plans that have impressed me over the years were implemented at the first and eighth grade levels by Mary and Ken. The appendix to this chapter contains a set of lessons for a unit in literature.

First Grade Unit on the Beach.   I was fortunate to witness the opening day of Mary's unit on beaches. As the result of some staff development work we were doing on problem solving, she decided that her traditional way of dealing with this unit—read and answer the questions at the end of the chapter—was not challenging enough. So she devised three questions that outlined her inquiry strategy:

"What do you know about the beach?" ("Full of sand . . . I go there every summer . . . lots of shells . . . I learned how to swim this year. . . .")

"What do you want to find out?" ("What are beaches like that haven't any shells?" (This question pleased the teacher and me because it illustrated Jenny's ability to envision the unusual or unexpected.) "Learn how to fish." (And this one may show some developmental differences with the first child's response.)

"How can we find the answers to these questions?" ("We can use the dictionary and encyclopedia like we did with studying Washington, D.C. . . . I can work with my friends.")

Mary was quite surprised with students' ability to apply prior knowledge to their inquiry and their interest in working with their friends. Her series of inquiry questions turned out to be a good diagnosis not only of their knowledge of the beach, but also how they transferred prior learning to new situations.

Eighth Grade Unit on Revolution.   Ken used a similar approach when he launched a unit on revolution in his eighth grade classroom. His content or stuff focused upon the concept "revolution," its nature, causes, and potential effects. (His concept contains historical significance, analytical potency, social as well as personal meaning. [What eighth grader has not already begun to think, at least semi-consciously, about rebelling against her/his parents?])

His objectives included having the students: describe the nature of revolution, analyze causes for revolution, in general and in particular the Russian Revolution, compare various revolutions—French, Russian, American, Industrial, Computer—suggest ways of preventing revolution (depending on student interest), and carry out other objectives that interest them.

This was a unit of several weeks' duration, so he needed a dramatic *initiating activity* to get his students intellectually and emotionally involved. Here is how he commenced his strategy:

On the opening day of this unit he walked into the classroom and made this announcement: "Starting today, all girls will get an A grade because they have been better behaved than the boys."

Obviously, after a pronouncement like this, students did not sit easily in their chairs. The class began to grow restless.

"That's not fair!" "How can you do that, Mr.—?"

At first, all the girls sat back and reveled in that quixotic decision, but then they began to reflect upon its arbitrariness, too. "Wait a minute! What are you going to do to *us* tomorrow?" "Today, it's great! But what's to prevent your picking on us next week?" And the negative responses grew from both boys and girls!

This, of course, was exactly what Ken expected and hoped for: fomenting a revolution right there in his Social Studies class. This was the opening gambit of his strategy to get students involved in considering the processes, causes, and effects of revolution, specifically the Russian Revolution. It is no wonder that his opening statement had the ring of a czarist ukase.

After his students had responded with predictable emotion (some even began to ask for an excessive number of passes, probably intending to report this to the office), Ken settled them down and moved on to the next phase of his plan: a consideration of their questions and concerns about revolutions in general and later the Russian Revolution specifically.

POINT TO PONDER: What made this initiating activity especially effective?

Ken was creating an emotion-laden discrepancy for his students: Classrooms are supposed to be run fairly with equal opportunity for all. Ken's statement upset all his students' perceptions about rights, rules, roles expected within the eighth grade classroom. Once he had fostered this kind of discomfort—or "violated expectation"—students began to identify problems they wished to inquire about:

What are our rights and how can we protect them?
What is a revolution and why do they happen? Are revolutions good, bad, or what? Who controls them?

How was the American different from the French and Russian? What makes a good leader?

What would happen if we (the students) actually conducted a revolution in this school? (One can see in the first question the growth of abstract thinking as defined by Piaget and others—the ability to articulate thoughts and feelings about nonconcrete abstractions and generalities that apply to people in general.)

These questions began the problem identification and solving portions of his strategy. Now, students wrote out all their questions and concerns as part of this *initiating activity*. These formed the basis for the rest of the unit, since Ken used them to supplement his unit objectives. Organized in advance, the activities that Ken introduced his students to followed this sequence of events:

1. Opening challenge to think.
2. Students' responses.
3. Students' questions and curiosities.
4. Organization and selection of objectives (from students' questions). Ken obviously knew in advance some of their concerns and was able to formulate a core of objectives from their initial curiosities and his own intentions planned beforehand.
5. The *core activity*. This involved establishing Research Groups around different objectives, thus providing students with elements of choice.
6. Research (conducted in library, resource materials, interviewing individuals, etc.). Here students gathered information (input) and processed it to make it meaningful. They took notes, created graphic organizers for concepts and chronological relationships, and held discussions in small and large groups under Ken's direction. For example, they read Pushkin's "Message to Siberia," viewed portions of *Dr. Zhivago*, played a simulation game focused on czar power, and read the writings of Karl Marx and Thomas Paine.
7. The *culminating activity*. Students took all the information they had been processing and began to find ways that facts and ideas connected and drew conclusions.
8. Reporting to the large group. Various forms of reportage were encouraged: written reports, panel discussions, aesthetic products depicting themes, role-playing problem situations. For example, in a "Meet the Press" format some students played the roles of Plato, Hegel, Marx, and Owen. These reports were Ken's assessment experiences. He could decide to give each group a joint grade or to evaluate students' work individually. He could also challenge students to evaluate themselves as members of a group and individually. (See Chapter 4.)

Ken's extension of the basic lesson planning format involves many of the concepts we have already discussed: creating the environment in which students can experiment, learn from each other, question and take risks; and share control with students over instructional objectives. The normal pattern is for the instructor to enter the classroom and say, "Today we begin a unit on Revolution; here's what we will be reading." Instead, Ken chose to give students some input into the kind of objective they pursued when he allowed their questions to become instructional intentions. They were in charge of the research phase; they made the meanings they uncovered, and they chose ways of sharing all these conclusions with their classmates. This is a vivid example of *sharing control with students.* (See Table 7.1.)

We haven't mentioned *transfer* and *metacognitive* phases of this plan, because I'm not sure Ken ever did anything with them. Nevertheless, it is not difficult to see how he could have used both very well:

TRANSFER   Where else in history do we encounter examples of revolutions and are they all the same? How does the process of revolution in history relate to any other subject area you know? How do these processes relate to your personal life? Where have you rebelled against authority?

POINT TO PONDER: How would you transfer the concept of revolution to other subjects and to your personal life?

Perhaps you thought of revolutions in science (Newton to Einstein), in mathematics (old to new math), the arts (from Impressionism to Cubism), and in our personal lives (getting married and becoming a parent).

METACOGNITION   What have you learned about your own thinking during the past few weeks? (Focus upon the data gathering and conclusion-formulation phases.) What have you learned about working with others? About your learning style in particular? How can you use any of these insights in other areas: school subjects and/or outside, personal life? These questions can be maintained in a Thinking Journal and not just at the end of the exercise. From the first day when students formulated their questions, they could begin writing responses to the following kinds of questions. (See Chapter 11.)

What is my task or problem?
How am I going about solving it?
Am I proceeding as expected? Do I need to revise my objective, strategies, etc.?
What am I learning about revolution? About my own thinking? About working in groups? What would I change, if anything?
What have I learned that I can use elsewhere? How?

EVALUATION   How did Ken evaluate students' progress? He had a number of different options including the following:

Student reports that included written documents, panel discussions, videotapes of revolutionaries playing different roles.

Students' written comments in their Thinking Journals.
Individual interviews with students during the unit.
Pupil self-evaluations.

And finally there should be in all units of study in schools an opportunity for students to pose meaningful questions: What are you now curious about? Where might this study of revolution lead?

Perhaps the most important aspect of this unit may be the students' encounter with the idea of revolution, its significance in history as well as in their own lives. Revolution as a concept is most important, because when revolutions succeed in different countries, they result in significant changes not only in leadership but in governance processes—as in the French, Russian, and American. They are also significant because one of the ideas we are focusing upon here is who controls the decision making. Revolutions have altered the control patterns within countries, and as the result of these shifts, persons have become empowered to take more control of their lives. So Ken's selection of an organizing concept certainly met several of the criteria mentioned above: subject matter significance and social value. It also relates to the developmental themes of adolescence—growing away from parental governance toward more independence.

POINT TO PONDER: How effective do you think these units were in terms of challenging students to think?

You might have considered the initial problematic situation presented in Ken's unit and Mary's respect for what students wanted to know as indicators that students would be highly engaged. What might have galvanized Mary's and Ken's students over such a long period of time was personal investment and commitment to a topic that had become meaningful to them through the strategy they selected: one of acknowledging what students knew and wanted to find out and one of confronting students' preconceptions about the fairness of life in classrooms. They presented them with situations that were nonroutine and authentic.

CONCLUSION

In this chapter I have focused upon disclosing problems to think about within various subject matters. In order to do this well, we must answer the questions "What is worth thinking about? What is worth spending time pondering? What concepts or skills are important enough to transfer into other subjects and into our personal lives?" I have suggested criteria for making these decisions, together with specific kinds of "discrepancies" or problems found within math, sciences, and humanities. Through the specific lessons and unit plans, I have attempted to exemplify all of these basic principles.

In the following chapter we discuss in greater detail the processes of problem solving and how this can be used in various subjects.

REFERENCES

Barell, John. 1980. *Playgrounds of Our Minds*. New York: Teachers College Press.

———. 1988. *Opening the American Mind, Reflections upon Teaching Thinking in Higher Education*. Upper Montclair, NJ: Montclair State College.

Beyer, Barry. 1988. *Developing a Thinking Skills Curriculum*. Boston: Allyn & Bacon.

Costa, Arthur. 1989. *Techniques for Teaching Thinking*. Pacific Grove, CA: Midwest Publications.

Fogarty, Robin, and Jim Bellanca. 1989. *Patterns for Thinking*. Palatine, IL: Illinois Renewal Institute.

Jones, Beau Fly, Jean Pierce, and Barbara Hunter. 1989. "Teaching Students to Construct Graphic Representations." *Educational Leadership* 46, 4:20–26.

Joyce, Bruce, and Marsha Weil. 1980. *Models of Teaching*. 2d. ed. Englewood Cliffs, NJ: Prentice-Hall.

Lieberman, Ann, and Lynne Miller. 1990. "Restructuring Schools: What Matters and What Works." *Phi Delta Kappan*. June, 759–764.

National Assessment of Educational Progress. 1986. *The Writing Report Card*. Princeton, NJ: Educational Testing Service.

Newmann, Fred. In press. "Higher Order Thinking in the Teaching of Social Studies: Connections between Theory and Practice." In *Informal Reasoning and Education*, ed. D. Perkins, J. Segal, and J. Voss. Hillsdale, NJ: Lawrence Erlbaum.

Perkins, David. 1986. *Knowledge as Design*. Hillsdale, NJ: Lawrence Erlbaum.

Perkins, David. 1989. "Selecting Fertile Themes for Integrated Learning." In *Interdisciplinary Curriculum: Design and Implementation*, ed. Heidi Jacobs. Alexandria, VA: The Association for Supervision and Curriculum Development.

Peters, Tom. 1987. *Thriving on Chaos*. New York: Alfred A. Knopf.

Polya, G. 1957. *How to Solve It*. New York: Anchor Press.

Resnick, Lauren. 1987. *Education and Learning to Think*. Washington, DC: National Academy Press.

Sarason, Seymour. 1982. *The Culture of the School and the Problem of Change*. Boston: Allyn & Bacon.

Schopp, Kenneth. 1982. "19th Century Revolutionary Russia: A Curricular Outline." Unpublished manuscript. Montclair State College.

Schrag, F. 1988. *Thinking in School*. New York: Routledge.

Sigel, Irving, Carol Copple, and Ruth Saunders. 1984. *Educating the Young Thinker*. Hillsdale, NJ: Lawrence Erlbaum.

Sternberg, Robert. 1985. *Beyond I.Q.: A Triarchic Theory of Human Intelligence*. Cambridge: Cambridge University Press.

———. 1987. "Questioning and Intelligence." *Questioning Exchange* 1, 1:11–15.

Swartz, Robert, and David Perkins. 1989. *Teaching Thinking: Issues and Approaches*. Pacific Grove, CA: Midwest Publications.

Tyler, Ralph. 1949. *Basic Principles of Curriculum and Instruction*. Chicago: University of Chicago Press.

Waterman, Robert. 1987. *The Renewal Factor: How the Best Get and Keep the Competitive Edge*. Toronto: Bantam Books.

APPENDIX: A MODEL FOR UNIT PLANNING

Goal.   Students will engage in problem solving about characters in an autobiography.

Rationale.   All characters in fiction and autobiography (as well as actors on the historical stage) engage in problem solving that lends itself to close analysis and, as a result, more comprehensive depth of understanding.

Content.   Nature of character, motivation, effects of behavior, problem solving, causal reasoning, and projecting consequences.

Time.   Two weeks.

Resource.   Richard Wright's *Black Boy*.

Strategy.

Lesson One

Objective.   To generate interest and engage in problem solving.

Content.   The dilemma Richard's mother faced when he killed the cat.

Initiate students into the study of this book by providing a thought-provoking incident that engages students in character analysis. This initial episode can be used to illustrate several of the major thinking processes associated here with character analysis—identifying significant character traits/attributes and using these to form an understanding of the people in the text.

These processes help us become familiar with a person's character by showing us his or her ways of confronting difficulties. Most significantly, we are engaged in gathering data from which to draw reasonable conclusions. We make judgments about character on the basis of actions within the text, and these pieces of evidence must then be related to each other in order to make valid inductive inferences.

Initiating Activity.   Read that portion of *Black Boy* wherein Richard hears his father tell him to kill a cat that is out on the front porch making a lot of noise. "I'm going to kill it," Richard tells his brother, who responds, "He didn't mean it!" Richard is determined to get back at his father, so he kills the cat by stringing it up from a tree. His brother is so appalled by this incident that he runs into the house and presumably tells his mother. Mrs. Wright comes out and exclaims, "What in God's name have you done?"

At this point stop reading the excerpt and ask, "What do you think was Mrs. Wright's problem at this point?"

Then: "How would you solve it if you were she?"

Students generate problem identification and solutions *separately*.

Then, they share in small groups to see if everybody defines the situation in the same way.

Then they hold large group sharing of problem identifications and solutions. Here you can illustrate how differently people see the situation and, by selecting one problem statement (e.g.: How to teach Richard a lesson about the value of life), illustrate that there are many different ways to solve a problem.

With four or five different solutions to the problem on the board, ask students to compare and contrast the solutions. Here they will identify significant attributes (e.g., external reinforcers versus more internal ones, force versus dialogic arbitration, etc.) among different solutions. Then ask, "Now, which would you choose and why?" This is the decision making move, and it will illustrate how we make decisions on the basis of criteria—in this case the attributes of the solutions previously identified. At this point we can ask, "Now, what does this solution tell us about the person who selected it?" This will elicit the character traits that are part of a character analysis.

Read Mrs. Wright's solution (one that filled Richard with terror) then ask, "Now what can you tell about her character from her kind of solution?"

Metacognition. "How did you decide what kind of person Mrs. Wright was?" Students may reflect upon the evidence, how it was used, and relate it to other pieces of evidence.

If you wish to test out students' abilities to identify problems, you can proceed in this fashion: "How did you decide what the problem was?" Students may reflect upon their ways of seeing the difference between givens and goals, between what is and what should be.

Transfer: "How do you go about forming judgments about other individuals?"

If you wish to continue with problem analysis, ask, "How do you go about identifying problems in your lives outside school?" Elicit a wide variety of strategies that will include such statements as "When something bothers me . . . when it doesn't feel right . . . etc."

Lesson Two

Objective.   Help students understand Richard's relationships with adults. Generate problem solutions.

Content.   Richard's listening to story of Blue Beard.

Strategy.   Read the passage where Mrs. Wright discovers the baby sitter reading the story of Blue Beard to Richard.

Ask comprehension questions: "What is the situation?" Elicit Who, What, When, Where. Discuss the meaning of the incident for Richard and his mother.

Ask, "If you were Mrs. Wright, how would you act toward Richard?" "What would you see as the problem, if any?"

"How would you solve it?" Elicit several different options.

Direct teaching of a thinking skill (see Beyer, 1988): "How did you generate solutions? What processes did you use (e.g., past experience, similar situations, put yourself into the situation, consider objective, etc.). (Metacognition.)

Ask, "What do these solutions tell us about you?"

Read Mrs. Wright's solutions and ask, "What does her solution tell us about her?" What conclusions can we draw? What is the evidence?

Practice: generate solutions to problems students identify in own personal life. (Transfer.) Discuss how their solutions reveal traits about them.

Initiate and maintain Thinking Journals where students generate their own reflections, questions, and relationships. See Chapter 5 and 11 for suggestions on students posing their own questions and problems.

Lesson Three

Objective.   Drawing valid conclusions.

Content.   Several incidents in Richard's life.

Strategy.   Midway through the book, for homework have students identify several incidents in Richard's life they think reveal most about his character. Give reasons for choices. Make all entries in Thinking Journals.

In small groups (or dyads) have students share incidents and look for commonalities. Ask, "What words do you think describe Richard's character after reading these incidents?" Challenge students to identify and agree upon several descriptors: courageous, rebellious, curious, hot-tempered, self-assured, etc.

In the large group, share these descriptors and make decisions about how well these apply to Richard. Identify criteria.

Take the descriptors/concepts used to describe Richard's nature and search the rest of the book for confirming and/or disconfirming episodes. This process of *relating* is very important: We want students to see episodes in relationship to each other so they can gather more evidence to support overall conclusions.

Draw tentative conclusions about Richard's character.

Metacognition. "How did we decide which we could say accurately described Richard?" Students should begin to identify these thinking processes: thinking of labels/concepts/descriptors, and then finding evidence to support one or more of these. The key intellectual process is identifying evidence that supports a claim or judgment.

Transfer. "How do you form character judgments about people you know?" Identify students' judgments formed in social situations and the evidence they have to support that. Ask, "Where else do you use the process of making judgments from observable/inferable evidence?"

(Note: from here we can stress other intellectual processes [for example, identifying assumptions or comparison/contrast] as well as significant ideas: growing up in the South; racial relations and how they have developed; dealing constructively with hostility; identity formation.)

Lesson Four

Objective.   Students engage in *culminating activity.*

Strategy.   With the help of students plan activities that engage students in analyzing the nature of one or more characters, perhaps ones not previously discussed in depth. These might come from Thinking Journals.

Create a role-playing situation wherein students place a character from autobiography in new situations and then discuss their analysis of the kind of person she or he was. Give reasons for choices with evidence to support.

Take Richard and place him in contemporary America and figure out how he would act. Discuss Richard's nature in this situation and relate actions here to others. (Can be separate essays/stories with rationale explaining what evidence supports your portrayal.)

Write stories that place major characters in novel situations. Provide reasons for choices.

Take an incident in the novel not discussed and have students engage in character analysis, providing support for conclusions and reflection on their own thinking (metacognition) and transfer to their own personal lives.

Any of these can be used for evaluation of students' facility with the processes and their using them to discuss main ideas within the novel: parental relations, race relations in the South, search for personal identity, etc.

Lesson Five

Objective.   Evaluate students' progress toward creating meaning and developing skills.

Strategy.   Create (alone or with student suggestions) experiences such as those above (Lesson Four).

Ask students to evaluate themselves. "How has your understanding of character and motivation changed during the reading of *Black Boy?* What have you learned most about why this is important to you? What have you learned about your own thinking?"

CHAPTER 8

Problem Solving and the Search for Meaning

OVERVIEW

In this and the three succeeding chapters I shall present significant elements of major thought processes: problem solving, creative and critical thinking, and metacognition. Identifying these elements and making suggestions for how they can be integrated within subject matter as well as taught directly should help us in our instructional planning. See Figure 8.1.

What do you suppose first and second graders consider to be the most important elements in their own problem-solving processes? When Mary Mulcahy asked her children, "How do you go about solving problems?" after an extended period of their doing just that in their classroom, she got answers such as the following: "Take the parts out of the problem that you don't really need—get to the main problem. . . ." "Make sure you know what you're trying to figure out before you start to do anything. . . ." "Make sure the problem makes sense. . . ."

These children have learned, through practice in trying to figure out what to do in a complex situation, that one of the most important aspects is *understanding the problem*. Researchers on problem solving have come to the same conclusion: that understanding the nature of the problem, or attempting to make it more meaningful, is one of the keys to figuring out what to do. The children identified many more rules for their own problem solving, and I shall return to them later in the chapter, but what interests me about their thinking is that these children zeroed in on the vital core of problem solving and decision making.

Consequently, in this chapter I would like to share with you different approaches to helping adults become more familiar with their own thinking. We will explore several strategies that help us understand the nature of difficult situations, so we can make better plans of action. Too often we act impulsively, identifying

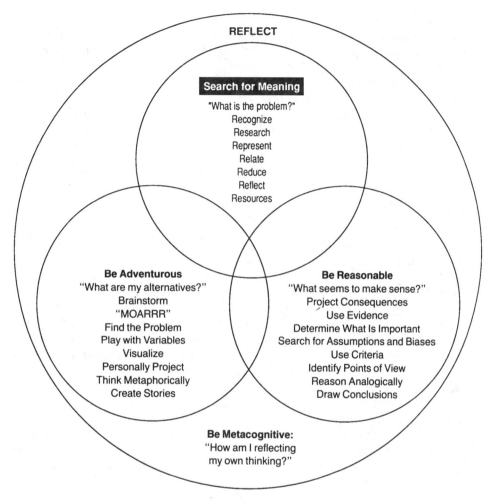

Figure 8.1. Overview of Intellectual Processes.

and selecting solutions that might not deal with the real situation. Let me present two different situations to illustrate my point.

Situation One: Imagine your friend hit a ball through the neighbor's window.

POINT TO PONDER: Now, if you had just learned this, how would you respond? Jot down your thoughts.

Some people say "I would run away!" or "I would go to my neighbor and make restitution for damages." Others say "I'd work it out with my friend" and still others say: "It's not my problem at all. It's his (or hers)!"

But usually there are a few folks who reject these alternative courses of action as being precipitous: "I don't have enough information yet. I'd have to ask some questions, such as: Where was I? What was broken? How well do I know the neighbor? Were there other people involved?"

These people realize that before we can act, we should conduct as much research to gather information as possible. Had others asked such questions, they might not even consider running away. They might not have a problem at all.

Situation Two: Imagine you and your colleagues have been asked by the superintendent to solve the problem of teacher absenteeism on Mondays.

POINT TO PONDER: What would you suggest your committee do? Jot down your thoughts.

You probably began by asking a lot of questions to determine possible reasons for such absenteeism, to look for patterns of behavior, and to understand local and other conditions that might have affected teacher attendance. However, when I have given this situation to adults to think through some have basically "solved" it in two minutes—make Monday payday or provide free breakfast on Monday mornings. There was little or no attempt to understand the nature of the situation before generating one or two solutions quickly, but then a great deal of time was spent discussing how to implement them. There was no checking out of assumptions that teachers were not present because there was something wrong with either the school or Mondays.

In both situations we have failed to heed Mary's students' advice—understand the situation before you act.

What I have tried to do is figure out ways of saying to myself, "Wait a minute. Are there questions I should ask myself before generating solutions and acting impulsively?" Figure 8.1 represents some of these questions we can ask before generating many different possibilities:

Do I understand the nature of this situation?
How does this situation make me feel?
Do I need to do more *research?* Ask for more information?
How can I *represent* the elements within the situation?
Can I *reduce* the problem to several different parts?
Can I *relate* this to any other problem?

These are questions I usually ask after posing problems to see how many participants thought of analyzing the situation in these terms. These questions help our students figure out the meaning and significance of any doubt or puzzlement during individual lessons or units. Figure 8.2 presents these questions and others under the heading "Search for Meaning" of a problem, because I believe this is what we should do before acting impulsively to arrive at a solution. When we say to students and to ourselves, "Now, think before you do anything!" these are the kinds of considerations that will help us be thoughtful. Therefore,

Search for Meaning and Understanding: WHAT KIND OF PROBLEM IS THIS AND WHAT CAN HELP SOLVE IT?

RECOGNIZE: What feelings do we have about the situation?

RESEARCH: What information do we need to solve this?

REPRESENT: Can we draw a picture or make a diagram?

RELATE: How is this related to other problems? What ideas or concepts do we recall from other problems? What patterns are evident?

REDUCE: Can we reduce the problem to several parts? Can we identify reasons why this problem exists?

REFLECT: What assumptions/biases/definitions should we question? Have we identified all significant information?

RESOURCES: Are there persons and things that can help?

WHAT DO WE WANT TO DO? Help students set/define a specific objective: "How to . . . " close gap between givens and our goals.

Be Adventurous: Generate alternative solutions; brainstorm alternatives. Go beyond the boundaries. Redefine problem. Challenge assumptions and definitions. Visualize, create model, personally project, play "What if?"

Search For Reasonableness: Anticipate results: If we do this, what will happen? Compare and contrast solutions using important characteristics. Select alternatives based upon criteria and good evidence.

Take Action and Monitor: How well are we doing? Do we need to revise our goals and strategies? Redefine the problem in new ways?

Be Reflective: Evaluate our ways of solving this problem: How well did we do? Why? What would we do differently next time? Why?

Figure 8.2. Problem Solving Processes.

these questions should be entertained—although perhaps not always—before we venture out to generate a lot of ideas and arrive at a conclusion about what to do or believe.

TEACHING PROBLEM SOLVING DIRECTLY

I will start here with problem identification, because it seems the most important; it is the basis of good problem solving and—as we shall see in the next chapter— the basis of good creative inquiry. This was where Karen and Mary Ellen started: What do you think Franklin's problem was?

Problem Identification

Problem Identification can be viewed from a number of different perspectives, but one that I have found helpful is this: Noticing the differences between what *is* and what *should be,* or the difference between the *givens* and the *goals.*

Givens and Goals.   This phrase was invented by Robert Barnes of Lehigh University, who uses the following framework with his students: (1) formulating the problem; (2) generating tentative solutions; (3) evaluating solutions; and (4) choosing a solution (Barnes 1988).

The stage of formulating the problem simply consists in helping students recognize the gap between the real situation and the ideal. This is classic problem identification strategy, and it is most useful for our purposes. In the ball-through-the-window problem, however, there are several ways of looking at the "givens":

The ball is in your neighbor's house now.
Your friend did it.
You are a friend of the person responsible.
There may be damage to the neighbor's house.

What might your "goals" be, or what is the "ideal" in this situation?

To have the ball on the playing field.
Your friend didn't do it. (Wishful thinking!)
To reestablish good relations with your neighbor.
To repair damages to the house.

As you can see, some of these hoped-for ends are easier to attain than others. But the idea of the difference between what we have and what we want is fairly obvious to see. How does Barnes's "goals and givens" help us with our students? For example, in geometry we have two triangles with angles and lines of specified dimensions (our given), and what we want (our goal) is to know if they are congruent and to prove it. Some students have real difficulty seeing a problem in terms of what we have (certain information) and what they want or need to do. Barnes's formulation seems to help here.

Franklin the turtle had a problem: The "given" was that he was afraid of small dark places; his "goal," we could assume, might be to become more comfortable with living inside (or outside) his shell. Adults who work on this problem see several other possibilities, such as his having the goal of "accepting himself."

"Givens" and "goals" can also be used to help students identify what *they* might be having difficulty with. What don't they understand in a given situation? What haven't they enough information about? This might not be the same as what they are being asked to do by a teacher or a textbook. For example, if we ask them to compare and contrast *Macbeth* and *Hamlet,* the problem might be "How do I go about it? Compare how? Contrast what with what?" If we want them to imagine themselves as sailors on Columbus's ship in 1492 and to write a diary of the voyage, their problem might be "How will I get information on the life of a fifteenth-century Spanish sailor?" Or it might be "How do I write a diary entry?" In other words, we ought to spend some time helping students understand what the "doubt, uncertainty, or difficulty" is for them. Too often we incorrectly assume that our problem identification is the same as our students'.

The Seven R Strategy.   The Seven R verbs help us delve into the situation in detail before we begin to set an objective and generate alternative solutions, to make reasonable decisions and be reflective. Figure 8.2 makes questions of them but here they are given as suggestions.

> *Recognize* the feelings we have in the situation.
> *Research* the kinds of information we need from whom?
> *Represent* the situation or problem internally through visual thinking and/or by drawing a picture, a chart, or a diagram.
> *Relate* this situation to others, if possible. How are they similar or dissimilar?
> *Reduce* the situation to a number of different parts. Can we identify reasons why this problem exists?
> *Reflect* on what assumptions, biases, definitions should be questioned. Consult *resources* who can help.

It is probably evident to you at first glance that posing these seven Rs helps us understand the problem and thereby makes it more meaningful. I have placed them in the order that seems most logical to me, but any order will do if it works for the student. That is the nature of a heuristic, a process that may lead to a good solution.

Recognize Our Feelings.   Why is this important? Many times the first indication of a dilemma is a feeling of dissatisfaction or annoyance. "I can't do this!" we hear ourselves say.

Recognizing—not hiding or repressing—our feelings is a principle of good problem solving, because if we fail to take note that we are suffering frustration and anger, we might do things not in our best interest. I used to spend lots of time trying to find a parking place in New York City; I would get angry and mutter uselessly to myself, and then all my ways of solving this problem just got clogged up like a drain. If I calmed myself down, saying "O.K., you're angry. Let's get beyond that," then I had a better chance of thinking clearly. Consequently, I would move on to an entirely new block and often be successful.

One of Rosemarie Liebmann's students once wrote in his Thinking Journal, "This problem scared me while reading it. It got better after I read it 6 or 7 times. I just took it step by step. . . ."

Perhaps the rereading and the writing helped Rich calm himself down. These were his ways of coping; other ways include sharing problems with a partner and discussing them with the whole class, so we can realize that we aren't alone in our bewilderments.

Teaching Strategy

> Pose questions: "How does this make you feel?"
> Encourage students to record feelings in Thinking Journals. (See Chapter 11.)
> Acknowledge your own feelings and invite others to share.

Research Facts. As noted above, too often we act quickly in complex situations. We are impulsive and fail to keep ourselves open to alternatives.

This suggests that we have not been trained to gather information before we start defining the problem. To be fair, most of us do not automatically think, Let me see, do I have enough information? What do I know about the situation and what do I need to determine? These questions serve as a kind of metacognitive stock-taking.

Teaching Strategies. With any complex situation, pose questions of this sort before solving or in lieu of solving to emphasize the importance of questioning: What do I know and what do I need to find out? What do I know and what do I *think* I know? (The latter challenges students to identify knowledge in the gray areas.) Encourage students to jot down the answers to these questions in their Thinking Journals, as they work through complex situations.

Represent the Problem in Other Forms. When a problem is presented in written or verbal form, good problem solvers find ways to translate it into some sort of internal or external representation. I automatically relate this to the algebra problem of two airplanes, one leaving New York City and the other leaving Chicago. At what point will they both have covered X number of miles? I always disliked these problems (and still do), because they seemed to have so little relationship to everyday life. In order to solve them I had to create a picture in my mind and/ or draw a picture. Hayes (1981) notes:

> To understand a problem . . . the problem solver creates (imagines) objects and relations in his head which correspond to objects and relations in the externally presented problem. These internal objects and relations are the problem solver's *internal representation* of the problem. Since people create them, different people may create different internal representations of the same problem.

Hayes's last statement suggests that each of us has different ways of aligning objects in relationships. Sigel (1990) speaks of "representational competence" as the ability to internalize experience and store it in "some type of symbol system." "All knowledge," he asserts, "is in some form of representation."

In the ball-through-the-window situation, some people visualize standing right there with the friend, but others see themselves in their kitchens observing from the window and others see themselves as far away (thus avoiding personal involvement).

In literature and history we can often resolve some dilemma by creating a picture of how ideas and concepts relate. For example, in Chapter 7 we discussed Ken's unit on revolution. Opportunities could develop where it might be easier for his middle school students to understand the relationships among the American, French, and Russian Revolutions if they drew diagrams relating causes/ processes/effects/key ideas, and so forth. Figure 8.3 gives an example of this kind of mapping.

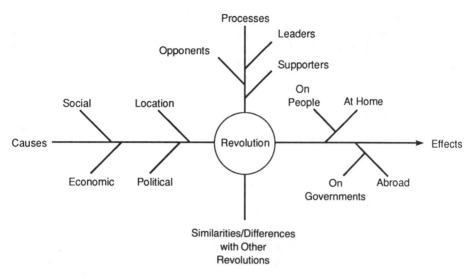

Figure 8.3

Hayes notes (1981) that drawing pictures or diagrams "can be enormously helpful in solving problems."

The power of visualization may be most evident in sports where athletes concentrate upon "seeing" the course they must run or the dive they must make. Football coaches' play diagrams are a well-known example. Olympic skier Vreni Schneider prepares for her downhill and giant slalom races by picturing a perfect run down the mountain (Nelson 1989).

Visualization in these instances does more than help the athlete picture precisely what she/he must do—out on the ice during a figure-skating contest, for example. Intense visualization sets up expectations that we can respond to almost unconsciously; it is a form of visual script that attunes our bodies and minds to perform as we wish under unusual or trying circumstances. Internal and external representation is not, in other words, merely an academic exercise we use to get good grades. People who market "success" materials in the form of taped speeches and written materials are always touting the power of visualization. It works.

Internal representation, or visualization, is how many productive thinkers have been able to figure out problems. Einstein was known for his thinking "more or less in clear images" (Ghiselin 1955) and Gamow, originator of the Big Bang theory of the universe's origin, used "intuitive pictures and analogies from historical or even artistic comparisons" (Barell 1980) to make problems comprehensible.

As one high school student wrote in his Thinking Journal, "I am learning that by keeping myself calm and *visualizing things* I can think more clearly." (Emphasis added.) Visualizing, in this case, has helped the student fashion the meanings he sees in the problem.

Teaching Strategies. Ask students to form pictures in their minds. "Please tell us what kind of an image you have, Jennifer, of the beach, of revolution, of Holden Caulfield, of the human cell. How is yours similar or different, David?" Examine each image or model for accuracy or fit, in accordance with evidence at hand.

Ask a group to draw a spider map to chart out major factors, elements, and their relationships. Then seek relationships, organize concepts hierarchically, and identify gaps in our knowledge for further research.

Challenge students to create their own models of photosynthesis or how radar works (Mayer 1989). See Chapter 9 for more details on model and metaphor making.

Relate This to Other Problems.   Reuven Feuerstein (1985) observed that students are often "episodic" in their thinking. By this he meant that they do not spontaneously relate one situation to another already studied or known to them. They think with intellectual blinders on. "What is this problem? What am I supposed to do with it?" are questions that drive some of us to distraction, because we think students should see the relationship between what's in front of them and what we did yesterday. But very often they do not. As Bransford (1986) notes, we possess a great deal of "inert" knowledge we do not seem to use where appropriate.

In every subject this process of seeking relationships is vital, because it affords us an opportunity to transfer key concepts and ideas from prior experience to a present situation and use it productively. Seeking relationships of this kind helps us find effective strategies and build upon them, helps us classify the problem (identify problem type) and thus understand something about its structure. "A sophisticated problem solver," notes Hayes (1981), "recognizes many problem types. . . ."

Teaching Strategies. How do we disclose these kinds of relationships? First, we have to search our memories for situations that are similar. We do this by asking ourselves:

> How is this situation like any others I know of (within the subject or in my personal life)?
> How are they similar (and dissimilar)? What are their important characteristics?
> What conclusions can I draw from these relationships?

We know from research (Mayer 1975 and 1989) that seeking internal and external connections improves our understanding and facilitates transfer to novel problem situations. Thus, we want to stress the conscious establishment of linkages, connections, and relationships within the subject and to students' lives beyond the classroom.

It is when we *relate* one problem type to another that we might *recall* vital concepts, principles, or ideas we encountered in an earlier situation. Hartman (1987) describes this step as asking, "What concepts, definitions, rules, procedures, equations, and principles might you need to solve the problem? Why are they needed for this problem? How could you use them? When?''

Recall is a very important step. The processes of problem solving are not more important than the conceptual content. Some of us too often make the mistake that the concepts of responsibility, friendship, or safety (in the ball-and-window problem) are less important than the processes I am writing about now. But recalling important concepts can make a problem meaningful. If we see how aggression, for example, was a causative factor in the Korean and Vietnamese conflicts, we might analogize between them and what happens in any other international hot spot where American interests are supposedly at risk.

Franklin's dilemma reminds adults of similar problems they have encountered with their own children and adolescents or at times in their own lives when unreasonable fears overcame them. Recalling such past difficulties can help put present-day ones into perspective.

A second strategy is to use our concept maps to help us see relationships. In regard to the concept map above (Figure 8.3) we ask:

> What characters, actions, results, objects are related to each other—within
>   the subject and in other areas? What patterns do I notice?
> Are there relationships I want to investigate further?
> How do these relationships affect my understanding of the situation? What
>   conclusions can I draw from perceiving these relationships and patterns?

A third strategy, therefore, involves searching for patterns. What, if any, patterns do I notice here—causal/motivational, spatial/geometrical, organizational/structural, sequential/historical, hierarchical?

Teach students the meaning of *pattern:* ''a combination of qualities, acts, tendencies, etc., forming a consistent or characteristic arrangement'' (Random House Dictionary 1967). And challenge them to find various kinds of patterns in their lives. This obviously leads to extensive comparing and contrasting to identify significant similarities and differences.

Reduce to Several Different Component Parts. ''A very powerful way to simplify the search for a solution is to break the problem into parts,'' notes Hayes (1981). Nicole went through several problem-solving exercises before her first grade teacher, Mary Mulcahy, asked her and her classmates how they went about solving these problems. ''You make them littler,'' Nicole said. Another student said, ''Take the parts out of the problem that you don't really need—get to the main problem.'' Without any direct instruction in breaking things into parts, first graders have realized, through varied practice (and this opportunity to reflect), that a good strategy to use with a complex problem is to ''make it littler.''

For example, in our ball-and-window problem, our thinking can be abetted by breaking it down into these parts: How to deal with the friend; how to deal with the neighbor; how to retrieve our ball.

For example, in the teacher absenteeism problem there are many facets: varieties of reasons for absence, each teacher's attendance record, school policy in the past, and possible solutions are some that come immediately to mind.

Dealing with these parts, of course, calls into question our priorities. Some who confront this situation wouldn't accept any of my problem statements above. "It's not my problem to begin with," they say. So they deal with only their own responsibility, and this simplifies it for them.

"Fractionation," as Hayes calls it (p. 35), is one good way of not being overwhelmed by a complex situation. Rosemarie Liebmann has been helping her high school students learn how to approach problems in mathematics by, among other strategies, breaking them into parts. One day she asked her students to identify a difficult problem outside school and to relate in their Thinking Journals how the strategies used to solve it may have helped. ("What was the problem? How did you solve it? Note your thinking processes.")

One student, Mark, noted that one day, while speaking with a friend, he used his problem-solving strategies. He wrote in his Thinking Journal:

> I got her to break down her problems into smaller ones, so that the sum of problems that she had made would not seem so overwhelming—like an incredibly hard algebra problem, where you take it one step at a time rather than all at once, which makes you depressed when you can't solve it.
>
> Then we discussed each problem separately and discussed different ways to solve it. . . . After we discussed each problem separately, we started to discuss her problems as a whole—like math again, where at the end you tackle the entire problem. . . . I got her to use a little metacognition, which I think is understanding and recognizing one's problems. She realized that she needed to be a little more positive about herself, and much more confident. . . .
>
> Although I personally did not do every step, I led someone else to doing it, and I'd much rather see someone else solve their problems with a little help from me than solve my own problems by myself.

Mark is an excellent example of someone who is beginning to internalize problem-solving processes and, in this case, helping someone else to carry out a similar process. It is also interesting to note Mark's identification of the role that feelings play in problem solving: breaking things down into manageable parts sometimes helps us overcome initial doubts and might increase confidence. "She realized that she needed to be a little more positive about herself" is the kind of knowledge of self that we shall discuss in more detail in Chapter 11.

Something else we see operating in Mark's little story: his ability to act as a "coach" for a friend, helping her think more clearly. He did this, according to Forman and Kraker (1985), by helping her become more metacognitive about her situation. Parents, teachers, and friends can play this role simply by listening and helping someone monitor his or her own thinking processes.

"Fractionation" requires analytic skill, so perhaps it's easier for students to practice a little bit on personal, practical situations first and later apply their learned skills to mathematics or literature. In any case, fractionation helps us deal with what might at first appear to be something that is overwhelming.

Teaching Strategies. Use our concept maps or graphic organizers as above. Use Thinking Journals wherein students can identify the problem and record how they reduced it to manageable parts. Teach students to think in terms of various human and natural situations: characters/objects; motives/causes/input; actions/processes; consequences/results/output; relationships: causal/spatial/emotional/historical/conceptual, etc.; environment/context/setting; sequence of events/plot.

Reflect on Assumptions or Biases and Definitions.   Here is where we can be both adventuresome and reasonable. Very often a problem will require a student to question his or her underlying assumptions about its nature. For example, in the ball problem, most adults naturally assume that the window is closed and that the ball broke it. However, someone sooner or later raises the issue: "Are we to assume that the window is closed or open?" As I noted above, some even question whether the window is attached to a house, a reflection that arose only after working on this situation with hundreds of people. An original insight, to say the least.

Most people assume that you, the problem identifier, are standing right there next to your friend, and not in your living room looking out the window from high atop a thirty-five-story apartment building. Indeed, most people assume that they are witnesses to the incident, but Hank, a math teacher, noted this in his initial set of questions: "Was I even there to witness this event? Perhaps I was in San Francisco and heard about it over the telephone." Thus, he took himself entirely out of the problem.

The above assumptions are representative of those that are present within any situation, from a physics problem to one involving a dispute between two nations.

Teaching Strategies. Consequently, we should learn to pose these questions:

> What must be true about this situation in order for us to make sense of it? (In other words, what assumptions must I make?)
> What assumptions am I making about beaches, revolution, about the characters in this book, about this physics problem?
> Which of these assumptions do I need to question?

If we learn to do this, we shall not fall victim to solving problems that need not be solved: If there is no broken window, we need not worry about expenses. There are other "content free" problems that challenge our underlying assumptions:

> Cut a bagel into twelve pieces, using three straight slices. (What assumptions do we need to challenge about the nature of a "slice," location of the bagel on the table, about the size of the resulting pieces?)
> Take six regular straws within their paper wrappers and create four congruent, equilateral triangles with no overlap (ruling out, thereby, the Star of David configuration) and no extraneous figures.

Identifying and questioning assumptions is significant because unless we train ourselves to pose some of these questions, we are in danger of leaping to identify solutions that might not meet our demands or those of the situation. Each of us should generate the kinds of question that help him or her the best, because how we analyze the situation directly affects the solutions we generate.

Setting an Objective.   Every situation requiring thinking demands that we, at some point, pose and answer the question, "What do I want to do here?"

The more we emphasize goal and/or objective setting as it relates to daily instructional problems, the easier it will be for students to relate these techniques to personal goal setting. The more we emphasize that students form their own questions—"What do I want to do about . . . ?"—the more we work toward empowering students to take some control and responsibility for their own education.

The objective we set should meet the following criteria: It should be specific—the more the better. It must be derived from the situation. It will probably lend itself to multiple approaches. Very often it can be stated in the term "How to."

If the objective does not meet some of these criteria, we might not be as precise in our thinking as we could be. For example, if our objective is "how to avoid blame" for the accident with the ball, we could choose a number of alternative actions: run, point the finger, turn the back, and so forth. The point is we must know what it is we wish to accomplish. Successful managers always explain their achievements by printing out the precise objectives they have set.

We should also remember that the students' concept of their objectives might not initially correspond with ours, because they see the problem differently or because they are experiencing difficulties with prerequisite skills.

Be Adventurous in Our Thinking

Generating Alternative Strategies or Solutions.   Generating alternatives may be the most practiced operation of all those mentioned here. We spend a lot of time in "brainstorming" exercises and in other kinds of experiences, designed to suggest multiple solutions that might be more or less adventurous, different from the norm or usual.

Here is one way of proceeding to generate alternatives:

M   Use *my* prior experience: "What do we know will work?"
O   Use *other people's* experiences: "What do we think might work?"
A   *Adapt* and combine different solutions. Play with possibilities: "What new combinations can we imagine?"
R   *Represent* the situation: "What picture can I create of the problem or a related one?"
R   *Relate* to similar problems or create an analogy. "How is this problem similar to another?"
R   *Reflect* upon assumptions: "What are we assuming here (as in the bagel or straw problems above)?"

Thus, we have an acronym for brainstorming that helps us do more than just say, "Think of lots of ideas." The word *MOARRR* might help to guide our generation of solutions.

Any of these means of generating an alternative can provide opportunities for good classroom discussion, because they will call forth our skills of weighing the pros and cons of each, identifying evidence in support and projecting consequences before we make our decision. (See Chapter 9.)

Students' Adventuring with Alternative Pathways.   In mathematics and science we most often use textbook problems that have a "right" answer. However, there are usually many alternative pathways to that right answer! It's a possibility that our students will figure out a wide variety of ways of reaching the intended destination, and we teachers must remain open to it. "What was the problem and how did you approach it?" are questions designed to help students focus upon their problem analysis and strategy generation. For example, with a problem for first graders like $8 + 6 = ?$ there are varieties of ways of solving it: "6 and 6 is 12, and 2 more is 14 . . . 8 and 8 is 16. But this is 8 plus 6. That's 2 less, so it's 14 . . ." (Peterson, Fennema & Carpenter 1989). It is important to ask for strategies to solve problems not only when there is a wrong answer, but also, and perhaps more significantly, when there is a right answer. This is what von Oech (1983) calls searching for "the second right answer." It is often "the second, or third, or tenth right answer which is what we need to solve a problem in an innovative way," he says.

For example, in first grade Karen used a very concrete problem with which to start her students thinking about problems and generating multiple solutions: "Suppose my finger was caught in my desk, and I couldn't get it out, what could I do?" "Use your other hand. . . ." "Have your partner help you. . . ." "Call the teacher. . . ."

Here Karen noted that an everyday situation "which they could relate to, allowed their minds to open up and come to understand the terminology." In order "to open up" we need to understand the situation and feel some comfort with it (Mahn 1989).

From the "finger" situation Karen moved on to role-play this dilemma with her first graders: "A bully is picking on a nice boy on the playground." Karen noted, "Once again the solutions were plentiful (walk away, tell the teacher, get a big brother to help, say something unexpected, call a name back, etc.). Videotaping this session, I realized that relating [them to] everyday situations . . . enabled [the students] to comprehend the terms problem and solution. Many of the youngsters experienced similar problems within their own lives, and could associate the actions and emotions which accompanied the situation (i.e., I got my hand caught in a car door and I cried. My brother always picks on me, and it's not fair)."

When we create within our classrooms opportunities for all students to share their diverse strategies as Karen has done, we create wonderfully enriching environments, where we can all learn from each other's creativity and insightfulness. We must attempt to pause after receiving the "right" answer and help students identify their thinking processes. How dull it is always to have one "right" way to solve every problem!

TABLE 8.1. Weighing Alternatives

Run Away		Point the Finger		Work with Friend	
Pro	**Con**	**Pro**	**Con**	**Pro**	**Con**
Quick; distances me from the action.	Cowardly.	Deflects attention.	Can cause bad feelings.	Maintain good relations with friend.	Might be harder.
Evidence		**Evidence**		**Evidence**	
I've done it before.	Adults say so. Feels bad.	Saw it work elsewhere.	Happened to me.	Strong feelings for friend.	Past experience.

The Search for Reasonableness

Anticipating Results/Projecting Consequences. "What will happen if I do this?" is a powerful question to ask, because it calls upon us to begin being reasonable by projecting consequences. Very often, when we project consequences, we find that they align themselves as pros and cons for each alternative. With such possible favorable and unfavorable consequences, we can then search for evidence that supports or contradicts these possibilities.

For example, in the ball-through-the-window situation we can say our objective is to avoid blame and we have three options: run away, point the finger, or work with our friend. (See Table 8.1.)

I have used this kind of chart with middle school students who were figuring out how to solve the problem of ozone depletion in John Borchert's classroom and with high school students determining the boys' problem in *Lord of the Flies* and the best plan of attack. Sometimes I ask, "How do we make a decision among all these alternatives?" and someone will say, "Whatever works best." Then you work with students to establish the criteria for a best solution; these may include efficiency, cost effectiveness, personally satisfying or long-lasting results.

Using these criteria, someone might select running away as the most effective solution, but then another student might retort that running away violates his or her personal code of ethics and that standing up to face the music is the best.

Karen Mahn discovered that this process of anticipating results grew quite spontaneously when her first graders came to discuss their solutions to problems. "As I sat in on group A's solution session, it wasn't so much the answers which amazed me, but rather the questions the children were asking concerning the responses [to the problem]" (Mahn 1989). After reading part of the story *Whose Mouse Are You?* (Kraus 1970), children were asked to figure out how to rescue a mother mouse from inside a cat.

Jessie's solution was to "Open the cat's mouth and take the mouse out," but Amy asked, "What if he was a mean cat—how would you get near it?" Jessie's response to this question was quite simple: "Kill him."

Sergio's solution was "Squeeze the tail and its mouth will pop open," but Jimmy asked, "How? What if the cat doesn't feel the squeeze?" Sergio's response was very direct: "Then take its eyeballs out."

Amy anticipated something about the cat's personality; Jimmy projected something about its physiology.

Karen discovered that her first graders had many different ways of examining the solutions generated by their friends. What is important here is to engage students in examining each other's choices, as Karen and Mary Ellen did with Franklin, to compare and contrast them. When we do this, we are identifying the important attributes of each, and these attributes then become the criteria by which we make a choice.

Selecting Alternatives.   Here we want students to state a preference based upon good reasons. These reasons should be supported by concrete, specific evidence as suggested above. However, some people's reasons are based primarily upon a set of values that are difficult to judge because they are subjective and emotional. Invoking such codes of ethics as the belief in a deity, for example, provides us with feelings, and these become our reasons.

Teaching Strategy.   Pose a dilemma. Challenge students to analyze it, identify the problem, set an objective, and generate alternatives. Then ask, "How do we make a decision among these alternatives?" If no one suggests looking at consequences or evidence, then suggest making a chart (Table 8.1).

Work through the chart and then have students, separately or in collaborative groups, make a decision and state specific reasons. Finally, pose the reflective question, "How did we solve this and what did we learn about our thinking in this kind of situation?"

Take Action

Here we put our selected option into effect. Of course, as we act, we may encounter unexpected difficulties, and these cause us, through our monitoring process ("How well am I doing?"), to revise our strategy and change to another option.

Be Reflective: "How Well Did I Do?"

This question is part of an "executive process" and, as such, is part of our metacognitive awareness and control of thinking (see Chapter 11). We should reflect soon after the event, so our memory has no time to fade.

Posing the question "How well did I do?" is an outgrowth of continually asking ourselves the monitoring question "How well am I doing?" We want to track our progress throughout, to know if we are achieving our goals, if they need to be revised, if our strategies are working. Then, at the end, we want to know:

Did I achieve what I set out to do?

How well did my strategies work? and Why did they work so well? or not
   work so well?
What would I do differently next time? Why?
What do I want to find out about now? Why?

These questions should become part of everybody's repertoire—an internalized script that we follow every time we encounter a problematic situation.

TEACHING PROBLEM SOLVING—STUDENTS
GENERATING THEIR OWN RULES

Up to this point I have assumed that these processes would be taught to students
directly. That is, a teacher can present numerous complex situations for his or
her students to respond to and determine their level of sophistication by the way
they analyze problems and resolve them. Subsequently he/she could select those
processes that the students need to become better at and then teach them directly
and continue to provide opportunities to use the skills acquired.

There is another approach.

We can ask students to develop their own rules for problem solving. We can
ask them to explain how they go about solving problems and making decisions.
What would be the value in proceeding in this fashion?

The suggestion was first proposed by Irving Sigel of Educational Testing
Service as we discussed problem solving at the elementary school level. Sigel's
own work with young children has focused upon helping them become better
thinkers (1984), and in this process he had been interested in the question of "rule
generation." We both thought that elementary school students were capable of
developing their own rules and that there would be much value in it for these
reasons:

1. What we create we own. If we discover ideas for ourselves, we will
    remember those ideas much longer than if they were imposed upon us
    by another. Research supports this contention. (See Hayes, 1981, for an
    extended discussion.) If we receive information and are asked to create
    pictures related to it, to pose questions, to arrange it in hierarchies, our
    own handling of the material will embed it in long-term memory. Thus
    students, asked to consider how they had solved a problem, would be
    thinking about what *they* had done and not the teacher.
2. It seemed to me that students would benefit from this process, because
    it could be internalized for future self-directed learning. If we are in the
    habit of asking ourselves, "What was the problem and how did I solve
    it?" we will have developed useful problem solving strategies on our
    own. To become better at any task, it is necessary to know how well we
    perform it, why we got the results we did, and what we might do differ-
    ently next time in order to improve. In other words, metacognition leads
    to improved performance in any field.

Mary Mulcahy's first and second graders generated a complete list of how to solve problems.

1. Think!
2. Take the parts out of the problem that you don't really need—get to the main problem.
3. Make the problem littler and littler.
4. Make sure you know what you're trying to figure out before you start to do anything.
5. Look at the problem from a different angle.
6. Make sure the problem makes sense.
7. Don't make the problem bigger.
8. Always try your best.
9. Work it out on a piece of paper—write it down in order, then list the best and worst solutions. This gets it better into your mind.
10. Ask someone to help you if the problem is too big.
11. When you're discussing a problem and you disagree with what someone else is saying, just jump in and argue. That helps everyone think.
12. Practice makes perfect.
13. Make sure the problem is clear to you.
14. If you're a bad thinker, try and think harder and read it over and over again.
15. Look at your solutions and see if they're good or bad.
16. It is not good to practice with a problem you already know a solution for or there is only one solution.
17. Try to do problems that are just right for you.
18. Break up the problem; solve each piece and then put it back together.
19. You can cut the problem in half.
20. Repeat what someone else says in a different way.
21. You can sometimes combine solutions.
22. Add on to someone's thinking.
23. Believe in yourself.

POINT TO PONDER: How would you assess these rules? How useful do you think they could be at your level?

One look at the children's list indicates that students already know that you need to *reduce* problems, to *research* them and gather information, to write it out (*represent*). They very clearly state that the problem must be clear to you (No. 13) before proceeding, and the implication is that you should not just act impulsively without thinking. This is a rather fine lesson to learn in first and second grade.

Mary posted all of these rules in the room on two large posters as reminders to follow while students were solving other problems. After they had finished each new problem, she returned to the posters for self-assessment: Most often the youngsters could find several steps that they had followed, usually "jump in and argue" (that is what they loved doing). This evaluative step, Mary found, was harder than generating the list, and it perhaps requires more experience and intellectual development.

In another school (River Edge, New Jersey) teachers examined their entire curriculum to find significant and appropriate problems for students to solve and then generate their own rules. Examples included:

Physical Education (Grade 6): There are seventeen people in this class; build a human pyramid using fifteen persons.

Special Education (Grades 3–4): On opening day in September: "The room has not been touched since you left it in June. How would you like to arrange it for the best learning opportunities?"

Grade 4: "A boy with red hair came to class, and most children made fun of him by calling him 'Carrot Top.' How would you deal with this situation if you were that boy?"

Grade 6: "How can we go about developing a time line for our study of astronomy?"

Kindergarten: "Here are many objects you find around the house [items that fasten one thing to another]. Which things seem to go together? [How would you classify these objects?]"

Each teacher developed a series of lessons centered around problem solving for most of the entire fall semester—in other words, about ten to fifteen lessons per teacher. I observed many of them and videotaped several myself. What did these energetic teachers demonstrate through this experience?

1. Some students initially have difficulty thinking about how to solve problems. In the pyramid problem, everybody worked individually with little or no sense of community and shared responsibility.

2. Most students initially had difficulty responding to the question, "What was the problem?" In the pyramid situation, for example, some students thought the major problem was that Timmy could not climb up over his classmates' backsides to get to the top—he kept pulling them down into a tumble on the floor.

3. In all grades students had difficulty with "How did you solve it?" especially since we wanted them to reflect on their thinking processes. In Grade 4 Carol Cutrupi decided to teach her charges directly to understand the word *process*. As a model, she used her own thinking processes and, as examples, getting to work and baking a cake. By the end of the semester her students had generated a number of different processes: identifying the problem; putting myself into the situation; making lists; thinking of many solutions; making decisions; and evaluating results. Mary Mulcahy's students did not, however, require this kind of instruction. Why? I am not sure.

4. Some students, especially some of the sixth graders, expressed frustration with this approach. "Why don't you just tell us the answer or how to do it!" was a comment more often heard. By grade 6 the hidden curriculum had fully coalesced.

5. Some students can transfer their rules from one situation to another and, therefore, use them for other perhaps more complex kinds of situations.

6. By the end of the experiment some of Carol's fourth graders were able to speak about what they had learned about their own thinking:

"I learned that you know more about the problem than the teacher. . . ." (When you "go up" to them, and they don't immediately give you the answer, you have to figure it out for yourself.)

"When you're home alone, you don't always want to call up your Mom and ask her how to make a peanut butter and jelly sandwich. . . ." (So you should think for yourself.)

"I think evaluating my answers is fun and important." (Why?) "Because I get better answers that way."

Why does this strategy work? I think the answer lies in the fact that, once confronted with a variety of problems, students discover in themselves all sorts of strategies for solving them. Sigel's original idea was a good one: Students will become more committed to and involved with a process where they have some *input* and *control*. All of the change literature (e.g., Fullan 1982; Sarason 1982) details the efficacy of involving those who will implement a change in its planning. We too often forget that students are capable of thinking about how to solve problems and can be made a part of the process. The strategy of challenging students to generate their own rules for problem solving should, therefore, demonstrate to all of us the value of involving even kindergartners in taking an increased measure of control over their own destiny.

STUDENTS IDENTIFYING THEIR OWN PROBLEMS

One of the most significant observations one can make about schools is that teachers identify the problems and students find answers to them. What would happen if we asked students to identify problems on their own and use some of the learned strategies to solve them?

Karen has done that in first grade. Her long-range strategy included starting with easily recognizable problems: the finger caught in the drawer and the bully on the playground. She then moved to problems in stories, like *Whose Mouse Are You?* (first without words and then with words) and finally to stories the students created themselves. Initially, students had difficulty creating their own stories, but eventually they succeeded. Karen's plan then called for them to read their stories to the assembled class and to ask for solutions, the best of which was to be selected by the author. Whichever answer he decided upon had to be backed up with a reason ("Why did you pick that answer? Why would that help?") Here is part of one such discussion about Mickey's problem.

MICKEY: What is the problem in my story?

ANDRES: The wolf is getting very close to you, and he might eat you.

JAHONNAH: The wolf may kill you.

MICKEY: Yup, my problem is that the wolf is getting too close to me, and I don't know what to do.

MISS MAHN: Mickey, ask the class if they can think of any solutions to your problem.

MICKEY: Does anyone have a solution?

SERGIO: Throw a stick, and the wolf will go the other way.

NICOLE: Put meat on the ground so the wolf won't chase you. He'll eat the meat instead.

RICHARD: Scream for help.

BRIAN: Go call for a hunter.

JAMIE: Run in your house and lock the doors.

MISS MAHN: Hearing these solutions, Mickey, would you pick one to help you or do you have an answer of your own?

MICKEY: I would run in my house like Jamie said, and maybe when I get in, I would call a hunter so he could come and kill the wolf.

MISS MAHN: Why would you choose these solutions?

MICKEY: Because my house is close to the mailbox, and I don't know if I have any meat.

Karen concluded that one element crucial to her success was creating "an environment where the students could identify a problem, think of ways to solve it, and explain reasons for their choices." What was essential, she noted further, was to create an environment "in which people can feel free to take risks, to experiment with alternative behaviors, to make mistakes without being chastised and to learn from failure" (Liebmann 1987).

CONCLUSION

In this chapter I have outlined some of the many different ways to introduce problem solving to students. Several ideas are very important to the teaching of problem solving.

First, we ourselves must be certain of what constitutes problem solving. What do we mean by "identify the problem"? What do we mean by "relate this to other situations"? What specific operations or processes are involved? How do these operations "work" in our own lives? Can we identify these operations in the ways we approach and analyze real-life problems? Second, whether we use a more direct or indirect approach, we must know what is involved in helping students become good problem solvers.

Students come to school with wonderful ways of identifying and solving problems already. If we can elicit some of these methods, we can enhance our instruction in any subject, by helping students use their own ways of dealing with situations. In order to elicit these methods, however, we must create the kind of environment described in Chapter 5. We must be open to all possibilities, be willing to take risks, and be persistent in our efforts to help students reflect upon their own thinking.

We all know that younger students' thinking is qualitatively different from that of older ones, high school level. We did not find, however, that the lack of "formal operational" logic or abstract thinking in elementary school students was too much of a hindrance to their identifying their thinking processes. Even first graders can engage in problem solving and—as Karen, Mary, and others have demonstrated—respond critically to each others' solutions. And as we have noted in Chapter 4, first graders like Mary Mulcahy's can reflect upon their thinking and evaluate it by noticing when they are copying others' thinking and when their thinking is good because "I understood the problem."

However we proceed, life in future classrooms will be markedly different for the Emilys of the nation, if we challenge students to use their minds as Marilyn's art students do: "The object sleeps until the mind invites it out for a dance" (Kuhlmann 1989).

REFERENCES

Barell, John. 1980. *Playgrounds of Our Minds*. New York: Teachers College Press.

Barnes, Robert. 1988. Personal communication.

Bransford, John, Jeffrey Franks, Nancy Vye, and Robert Sherwood. 1986. "New Approaches to Instruction: Because Wisdom Can't be Taught." Paper presented at a conference on Similarity and Analogy. University of Illinois. June.

Feuerstein, Reuven, Mogens Jensen, Mildred Hoffman, and Yaacov Rand. 1985. "Instrumental Enrichment; an Intervention Program for Structural Cognitive Modifiability: Theory and Practice." In *Thinking and Learning Skills: Relating Instruction to Research,* Vol. I, ed. Judith Segal, Susan Chipman, and Robert Glaser.

Forman, Ellice, and Myra Kraker. 1985. "The Social Origins of Logic: The Contributions of Piaget and Vygotsky." In *Peer Conflict and Psychological Growth. New Directions for Child Development,* ed. M. W. Berkowitz. No. 29. San Francisco: Jossey-Bass.

Fullan, M. 1982. *The Meaning of Educational Change*. New York: Teachers College Press.

Ghiselin, B. 1955. *The Creative Process*. New York: New American Library.

Hartman, Hope. 1987. Personal communication.

Hayes, John. 1981. *The Complete Problem Solver*. Philadelphia: Franklin Institute.

Jones, Beau Fly, Jean Pierce, and Barbara Hunter. 1989. "Teaching Students to Construct Graphic Representations." *Educational Leadership* 46, 4:20–26.

Kraus, Robert. 1970. *Whose Mouse Are You?* New York: Macmillan.

Kuhlmann, Marilyn. 1989. "Creative Success Enhanced through Critical Thinking." Unpublished manuscript. Montclair State College.

Liebmann, Rosemarie. 1987. "How Important Is Environment?" *Cogitare,* 2, 3:1.

Mahn, Karen. 1989. "Mr. Detective, Can You Help Solve This Problem?" Unpublished manuscript. Montclair State College.

Mayer, Richard. 1975. "Information Processing Variables in Learning to Solve Problems. *Review of Educational Research*. 45:525–542.

————. 1989. "Models for Understanding." *Review of Educational Research* 59, 1:43–64.

Nelson, Janet. 1989. "A Confident Schneider Rolls Along." *The New York Times*. February 6. p. C7.

Perkins, David. 1989. "Are Cognitive Skills Context-Bound?" *Educational Researcher,* January–February, pp. 16–25.

Peterson, Penelope, Elizabeth Fennema, and Thomas Carpenter, 1989. "Using Knowledge of How Students Think about Mathematics." *Educational Leadership* 46, 4:42–46.

Sigel, Irving. 1986. Personal communication.

————. 1990. "Representational Competence: Another Type?" In *Criteria for Competence: Controversies in the Assessment of Children's Abilities,* ed. M. Chandler and M. Chapman. Hillsdale, NJ: Lawrence Erlbaum.

Sigel, Irving, Carol Copple, and Ruth Saunders. 1984. *Educating the Young Thinker.* Hillsdale, NJ: Lawrence Erlbaum.

von Oech, Roger. 1983. *A Whack on the Side of the Head.* New York: Warner.

CHAPTER 9

Adventures in Imaginativeness

OVERVIEW

Adventurous thinking helps us go beyond boundaries and constraints we place upon ourselves. In thinking adventurously, we may exercise more personal control than in other aspects of searching for meaning and reasonableness. Here we shall explore several distinct pathways to remove us from the ruts of everyday thinking: problem identification, playing with variables, visualization, personal projection, metaphoric thinking, and story creation. See Figure 9.1.

Mary Mulcahy's children, in discussing their ways of solving problems said, "Look at the problem from different angles."

Gordon, a high school student, once described his thinking this way: "What is important to me is expressing myself and to do this you have to let your imagination go . . . take what you perceive and do something wild with it" (Barell 1980).

Einstein spoke of engaging in "combinatory play" with ideas and images, before he thought logically in words.

These are examples of being adventurous while we are identifying and solving a problem. Mary's students know from experience that sometimes you have to turn a problem around or upside down in order to get at the real issue or generate alternative solutions. Gordon reflects upon his propensity for using his imagination as the forge upon which to transform what he perceived, much as Stephan Dedalus, the young artist, saw himself as "the artist forging anew in his workshop out of the sluggish matter of the earth a new soaring impalpable imperishable being" (Joyce 1956).

Einstein used his imagination to conjure images and play with them as a way of thinking through problematic situations. For him, imagination was more important than absorbing positive knowledge.

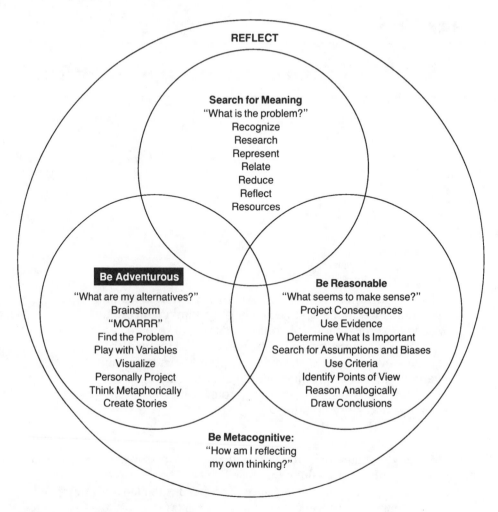

Figure 9.1. Overview of Intellectual Processes.

In this chapter I shall discuss various ways of using our imagination in the service of problem solving. Once we have identified the doubt, perplexity, or conflict, there are numerous ways of carrying it into new territories and making significant discoveries about it while cavorting upon the playgrounds of our minds.

IMAGINATIVE THINKING DEFINED

The definition of imaginative thinking I use, again, derives from Ryle (1979):

> Pathfinding is trying to better one's instructions . . . [it is] trying out promising tracks which will exist, if they ever do exist, only after one has stumbled exploringly over ground where they are not.

Here is a key to imaginativeness and adventurous thinking: exploring new territory in order to get ourselves out of the ruts of conventionality and tradition. Similarly, scientist and artist Jacob Bronowski (1978) saw imaginative thinking as the reason why humankind has progressed to such an extent over so many years. Imagination is . . .

the opening of the system so that it shows new connections. . . . All those who imagine take parts of the universe which have not been connected hitherto and enlarge the total connectivity of the universe by showing them to be connected.

He further noted that when we engage in the exploring necessary to seek new relationships, we take "the closed system and push its frontiers imaginatively into the open spaces where we shall make mistakes."

We seek these kinds of connections in different domains: Bohr's analogizing between the solar system and the atom; Keats's comparing the reading of Chapman's *Homer* to a "watcher of the skies when a new planet swims into his ken; seeing discussions with dictators as if they were examples of Chamberlainlike appeasement. Here we are comparing, seeking what Bronowski called "hidden likeness," making analogies, thinking "as if." All of these involve imagination.

Imaginativeness, More Specifically

There are several ways in which thinkers use their minds in order to reach productive, creative ends. We will focus upon these processes:

Problem finding—redefining, relocating the problem.
Playing with variables—reorganizing the elements by what-if questions.
Visualization—representing the situation in pictures, internally or on paper, and modifying as we obtain more information.
Personal projection—investing ourselves personally in a problematic situation.
Metaphoric thinking—analyzing and creating metaphors, analogies, and models, seeing "as if."
Story creation—placing facts, ideas, and situations within a story context.

These are some of the processes people engage in as they create their own pathways, and I am labeling them as imaginative because they do help us discover and create those hidden likenesses that might otherwise remain behind the all-too-rigid boundaries of our conventional ways of perceiving. Figure 9.1 suggests how these processes fit into our overall problem solving processes of searching for meaning and reasonableness.

PROBLEM FINDING AND REDEFINITION

Characteristically, the creative person has the ability to look at a problem from one frame of reference or schema and then consciously shift to another frame of reference, giving a completely new perspective. This process continues until the person has viewed the problem from many different perspectives. (Marzano 1988, p. 26)

This flexibility of thinking results from reframing the problem, looking at it from a different vantage point. Perkins (1981) reports on the problem-finding capabilities of good artists. They spend time analyzing a given aesthetic problem, manipulating the subject, playing with angles and composition, color and tone, and in this process figuring out how they wanted to represent the theme. Even after commencing work, they are open to restatements of the original problem (p. 185).

In our teacher-absenteeism situation one way to define the problem is to ask how to keep teachers in school. This may suggest solutions that depend on external motivations, such as Monday paydays. We can, however, shift our focus from such externals by redefining the situation as a question of how teachers can create a school that meets their needs. This definition might focus our attention on such internally rewarding solutions as school-based management, shared decision making, and openness of communication.

Practical Application

After reading the story of *Franklin in the Dark* (Chapter 2), Karen and Mary Ellen asked the question, "What was Franklin's problem?" The second graders said, "He was afraid of small dark places." This is a good recollection of what the story says almost literally.

When this story is used with adults, however, their breadth of experience allows them to locate the problem in several different areas or within a wider diversity of schemata. In other words, the adults offered very different versions of the problem: how to accept himself, how to overcome a fear of the unknown, how to learn to live without a shell for protection, and how to stop equating darkness with danger.

In a fifth-grade class studying dinosaurs, one student asked, "What are the dinosaurs like that we haven't discovered yet?" (This reminds us of Jenny, who asked "What are beaches like that haven't any shells?") This is beautiful to play with, because it opens so many possibilities for reasoned speculation: "How would you go about figuring out what these unknown dinosaurs would look like?" This question calls for much knowledge of currently known dinosaurs (a fairly vast subject all by itself), geological time and organic development patterns. The student would have to analyze the problem, collect information, then project possible consequences that are more or less likely, depending upon the evidence he or she collected.

In a high school chemistry class I heard a similar question: "What are the elements of the periodic table like that have not yet been discovered?"

What are these students doing? They are refocusing their attention away from the obvious toward those parts of the situation often overlooked or not looked at at all.

Teaching Strategy. How do we help people become better at redefining the problem?

1. State the major concept (revolution) and the problem connected with it: How to avoid revolutions in the future.
2. Create a graphic representation to reduce the problem to its several parts. Or use our Thinking Journals to write about different elements.
3. Identify most common focus: causation, participants, etc.
4. Refocus attention by reversal of relationships or inquiring about over-looked elements of the problem. The key questions will be: "What if we look at those concepts that are usually neglected [e.g., the opponents of revolutions]? What would we disclose about revolutions as a result?"

So what we do is start by reducing the problem to its parts and then identify those parts that may have been overlooked. Or we factor in parts not previously connected.

For example, in Ken's unit (see Figures 7.2 and 8.3) the most common kinds of questions about revolution might be "What is a revolution?" and "What causes them?" After identifying several parts (causes, effects, leadership, life-styles before and after, revolutionary processes, location, opponents, etc.), students might refocus their attention from causes to ask, "Who opposed the major revolutions and how were they alike?"

Or another question might be "What do revolutions cause?" This question results from one of de Bono's "lateral thinking" processes: reversal. You take the parts and reverse their polarity.

Another means of helping students redefine the problem is through their Thinking Journals. Rosemarie Liebmann's students are continually using their journals to figure out the elements of a problem in mathematics or their own lives and how they can be arranged in their own minds. Shannon's journal entry one day reflected her concern with a teacher who "obviously favors me. . . . I am getting the 'teacher's pet' image which I absolutely hate!" Her first thought was to put up with it, ignore it. She analyzed this, weighing the pros and cons of discussing it with the teacher (e.g., fear of offending her and of grade penalization) and then she shifted her focus: "I guess the real problem is myself. I must be doing something that encourages it." This realization enabled her to examine her own behavior rather than blame the teacher. (See Chapter 11.)

Problem relocation or reframing is one specific way we bring a fresh and perhaps imaginative perspective to a situation. The processes described above may have contributed to William Blake's writing, in "Auguries of Innocence," "To see the World in a Grain of Sand, And a Heaven in a Wild Flower; Hold Infinity in the palm of your hand, And Eternity in an hour."

PLAYING WITH VARIABLES

After mapping out the variables in our minds, we play with them. Einstein referred to his propensity for "combinatory play" as a part of his productive thinking. He played with "more or less clear images" as do many thinkers. At an early point in his career, perhaps as young as sixteen, he posed this question for himself: "What if I were to ride along a ray of light and look back upon such a ray? What would I see?" In 1916, as a result of this kind of thought experiment (he called them *Gedanken*), he was able to design the special theory of relativity. We engage in this kind of activity all the time when we ask, "What if I were to do this?" "What if things were slightly different?" What-iffing can identify elements of the puzzle, rearrange them in our minds, seek those new connections Bronowski spoke of.

Practical Application

Playing with variables and asking what-if questions can enhance our problem solving in a number of different ways:

Identifying New Problems.   Jenny's question, "What are beaches like that have no shells?" opens our eyes to the concept of a different kind of beach. We can then explore causes ("How could a beach lose its shells?") and preventive measures ("How could we prevent this in the future?"). It seems that Jenny knows of beaches that have shells; she may be using her imagination, through what-if questions, to think of a contrary-to-fact situation. She has reduced the complex situation to this variable for now.

Examining existing patterns and challenging their necessity is another way we play with variables: "What if classroom seats could not be in rows facing the front?" By considering this question, we examine *what is*. We can then assign reasons *why* classroom seats are so often in rows and consider alternative possibilities. And finally we might want to change what is to *what should be:* "When would it be appropriate to use a different formation?" (Sarason 1982).

We can also play this kind of game with scientific reality as we know it: "What if oxygen and nitrogen had not existed in our atmosphere in exactly the proportions they do now? How might human life have developed differently?" When we pose this question in science class and proceed to consider all the possibilities, we test our understanding of the relationships of these two elements and their effects upon our lives. With the depleting ozone layer, there is the possibility that life as we know it will not remain the same, and we should become good at considering alternative conditions.

We can do the same in history. Take the statement usually accepted as true: Columbus discovered the New World in 1492. Consider all the elements we can rearrange in our imaginations:

> *Location:* "What if he had landed in Tierra del Fuego?"
> *Persons and Time:* "What if [current U.S. President] had commanded the ships? How would he have handled the crew's dissatisfaction?" "What if Columbus had not held typical fifteenth-century views on converting the natives and enslaving them?"
> *Action Words:* "What if Columbus had realized he had found an entirely new continent?"

Complete Reversal: "What if native Americans had sailed east and discovered a New World?"

All of these what-if questions are ways of exploring possibilities, of disclosing new problem situations and new perceptions of our world. As Ryle noted, thinking opens our eyes to new and overlooked dimensions of reality. As one student responded to the last question about Columbus: "We would have a lot of reservations about the English."

Such questions get us out of our intellectual ruts, as evidenced by a *New Yorker* cover some time ago. It depicted the landing of the Mayflower at Plymouth not from the perspective of John Alden and Priscilla Mullins on board, but from the perspective of two quizzical turkeys standing on the shore looking out across the bay at the strange arrangement of planks that was arriving.

The what-if question is effective in any discipline (Barell 1980). It enhances our power in mathematics if students develop the script: "What if I rearrange the elements of this equation?" It is at the heart of artistic creation when the novelist asks, "What if we put a very self-conscious adolescent [Holden Caulfield] in the company of nuns who teach *Romeo and Juliet?*"

Generating Solutions.   Suppose students in Ken's class wanted to think of ways of preventing revolutions, to ensure more orderly transitions of political power. How could they engage in playing with variables or asking what-if questions? By returning to our graphic of revolution (Figures 7.2 and 8.3), we notice other elements: leadership, effects, other countries, processes, participants, social-political-economic environment. All these are elements to play with. Which might we question or seek new relationships among?

What if we alter the economic environment? What effect will that have?

What if we empower the participants early in the history of a nation?

What if we got the proponents and opponents together to figure out an alternative course of action?

You can see how extensive our network of associations can be within a hypothetical framework.

Teaching Strategy

Think aloud: "When I think about revolutions, I sometimes wonder 'What if they proceeded backward?' "

Examine the thought processes of scientists, poets, historians and mathematicians. (See Ghiselin 1955; Perkins 1981; John-Steiner 1985.)

Give students practice posing what-if questions in their journals, as part of nightly reading assignments or while studying graphic organizers.

This question and the process of playing with variables can be fun when we pose silly questions ("What if everyone had three hands?") or it can be very serious as when we ask, "What if our Bill of Rights were totally suspended?" Interesting reactions can occur when a student asks the popular question "What if there were a lady President?"

VISUAL REPRESENTATION

We have already spoken of the potency of representing a problematic situation to oneself in Chapter 8. How we graphically, symbolically, or mechanically represent a problem determines the kinds of strategies we will be able to employ (Hayes 1981). Furthermore, this self-created picture represents our understanding of the situation and often clarifies it for us. We create meaning for a situation as we create a representation of it. We can draw our pictures with lots of information at hand and compare them, or we can draw an initial impression and see how it changes as we acquire more facts.

Practical Application

Here's how we use representation in inventive ways in different subjects:

Science

> Draw your representation of the human cell under normal and diseased conditions. Then compare with a neighbor.
>
> Create a model of the atom . . . the carbon molecule. . . . "charmed quarks" [a longer-term project].
>
> Act out the relationship between amperage and watts, between mitosis and meiosis, between igneous fusion and the earth's crust, between fission and fusion, between energy and entropy, etc.

Mathematics

> Create a model of the wrapping function going from −4 pi to +4 pi (Barell 1980).
>
> Find geometric shapes within the contemporary art of Kandinsky, Rothko, Klee, or Calder.
>
> Take any word problem and draw a picture that shows how you understand the action. (E.g.: A car can average 20 mph up Pike's Peak and 60 mph down the same road. What is its average speed for the entire trip?).
>
> Imagine yourself as the tangent to a circle. What is your main goal in life? What do you fear? What would you like to become?

Literature

> How would you represent Macbeth's "vaulting ambition" in a drawing, a sculpture, a building, a haiku, or a puppet show? (Do for homework and share: identify similarities and differences; search for reasons why drawings are different. Which do you like best and why?)
>
> Create a visual image of Walter's dilemma in *Raisin in the Sun*.
>
> Draw a picture illustrating how Franklin might solve his problem.
>
> How would you act out the relationship between a mysogynist and a bigamist? Between slim and skinny? Between theme and plot? (A game for review prior to a test or as learning experience after homework.)

History

> Draw a picture representing how Napoleon planned his invasion of Russia.
> What do you think Hannibal looked like? Describe him on the basis of evidence presented in your textbook. Draw a picture of what his major goal in life was. Compare this picture with that of Alexander the Great's major goal in life. (Homework assignment and then share in small groups.)
> Create and share with others a visual image of the troops at the battle of Lexington.
> How do you visualize the building of the Pyramids or Stonehenge?

These are various ways of representing concrete and abstract concepts. Following such activities, we should pose questions of the participants and the observers:

> What were you trying to represent? (Identify concept/person, etc.)
> How did you do it? (Describe specific actions/elements of drawing, etc.) How did you feel about the process of drawing, or about the image itself?
> How well do you think you did? Why? (Evaluate how well the drawing reflects specific characteristics as identified above. Search for reasons and evidence concerning the drawing, for example.)
> How might you do it differently next time? Why? (Suggest alternatives, with reasons.) How did your image change over time? Why?
> What have you learned about the concept/person from your representation? From others' representations?

My point here is not only to evaluate the experience but to make it as metacognitive as possible (Chapter 11).

I included acting (under "science") as a part of how we might represent something, for that is what any actor does playing Hamlet or the life of a "charmed quark." She/he thinks of what this object or person means and how she/he will create a representation that communicates the essence of it to an audience. As in creating a metaphor (see below), we communicate our understanding of these critical attributes by the inventiveness of our approach.

Penny is a high school social studies teacher who once challenged her students to draw a picture of the concept *ethnocentrism*. Upon seeing Barbara's representation I asked her, "How did you figure that out? What was your thinking?" With a little hesitation, she proceeded to share her thinking with me: Figure 9.2 reproduces her representation as well as her thoughts.

Unfortunately, we rarely challenge our students to use their powers of imaginative representation to illustrate the concepts they are studying.

Teaching Strategy. Now, how can we teach students to use their intellect and feelings to create a visual representation? Here are some specific suggestions:

> Think of the person, object, or concept you wish to represent—for example, liberty. Think of your feelings and all the information we know about the subject.

other
countries

We rule
We are
the best
decided which to do

① I thought of definition

② people - thought

③ decided to draw 1 person + not a lot of people.

④ Not good drawer easy stick figure.

⑤ Drew shirt because I couldn't use words.

⑥ Wrote the words. The world rule came from
around.

⑦ Other countries - dirt on ground low/stepped
on. Dirty

Figure 9.2.

Identify the major attributes. What is important here? (E.g., freedom from
constraint, self-expression and direction.)

Decide which attributes and feelings you wish to portray. What do you see
in your mind's eye when you think of freedom from constraint? I see people
romping through fields of gently blowing flowers; I see inhabitants of Plato's allegorical cave turning and moving toward the light of knowledge,
etc.

Draw, sculpt, act out your image.

Reflect and evaluate.

Art, therefore, is one of our most significant ways of communicating the
meanings we are fashioning out of our experience. Without aesthetic experiences,
the world would indeed be dreary.

Visualization and Problem Solving

When do we engage in this kind of imaginative thinking? There is obviously no set time, but it is usual to engage in visualization at the beginning and end of a unit—on, say, photosynthesis or *Inherit the Wind*. Visualization can be used as rough pre- and posttests of our understanding of concepts and relationships. How do we see the photosynthesis concept initially and after we have studied it in depth? What changes in our representation of it?

Obviously, when we read a novel or short story, our powers of visualization are engaged throughout. We are constantly creating images and following the action in our mind's eye. As teachers we can check students' comprehension by closely monitoring their visual images for accuracy, vividness, and insights.

We will probably also use visualization at the end of a unit to give students a moment of creative expressiveness, to check their understanding and to provide yet another means for them to share their ideas. (Creating a picture of ethnocentrism is how Penny ended her unit in social studies.) Creating a visual or symbolic representation of an idea can, of course, be done in small problem-solving groups and could be a logical way of reporting findings for our work on revolution. (See Chapter 7 and Ken's unit plan.)

IMAGINATIVE PROJECTION

Imaginative projection is something we do every day. We think of what it would be like to walk in the shoes of a friend or the person sitting across from us on the bus. Or we dream of flying across the universe like a giant petrel. It is a skill that recent research indicates our students are not very good at (NAEP 1986). It is also a skill that allows us to become more empathic with other persons, to imagine how they think and feel, and to figure out how one person can reason as she/he does in a particular instance. In playing with the ball-through-the-window problem, we use imaginative projection to think of how the friend and the neighbor are probably responding to the incident. In Ken's unit on revolution, students imaginatively project themselves into new situations when they ask, "How am I going to respond when the same conditions affect me?" In a unit on the human cell, it would be helpful for students to project themselves into the cell to see how their environment affects their behavior.

I recently conducted an in-service workshop in which we read material from a textbook on prerevolutionary France, especially about the bourgeoisie and the common people who made up the third estate. (The clergy comprised the first estate and nobility the second.) I then told the participants to imagine themselves as members of the third estate (comprising 99 percent of the population) and identify their problems after Louis XVI locked them out of the meeting with the other estates in 1789. What solutions could they generate? They worked alone and then in small groups to achieve consensus if possible.

Subsequently, I asked them what thinking processes they were using to respond to this challenge. They told me problem identification, solution generation, comparing (one solution with another), and establishing criteria (with which to make a choice).

And one assistant principal, Stewart, concluded by saying, "I had to project myself into the role of a [French peasant] and try to imagine my life, without much power, paying all those taxes to support the clergy (first estate) and nobility (second estate). And believe me I didn't like it one bit." Thus, imaginative projection helped Stewart identify the problems of a whole class of people in the past.

A philosopher of history, R. G. Collingwood (1939), suggests that the study of history involves just such "rethinking" the thoughts of those men and women who were the actors upon our historical stage. "Political history is the history of political thought. . . . Military history . . . is a description of plans and counterplans: of thinking about strategy and thinking about tactics, and in the last resort of what the men in the ranks thought about the battle" (p. 110). For example, in studying the battle of Trafalgar, Collingwood comes upon words uttered by Lord Nelson: "In honour I won them, in honour I will die with them." The historian wants to rethink Nelson's thought: Should I make myself less conspicuous to the enemy in the rigging of their ships by removing these medals? Nelson's thought, as Nelson thought it and as I rethink it, is certainly one and the same thought . . ." The major difference, of course, is one of context.

Collingwood's "rethinking" involves projecting ourselves into Lord Nelson's mind at that moment when he faced the enemy from the deck of H.M.S. *Victory,* considering the problems he faced, his options, and the course of action he would take.

Similarly in science, productive thinkers have engaged in such imaginative projection with the objects of their study. Joshua Lederberg (quoted in Judson 1980), a Nobel Prize-winning geneticist, reflecting on the nature of scientific inquiry, noted "the ability to imagine oneself inside of a biological or other situation" is one of the several talents required.

> I literally had to be able to think, for example, "What would it be like if I were one of the chemical pieces in a bacterial chromosome?"—and to try to understand what my environment was, try to know *where* I was, try to know when I was supposed to function in a certain way, and so forth. (p. 6)

POINT TO PONDER: Why do you think rethinking history and imagining oneself inside a biological phenomenon are likely to be productive?

One reason might be that we so invest ourselves in the object of our study that, as Lederberg noted, we identify with him or it to an extraordinary degree. We can then figure things out; why Nelson decided upon his course of action and why the chromosome behaves as it does. We, in effect, become one with the object of study by means of our ability to project ourselves imaginatively into a novel situation. This, of course, is what every actor does.

Emphasizing Empathy

Projecting ourselves into the mind and heart of another individual in order to become more empathic involves using our own thinking as a model and might proceed in this fashion:

> Collect as much data/information about the person (or object) as you can.
> Identify major characteristics/attributes about persons/objects.
> Select those characteristics that define major aspects of persons' identity.
> Visualize that person within a specific context: Nelson on the *Victory,* Hamlet seeing the ghost of his father, Franklin speaking with the elephant. Conjure images of the details of the surroundings: guns blazing, the castle and its environment. If you are dealing with objects like igneous rocks within the earth, imagine the pressure and heat of the surrounding rock.
> Ask yourself questions like the following: What do I see in my surroundings? How do I feel and why? What action is likely to take place? What if something changes in my surroundings? (Fill in specific details, like increased pressure, missing or deformed parts of the cell.) What would be the consequences? What would create a problem for me in this situation? How would I—as a chromosome or igneous rock—likely respond?

Then draw conclusions from your visual excursion about the general nature of the object and about how you would feel.

These processes for imagining ourselves as someone or something else are very similar to those used by an actor when he or she prepares to play the role of a certain character or, as in drama classes, of an animal or other object. We must immerse ourselves in the nature of that person or object. A very good way to begin to understand the person or object is to create, once we have some information, a visual image that we continually modify as we gather more facts.

Imaginative projection allows us to become one with our dilemma or the object of our study (thereby more thoroughly understanding it).

Good thinking in all subjects, therefore, demands this kind of imaginative thinking, and it is not only the domain of playwrights and poets. It is the very stuff of being a thoughtful person.

METAPHORIC THINKING

As Macbeth's scheme to acquire power begins to unravel before his violence-weary eyes, he says:

> *Life's but a walking shadow, a poor player*
> *That struts and frets his life upon the stage*
> *And then is heard no more*
> *It is a tale*
> *Told by an idiot, full of sound and fury,*
> *Signifying nothing. (Act V, scene 5)*

Shakespeare created two of the most famous metaphors in all of literature when he compared life to shadows and tales told by an idiot. This is what a metaphor is—a comparison between unlike objects or phenomena. Metaphors are very powerful uses of figurative language, because they deepen our understanding of one element (life) by relating it to the other (shadows and stories). Ortony (1979) describes metaphors as "interactive" constructions that disclose meanings and can help us acquire new knowledge. Thus, metaphor, far from being a simple substitution of one term for another, is a means of bridging the gap between the known and the unknown. In Emily's mind, her life in the classroom was being lived as if she were a tape recorder, mindlessly recording and playing back sounds.

Metaphors, then, are one means of seeing "as if" one thing were similar to another: brains as sponges, computers, or interactive networks. In other words, metaphors are ways of creating adventuresome and reasonable meanings, encapsulating the three elements of the thoughtful process (meaningfulness, adventuresomeness, and reasonableness) mentioned in our definition (Chapter 2).

How do we use metaphors in everyday instruction?

Students' Own Metaphors

Several years ago I initiated a project in several inner city schools that was designed to challenge students to develop their metaphors for the fundamental concepts within a particular subject. This project was based upon a notion (Barell 1980) that if students could create their own metaphors, we would have excellent opportunity to evaluate how well they understood a concept, such as imperialism. This project was also predicated upon the fact established by Mayer (1975) that, when challenged to relate subject matter concepts to the whole range of their experience, students' abilities to retain these concepts and use them in future problem solving was enhanced. The study and creation of metaphors thus became a model for good instructional practice: Take a subject matter concept like imperialism and find models or vivid expressions of it within your own experience. You will, thereafter, remember and understand these concepts better for doing so.

To commence our study and creation of metaphors, we engaged our imaginations by studying the meaning of "Life's but a walking shadow" and similarly famous statements. We then expanded our own thinking by completing statements such as "School is . . .", "Mondays are . . .", "Thinking is. . . ." Teachers played with these ideas, and then they engaged their students in metaphoric thinking and obtained results like these:

> "School is experiencing a day on a desert. You are out there with nothing to do but try to find your way home."
> "Thinking is a form of alcoholism, because if you cannot control it, your life could be hazardous."
> "Thinking is observing a bird's nest. When you observe a bird's nest, you can see the quality that the birds have in building their home, and thinking helps to find the qualities in all things." (Sutton 1982)

We then asked teachers in all subject areas to select a significant concept in the unit they were studying and follow a sequence of steps for students to create their own metaphors:

Identify the concept, e.g., imperialism.
Identify attributes of a concept.
Select one or more major attributes of concept.
Find object or phenomenon that has similar attributes and create metaphor.

In actuality, students followed one of two similar patterns. They either found words that define the concept of imperialism—"Imperialism is expanding your power"—or they went right to creating the metaphor without formally identifying the attributes—"Colonialism is a pimp who takes all the money."

Several other examples of the metaphoric statements these tenth graders created:

English: "Theme is getting to the middle of an artichoke. You get to the middle and you see what made all the leaves. That is the root of it." "Theme is the axis of a globe; everything revolves around it."
Science: "Hypotheses are astrological predictions."
Math: "Factorization is like slicing a cake and eating it piece by piece."
Social Studies: "Democracy is a parking lot." "A coup d'état is like cancer."

Once students had created their metaphors, I asked them to justify their comparisons to their classmates, to see how reasonable they seemed to be. The purpose of this phase was to test out what some call the "fit" of the metaphor: Does a "theme" really resemble getting to the heart of an artichoke? In what ways does the latter term, "the vehicle" (the artichoke), deepen our understanding of "the topic" (theme)? Leslie interviewed her student who saw democracy as a parking lot, and he said, "Each car in a lot has equal space just as in a democracy all rights for people should be equal. . . . in a parking lot everyone pays the same amount of money . . . so there is justice in both." (In short, this student sees democracy as an expression of "equal" but not necessarily of "free.") (Jenkins 1982.)

Factoring is like slicing a cake and eating it, because in factoring you take numbers apart "making them smaller just like slicing and eating cake. The more you eat, the smaller it gets. In factoring, the more you take the numbers apart, the smaller they get." (Samuels 1982.)

After an extensive debriefing on this metaphor Leslie's student reflected, "You know I've never thought so much about my own thinking." This, of course, was one of our objectives: to make our thinking about language and thought much more explicit and fun. Playing with ideas, as these students experienced it, was enjoyable because they were in control of the creative process.

If, as Galda asserts (1981), understanding metaphor "requires the ability to entertain multiple attributes," then we were challenging students to develop their thinking to a fuller maturity.

Metaphors and Problem Solving

Critically examining metaphors and analogies can uncover problematic situations. For example, Leslie taught tenth-grade social studies, and she decided in one of her units to focus upon the metaphoric statement "The United States is a melting pot." During the several lessons that comprised this unit, she challenged her students to evaluate this statement critically: "This country is a true melting pot where many groups of people are transformed into a new race of human beings." The activities she engaged her students in involved:

> Determining the meaning of the original metaphor.
> Critically analyzing the attributes of the major elements: the United States and a melting pot.
> Evaluating the metaphor, examining its critical attributes and relationships.
> Creating a better metaphor that more truly reflected how her students saw life from the inner city.

In our planning discussions for this unit, Leslie and her colleagues seemed to favor this metaphor for themselves: "The United States is a stew of different peoples." In this metaphor there is no melting away of the distinctiveness of different elements—only a blending in which the meats and vegetables retain their color, shape, and much of their distinctiveness while contributing to the overall flavor.

Thus, Leslie saw a problematic situation in a commonly accepted (and often misquoted) metaphor about the United States. We can do the same in science with statements such as the following:

> The brain is a computer.
> The atom is a miniature solar system.
> Photosynthesis is a factory operation.
> ". . . gravity is the glue holding us onto the earth" (Stephen Hawking 1988).

We can do the same in literature by identifying metaphors in the books and poems we are reading:

> "When you write, you lay out a line of words. The line of words is a miner's pick, a woodcarver's gouge, a surgeon's probe" (Dillard 1989).
> "Much have I travell'd in the realms of gold. . ." Keats.

Here we are taking the comparisons of someone else and determining if they present a problem for us as they did for Leslie and her students. In her case we were engaged in what Heidegger, the German philosopher, called "unthinking" a common understanding. We were also engaged in what the historian Lukacs (Mee 1976) calls a rethinking of history that helps reveal the meaning of historical events.

Another way to use metaphor in problem solving is as a tool for *relating* and *representing* the problematic situation. Confronted with the situation of the ball through the window, we can ask, "What is this situation like?" Confronted with the teacher absenteeism problem, we can ask what this situation is like and respond, "It's a sturdy tree with roots spreading in many directions."

In another problematic situation, *Franklin in the Dark:* Franklin's problem was facing himself in the mirror (of his identity) or looking himself in the eye.

In the dilemma Ken presented his students (Chapter 7), they could frame their problem in these ways: "We are the dust under everybody's feet."

When metaphoric relationships like these are created as part of the problem identification, we can then formulate strategies to emancipate themselves from slavery or become the "mountains of strength" upon which others base their confidence.

Thus, metaphors help us uncover problematic situations to think about ("The United States Is a Melting Pot") in terms of their meaning. Metaphors reveal our understanding and help us create new meanings from our own experience. Metaphors help us frame the dilemma in such a way that solutions appear ("We are dust . . .").

Metaphoric thinking, in conclusion, is an excellent way to engage students in the three aspects of thinking: searching for meaning; being adventuresome in establishing unique relationships; and being reasonable by examining the fit between terms ("Life" as a "tape recorder" and as "walking shadows"). Both Shakespeare and Emily observed life and designed reasonable and meaningful images that transcend the separate words themselves.

CREATING STORIES

No one can read or listen to Joseph Campbell speak about mythologies of the world and how each seems to represent humankind's deepest strivings and feelings without thinking that here is a great wellspring of imaginative activity. Myths are stories created to solve great mysteries of our experience: how we were created, what is the meaning of lightning and thunder, and how does a boy or girl become an adult? When you write a story, you are usually posing a lot of questions, some of which the story will answer.

Practical Application

Perhaps story telling helps us not only pose certain meaningful questions but also to resolve some of them, at least temporarily. Telling a story in any subject provides us with wonderful opportunities to explore meanings and relationships in a very different form. Here are some examples:

Mathematics

Create a story about how one estimates the number of jelly beans in the jar. Write a story of how two triangles relate to each other: one isosceles and the other scalene.

Science

Write a story showing how two atoms join to form a particular molecule.

Tell a story of what would happen if we could see all the stars during the daytime.

Create a story telling what you would do if you found a live dinosaur that was supposed to be extinct.

History

Write the story of Napoleon's feelings and actions while his army was invading and retreating from Moscow.

Invent a story to explain the significance of the drought of 1988 in midwestern United States.

Literature

Rewrite the story of "The Fox and the Grapes" to convey a different idea.

Write a story about you and Holden Caulfield after he comes to New York from Pency Prep.

Write a story of how tragedy was first created by the Greeks.

In story writing we are not only inventing; we are explaining how persons and situations are related. We know from research (Hayes 1981) that stories and similar elaborations enhance memory of information, because they are our own creations, our own establishing of linkages among a wide variety of pieces of information.

I know one science teacher who engaged his students in story writing. He told his students to identify a phenomenon they were curious about: why smoke rose and turned to turbulence at a certain height; how come the sun appears larger when it sets; why some beaches have no seashells. He then told them to write stories about scientists figuring out these puzzles: "What would be their hypotheses? How would they go about proving and disproving them?" The students loved the activity, but their parents saw no relationship between this activity and what was in the textbook.

Teaching Story Telling

The major strategy would be to give students opportunities to practice telling and writing stories. Every story has characters, setting, and action, which can be used to pose questions. There are also themes, major ideas, or a point that we can ask students about.

One way to start a story is to identify a problem and figure out how to solve it through a narrative with characters whom we know or invent. This is what professional short story writers do: identify a problematic situation and create living characters to go with it, who attempt to solve their difficulties, overcome the obstacles, and find solutions. Many teachers mentioned here—Mary, Karen,

Ken, and Doreen—have successfully tapped into students' natural ability to spin a yarn.

Thus, through our modeling and affording students opportunities to share their stories in small cooperative groups, we can tap into a potentially powerful process students already excel at.

CONCLUSION

Being adventurous and imaginative in our thinking is not all about romantic episodes of being inspired by the Muses visiting us from distant Mount Helicon. Imagination as conceived here is about creating meaning, seeking, finding, and fashioning new relationships. In one sense all acts of thinking are inventive; they represent creating our own pathways through the myriad kinds of experience we encounter in life. In this sense, every one of our classrooms is daily teeming with creative or inventive thoughts, for every student figures out the meaning of situations in her or his own way. For example:

One day Viola Stanley and I asked her students to jot down things they wondered about (subjects or life). Caitlin wondered, "Why does the earth spin?" She was then asked to figure out how to answer her own wonderment. "Ask astronomers. . . . Get involved with the space program and do research. Since gravity is like magnetism, there might be north and south to gravity, so if the night repels one side of the earth . . . it turns [as a result]."

Caitlin's wondering is just one example of so many I have encountered, wherein students use their imaginations to help solve a problem or to identify a newer, undisclosed one. She was adventurous in creating a relationship between gravity and magnets, and this is the kind of thinking we need to encourage.

This is why asking such questions as "How did you think of that question or answer?" and "How would you figure this out?" will elicit creative thinking. It is creative for the student in the same way that Ryle (1979) claims that the child spelling the word *CAT* for the first time is thinking, creating her own pathway.

We are what we are as human beings by virtue of this ability to envision alternative futures and horizons that lie beyond our todays. Imaginative thinking takes us away and celebrates our control over our own destinies, allowing us to transform our tape recorders into more adventurous pioneering spirits.

REFERENCES

Barell, John. 1980. *Playgrounds of Our Minds*. New York: Teachers College Press.

Bronowski, Jacob. 1978. *The Origins of Knowledge and Imagination*. New Haven: Yale University Press.

Collingwood, R. G. 1939. *An Autobiography*. London: Oxford University Press.

Dillard, Annie. 1989. *The Writing Life*. New York: Harper & Row.

Ghiselin, B. 1955. *The Creative Process*. New York: New American Library.

Galda, S. Lee. 1981. "The Development of the Comprehension of Metaphor." ERIC, ED 201 962.

Hawking, Stephen. 1988. *A Brief History of Time, from the Big Bang to Black Holes*. New York: Bantam Books.

Hayes, John. 1981. *The Complete Problem Solver*. Philadelphia: Franklin Institute Press.

Jenkins, Leslie. 1982. "Teaching History with Creative Metaphors." Unpublished manuscript. Montclair State College.

John-Steiner, Vera. 1985. *Notebooks of the Mind, Explorations of Thinking*. New York: Harper & Row.

Joyce, James. 1956. *Portrait of the Artist as a Young Man*. New York: Viking Press.

Judson, Horace Freeland. 1980. *The Search for Solutions*. New York: Holt, Rinehart & Winston.

Kundera, Milan. 1980. *The Book of Laughter and Forgetting*. New York: Penguin Books.

Marzano, Robert, et al. 1988. *Dimensions of Thinking*. Alexandria, VA: Association for Supervision and Curriculum Development.

Mayer, Richard. 1975. "Information Processing Variables in Learning to Solve Problems." *Review of Educational Research*, 45:525–542.

Mee, Charles. 1976. "The Last European War. *Horizon* 18:104–105.

National Assessment of Educational Progress. 1986. *The Writing Report Card*. Princeton, NJ: Educational Testing Service.

Ortony, A., ed. 1979. *Metaphor and Thought*. NY: Cambridge University Press.

Perkins, David. 1981. *The Mind's Best Work*. Cambridge, MA: Harvard University Press.

Ryle, Gilbert. 1979. *On Thinking*. Totowa, NJ: Rowen & Littlefield.

Samuels, May. 1982. "Mathematics and Creative Metaphors." Unpublished manuscript. Montclair State College.

Sarason, Seymour. 1982. *The Culture of the School and the Problem of Change*. Boston: Allyn & Bacon.

Sutton, Sarah. 1982. "Metaphor: An Educational Tool." Unpublished manuscript. Montclair State College.

CHAPTER 10

The Search for Reasonableness

OVERVIEW

Reasonableness is an objective of all thinking, and here we
explore various elements: arriving at conclusions by using good
reasons, identifying assumptions, taking another's perspective
and analogical thinking. Finally, we examine some of the
feelings often associated with critical inquiry: not wanting to
question authority and hesitancy about questioning someone's
reasoning process.

Mary Mulcahy's students, faced with the problem of graffiti on their bathroom
walls, had a number of different solutions:

Speak with the principal about it.
Post guards outside each bathroom and check entrants for pencils.
Place a videotape recorder inside and make a tape to see who writes on the
    walls.

When the second suggestion was made, there was much discussion and argument about what first-grade guards could do with sixth graders who wanted to
enter the bathroom. (The graffiti was in script, not printing, so the youngsters
had inferred that the culprits were older children.) And when the last suggestion
was made, one girl spoke up rather loudly: "Why would you want a videotape
of that stuff!" The debate quickly shifted to other matters.

Mary's students often just jumped in (as one "rule" had urged) to argue a
solution they didn't agree with or had questions about. They seemed to know that
certain ideas are not reasonable—like having videotapes. And certain ones, like
asking sixth graders to empty their pockets to find pencils, might be impracticable.

These students had some criteria for reasonableness, including feasibility and practicality, appropriateness, and whether or not it seemed to solve the problem at hand. We might add one other: Does it take into account other factors or contingencies? Does it have unforeseeable and unacceptable consequences?

Sitting on their rug in the corner of the classroom, Mary's students illustrated what McPeck (1981) calls critical thinking:"a certain skepticism or suspension of assent toward a given statement, established norm, or mode of doing things." This skepticism involves knowing "when to question something and what sorts of questions to ask."

These students were in search of reasonable solutions to the problems they were discussing, and this search involves what many people call critical thinking skills. The search for reasonableness suggests to me a disposition to question possible solutions, interpretations, and claims, a willingness to suspend belief or acceptance pending our reflection on the kinds and qualities of reasons and evidence used, assumptions made, and biases involved. It also involves striving for clarity of meaning by asking for definitions and avoiding ambiguity and over-generalizations.

Thus, being reasonable and searching for meaning are very closely related. Indeed, being reasonable as we shall describe it here is an integral part of problem solving and is not limited to identifying which solution is best. Figure 10.1 illustrates the processes we shall consider:

Knowing what is important and what is unimportant.
Using evidence to support claims, causal explanations, and predictions.
Searching for assumptions, inferences, and biases.
Using appropriate criteria.
Identifying points of view and possibilities different from your own. Considering evidence contrary to our favored point of view.
Taking others' points of view and being able to reason therefrom.
Reasoning analogically.
Drawing reasoned conclusions or making judgments.

As we have noted all along, every mental operation is accompanied by feelings and dispositions. We shall explore these in this chapter as well, for example the disposition to maintain an open mind.

DRAWING CONCLUSIONS OR MAKING JUDGMENTS

James Harvey Robinson wrote in *The Mind in the Making* that "most of our so-called reasoning consists in finding arguments for going on believing as we already do" (1967). He called this "rationalizing," and it is important for our discussion to consider his words, because too little of our time in school is spent in helping students formulate reasoned judgments and to figure out how we all have arrived at our conclusions. Therefore, our discussion will begin with the process of draw-

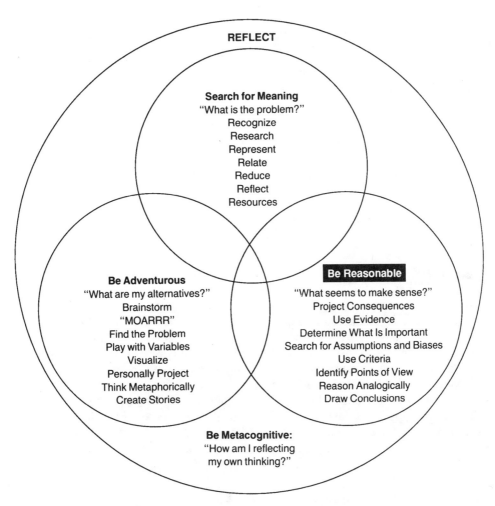

Figure 10.1. Overview of Intellectual Processes.

ing conclusions, because it seems to me that this is what we are attempting to be reasonable about—our conclusions, solutions, interpretations, etc. Figure 10.2 is an attempt to show how some of the processes listed above are related to drawing conclusions.

I think such an image is appropriate because so much of what we hear in classrooms are the conclusions students have reached:

"*Black Boy* is a great book."
"This is the way to solve it."
"Churchill could have prevented World War II from happening."
"I love this class."

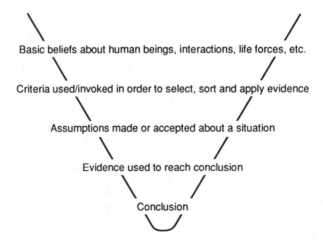

Basic beliefs about human beings, interactions, life forces, etc.

Criteria used/invoked in order to select, sort and apply evidence

Assumptions made or accepted about a situation

Evidence used to reach conclusion

Conclusion

Figure 10.2.

In the above judgments students are sharing with us the results of their thinking and experience, and if we are interested, we can explore this thinking through quality responding to discover their reasons, the kinds of evidence they used to support them, any assumptions and definitions they might be using, their evaluative criteria and undisclosed beliefs about human beings.

Our search for reasonableness will include all of these processes, because they will disclose those aspects and elements of students' thinking that too often go unspoken and unchallenged. The same, of course, is true of adult conversation.

Let's start with deciding upon what is important.

KNOWING WHAT IS IMPORTANT

A history professor colleague of mine, when asked what students had difficulty with in history, remarked, "They have the darndest time knowing what's important. You look at their textbooks, and they're all underlined." These college students cannot tell which facts are more important than others and probably a lot of their friends have this same difficulty.

This means that many students have difficulty doing what Sternberg (1985) calls "sifting out the 'wheat from the chaff': recognizing just what information in the passage [or problem] is relevant . . ." (p. 225). Sternberg's term for this process is "selective encoding."

Determining what is relevant and important, of course, depends a great deal upon the nature of the problem and the background knowledge we bring to the situation. For example, if, in a paragraph on the Appalachian Trail, you are to identify the main idea behind it, you must know something about geography, trail making or maintaining, and perhaps the culture of populations along that trail.

We seem to think that getting the substantive idea from our reading is a mechanical matter of finding the "topic sentence." It is not so easy, because this task involves finding important pieces of evidence, relating them, and drawing a conclusion— an inferential process.

We can challenge students by asking such questions as "What information [evidence] do you think is important in this passage?" "Why do you make that selection? What are your reasons?" "What criteria are you using to make that decision [for more advanced students]?" "Now, how do you relate all this information? Do you see a pattern or organizing principle?" "What conclusions can you draw as a result?"

These questions can be answered correctly only if the student knows something about the subject—or is very good at using the clues learned in school about finding relevant information. The first clue we learn was echoed by the principal of a middle school when he and his teachers were analyzing students' thinking skills:

"You ought to know to look for the bold letters in the text. That's your first clue."

Students learn to look for chapter headlines, bold print, starred items, and so forth. But beyond this we must know which information will add up to the main idea. Here are some other ways of finding this out:

> As in a court of law we look for the *preponderance* of evidence. What ideas or concepts are mentioned repeatedly? Where is the emphasis placed?
>
> Which evidence is *relevant* to whatever is being discussed or to the problem at hand?
>
> How can we tie them together or *relate* them to yield a main thought or inference? For example, in the sentence "He crossed the lake and tied up at the pier," which pieces of evidence will lead you to make an inference about his mode of transportation? Notice that you also have to use your background knowledge about "crossing" bodies of water, about vehicles that one can "tie up" at a pier, and so forth. If we don't know anything about boats and seaplanes, we will have a hard time figuring out what that passage is all about.

How do these considerations relate to problem solving?

With my roadblock problem (Chapter 2), what seemed relevant? The fact that it had occurred before, and over time I had learned that signs and oral directions can be misleading.

In *Franklin in the Dark,* relevant and related information includes the facts that he feared small places and that he sought advice from other animals, not necessarily the color of his shell or the kinds of animals he spoke with.

In Mary's graffiti problem, it was obviously very important that it was first graders who were working on it and that they had reasoned (because the writing was in script) that it was fifth and sixth graders who were making the graffiti. People's names and what they actually wrote didn't seem important to the problem solvers.

One final note: In each situation above a person's (or animal's) values and beliefs can determine what is important. Time and self-esteem seem important in these instances. Similarly, in the situation with teacher absenteeism, the superintendent might deem any absence as a reflection on his or her leadership. The teachers, on the other hand, might be absenting themselves because of work conditions, including lack of opportunities for being heard and participating in significant decisions. Such "messy and indeterminate" situations will often reflect conflicting value perspectives which need to be determined and acknowledged before solutions can be achieved.

USING EVIDENCE TO SUPPORT CLAIMS, CAUSAL EXPLANATIONS, AND PREDICTIONS

Students often have difficulty providing evidence for their conclusions, as a National Assessment of Educational Progress (NAEP 1986) report asserts. Adults also have this kind of difficulty. Ask someone why he or she believes in astrology—what evidence do you use to base your belief upon—and you might hear, "Well, what they say about Pisces and Capricorn seems to be true."

"Is there any other evidence that the motion and position of the planets influences human behavior?"

"People are affected by the weather."

"What leads you to believe that our weather is related to the positions of the planets and when you were born?"

"It just seems that way."

Some might consider this insufficient evidence to support a belief in the power of astrology. But I have had this conversation, and it seemed to confirm what others have observed: We human beings often believe in something unsupported by much substantiation.

On the other hand I have found seventh and eighth graders in Beth Friedman's class quite good at analyzing literature from chambers of commerce for several key elements: the believability of the source, the misleading use of language, the accuracy of data presented, and what's missing ("The truth," one girl said). Students recognized all these elements without my telling them directly, and this demonstrated to me that some of them were quite sophisticated at evaluating the information they were confronting. They were—perhaps not surprisingly given the media to which they are exposed—good at recognizing the possible bias or vested interest of the source, the misleading evidence skewed to show everything in its best light, the absence of a lot of potentially contradictory information, and the highly suggestive nature of the language. One state advertised itself with a lovely picture of the full moon framed between two naturally beautiful rock outcroppings, not usually associated with that state, and the slogan "Linger Longer."

In both of these cases, of astrology and chamber of commerce information packages, we want to arrive at a conclusion in order to know what to believe or do. For example, very often when we confront a dilemma or perplexity, we want to figure out reasons why it existed in the first place: a car that won't start or a squirrel in your house. The latter incident happened to my wife and me recently. We returned to our home after an absence of two weeks to discover the living room in great disarray. Lamps, candles, and plants had been knocked over and there, perched above the windows that had been gnawed around the edges and a wooden window shade with a gaping hole in it, sat a nervous-looking squirrel. After spending over an hour with a broom and a little anger, we managed to shoo the little rodent out the front door. It was indeed a test of overcoming impulsivity.

But now the larger issue remains: What caused this situation, and here we need evidence in order to find the explanation. Here is one way to proceed:

> Generate a number of possible hypotheses (causes).
> Identify evidence that supports one or more.
> Examine evidence that counters any or all but one hypothesis.
> Weigh evidence that supports and/or refutes.
> Draw conclusions.

My initial explanation was that the squirrel entered the house when I carelessly left open a screen door. Subsequently, people with experience have caused me to challenge this assumption and to find other hypotheses: down the chimney, through a very small opening in the wall, etc. Finding evidence that proved my initial hypothesis was very difficult. Eventually, all evidence (e.g., fur on top of the chimney flue) pointed to one conclusion—it descended the thirty-five-foot chimney.

This example is patterned after one Robert Swartz (in press) has presented many times: a dead mouse in the garage. He uses it to illustrate how we search for evidence to support our conclusions. Swartz elaborates: This process entails gathering

> *accurate* information and call[ing] up relevant bits of knowledge we already have so that we can make a *reasonable* judgment. This evidence should, of course, be certified as accurate and that's a matter of calling for the use of another cluster of basic critical thinking skills focussing on . . . the *reliability* of the sources of the information, including our own observation capacities. (Emphasis added.)

At some point Swartz notes we may have to say, "I can't arrive at a reasonable judgment because I do not have enough evidence." Avoiding "premature closure" is crucial to such investigative inquiry and, notes Swartz, "cannot be underscored enough."

We also use evidence to predict consequences or possibilities. In a fifth-grade classroom, I asked a small group of youngsters, "What do you think will happen in the following chapters of Madeleine L'Engle's *A Wrinkle in Time?*" Students then predicted what they thought would occur. "What do you base your conclusions on?" I continued. Students had reasonable evidence from prior reading to agree upon certain predictions. Their subsequent reading would prove or disprove these predictions.

Teaching Strategy. Arriving at conclusions after a considered and reasoned identification and assessment of information is something we should always be encouraging within the classroom. In our teaching we could ask ourselves and our students questions like these:

"What is my objective: find main idea, causal explanation, etc.?"
"What are possible main ideas, hypotheses, or explanations?"
"What kinds and qualities of information do we have/can we obtain through research to support or refute any of these possibilities? Is the evidence objective, relevant, accurate?"
"Which of our suggested possibilities seems to be supported?"
"Why do you draw that conclusion?" (Focus here upon the reasoning process.)

UNCOVERING UNSTATED ASSUMPTIONS OR PRINCIPLES

If we look back at the believer in astrology, we can find some interesting assumptions that led to the conclusion: "People are affected by the weather." This person seems to be operating from an assumed relationship between weather in earthly environments and the planets.

Almost any conclusion a person arrives at, upon the investigation of some evidence, involves reasoning from certain unspoken assumptions or principles. What's fun is to try to figure out what someone else (or yourself) must believe to be true in order to arrive at a certain conclusion. For example:

It is now snowing in New York City as I write.
The radio says it is no longer snowing in New Jersey.
Therefore, it will stop snowing here in the city within a couple of hours.

What must I believe to be true in order to have reached my conclusion?

That weather patterns generally move from west to east.
That this storm follows the usual pattern.
That weather systems often follow a certain "logic," if we can call it that.
That the person on the radio is a reliable reporter of whether or not it is snowing.
That the present weather system is moving at such a rate that it will move beyond the city within a couple of hours.

And we could identify a few more scientific principles that must be true for me to reach my conclusion. These kinds of assumptions are very rarely if ever disclosed in our classrooms. Why? One reason may be that few of us were educated to engage in this kind of dialogue with another person. Another reason may be the time it takes to "unpack" such underlying ways of thinking. Surely, another reason is probably our emotional discomfort at what is perceived to be challenging another person's thinking. This makes some of us very uncomfortable.

Teaching Strategy. Through modeling and questioning, we help uncover assumptions. In the ball-through-the-window problem what did many of us assume? Or, evidencing our impulsivity, take for granted without too much thought?

> That the window was closed.
> That you were playing with the friend and observed the incident firsthand.

Another example:

TEACHER: Franklin was afraid of the dark—of small dark places. What else might we say he is afraid of? (What else can we assume to be true about this turtle? See Chapter 3.)

STUDENT: That he is afraid of being in a cave.

STUDENT: That he has no friends.

TEACHER: Why might that be true, Jennifer?

STUDENT: Because most turtles like their shells! (Therefore, he is sufficiently different from others to make them wonder about him and his "weirdness," perhaps.)

And a final example: In Ken's unit on revolution, what assumptions are there to be identified at various points in the investigation:

> That all revolutions are violent.
> That revolution leads to desired change.
> That all revolutionaries are young, hotheaded zealots.

POINT TO PONDER: Now, why spend time identifying underlying statements that we often take for granted? What purposes does this exploration serve?

Some of you might say that by doing this we uncover assumptions that aren't true: for example, the window might be open. Therefore, our thinking in this situation will be affected: Why run away if no glass is broken? Some of you might say unstated and inaccurate assumptions unnecessarily narrow our thinking: If all revolutions aren't violent by nature, then we can see certain political events as revolutionary (for example, the tearing down of the Berlin wall). And some of you might notice that, if we are in the habit of questioning unstated assumptions, we get better at challenging established ways of thinking and behaving. If all seats need not be in rows all the time, and if learning is not always facilitated by having everybody doing the same thing at the same time, then we can arrange our students in physical formations that suit a variety of individual and small-group purposes.

By examining such patterns of behavior (Sarason 1982) and questioning them, we identify solutions to problems that no longer exist.

USE OF APPROPRIATE CRITERIA

Matthew Lipman (creator of Philosophy for Children) has defined critical thinking as reflective thinking that is concerned with criteria, sensitive to context, and self-correcting (1988). He asserts that when one forms a judgment, he or she is using criteria as reasons by which to make that judgment. Architects use criteria such as beauty, functionality, appropriateness, expense, and style to evaluate buildings; poets use form, style, imagery, and expressiveness to assess their work. Reasons can be based upon ideas, principles, values, concepts of what is of worth within a discipline (e.g., balance in math and literature).

For example, one of my students said her brother was a good thinker because he took his time to think out a lot of things first. I asked her what other criteria she used for a "good thinker." Since we hadn't discussed "criteria," she was stymied. "I don't know what you mean," she said.

So we proceeded to analyze another student's favorite book, *Native Son* by Richard Wright. "Why do you think this was the 'best' book you ever read?"

"Oh, because I got right into it quickly—the plot was good, and it was very graphic—I could see all of the characters. I also thought the theme was important."

Right here she has given us several criteria: a suspenseful plot, Wright's ability to create very vivid characters, and the significance of the theme. Once these were identified, we could, if we wished, discuss them as appropriate criteria for evaluating a novel. Here criteria might be much more subjective than they would be in assessing, for example, the quality of an experiment in science.

On another occasion I asked Beth Friedman's eighth graders who were involved in a unit called "Adopt a Town" what their definitions of a good town were. They said:

> no heavy industry
> people can trust one another
> ample space for skateboarding
> good schools and shops

With these characteristics, or criteria, we were able to ask, "What kind of evidence would indicate to you that people trusted each other?"

> "If you ran out of money at the store, they'd give you credit."
> "People wouldn't have to lock their doors all the time."

This experience provided a natural progression from their general conclusion ("Such-and-Such is a good town") to their reasons ("People can trust one another") to more specific information in support of their reasons ("You can leave your doors open at night").

Why is it important to consider criteria? For one reason we are always making judgments about the quality of things and people: books, towns, classrooms, friends, solutions to problems. Mary's students used a set of criteria to reject setting up videotape in the bathrooms and select a meeting with the principal. Perhaps they could be called feasibility and appropriateness.

In order to become good at identifying criteria, we must possess the general ability to analyze concepts by identifying their significant attributes. These attributes—good plot, trusting people—can then be generalized to form the reasons we use to evaluate the book or town.

OPENING OURSELVES TO OTHERS' POINTS OF VIEW

I was speaking with a friend of mine recently, and she was complaining of how a supervisor was treating her department in school. She had a lot of good evidence to suggest that the supervisor was not handling situations with the best interpersonal skills. At one point I stopped her and asked, "What do you think are his reasons for acting this way? Put yourself in his shoes and see if you can see why he is behaving in this manner."

This caused her to stop and to admit finally that this challenge was quite difficult and one she was not used to performing.

On another occasion I was discussing the South African political situation with a professor of political science at a Midwestern university. I asked him where he stood on the matter of American divestment as a way of putting pressure on the South African government to alter its apartheid policy. He gave me his position. I then asked, "Could you outline the reasons *against* your position, since I am not really certain what they are?"

He thought for a moment and then said, "No, I really can't."

Finally, if twenty years of marriage has taught me anything, it is that one of the best ways of overcoming stress and differences of opinion is to put yourself in the other's shoes and try to see the situation as she/he does. For example, I recently walked into the bedroom where my wife was ironing and watching an old movie on TV. I turned the TV down and turned to ask her a question about some architectural plans for our house. She promptly told me that I was rude and inconsiderate, and I had to agree that I had acted peremptorily and without thinking of her interests. I had just assumed that she would want to help with a family project at *any* moment, and I was incorrect. She deserved and received an apology for my inability to take her perspective.

All these examples illustrate our difficulty with two skills: knowing what another point of view is and being able to reason from that point of view. It obviously involves a high degree of an ingredient missing from much of human discourse: empathy.

David Perkins of Harvard has done extensive research on informal reasoning, and one of his findings is particularly important here. He found that, whether at the high school, undergraduate, or graduate level, students had a great deal of difficulty identifying and/or defending a point of view different from their own. He posed timely "ill-structured" dilemmas such as the following: "Would restoring the military draft significantly increase America's ability to influence world events?" Typical renderings are the following:

"Yes, because a draft would give the U.S. more manpower in the army. The U.S. would have a bigger stick to wave, and foreign nations would be impressed."

"No, because a draft would trigger widespread protests, as it did during the Vietnam war. . . ."

Perkins' analysis of these arguments follows.

> As must be plain, the principal trouble with such arguments is incompleteness. Each puts forward a point worth pondering. A really good reasoner would make all these points and many more besides, pulling out of the whole some balanced appraisal of the pros and cons. In advancing the various lines of argument, *the good reasoner also would note counterarguments that qualify them and would make appropriate hedges. Instead, the typical argument in our sample concentrates on one side of the case, does not develop that side very fully, and neglects relevant counterarguments and appropriate hedges.* . . . An argument typically fails not because a person cannot think of an argument or because the argument a person generates has no logical bearing but rather because a number of other lines of argument, some of them independent of the given argument, need consideration too. (1985, emphasis added.)

This research obviously places a heavy emphasis upon the value of seeing two sides of the coin—of being able to put yourself in the other person's shoes and to see the kind of evidence that leads him or her to different conclusions from your own.

Obviously, if we wish to enable students to think of arguments contrary to their own, we must provide experiences that challenge them to do so.

Teaching Strategy. Here's one way in which I have attempted to encourage what some have called perspective taking:

Tom says, "I think the evidence supports my contention that a world government is our best bet for extended global peace."

Judy disagrees. "The evidence suggests that such a solution will never work and that all nations must learn to work together as independent entities."

After each has had an opportunity to present conclusive evidence to support a point of view, I say, "Tom, will you try to argue Judy's case? And, Judy, will you please try to see the situation from Tom's point of view?" The idea here is to see how she/he has come to a conclusion.

Finally, after they have gone through this exercise, I ask them, "Now, what have you learned? About your own thinking? About the other's position? About your initial conclusion?" This is the reflective, metacognitive question.

The objective is not to change a person's mind but rather to engage in reflective thinking about how we think: to become more metacognitive. One result of this technique is that people will often say, "Well, I still believe as I did, but

I do see the other side and can better understand why she feels that way." Or they might conclude, "Now I have an expanded outlook. My thinking isn't quite so narrow."

POINT TO PONDER: What does this require of Tom and Judy?

Here are some considerations:

Thoroughly understanding the situation: knowledge of information.

A suspension of one's own egocentric point of view to attempt to empathize with the other side.

The ability to visualize or construct a model of the other's position and the data that supports it.

Perhaps a willingness even to find information that supports the other's point and, consequently, refutes one's own position.

Piaget has suggested that children about age nine begin to see experience from another's point of view. However, more recent research (Goleman 1989) suggests that even young children can be empathic and respond to the situation of another person. With increasing age, this ability seems to advance the objective of improved problem solving and probably our understanding of other people's positions.

Obviously, if we wish to enable students to think of arguments of others and those contrary to their own, we must provide experiences that challenge them to do so. Role reversal and role playing exercises will provide such opportunities.

ANALOGICAL REASONING

It was said in 1990 that Saddam Hussein was another Hitler. Do you agree with this comparison? Why or why not?

"I'm going to cut down this cherry tree," said John. "Why?" asked Nancy. "Because it's old and diseased," replied John. "Would you cut down old people because they're old and diseased?"

Both of these are examples of analogical reasoning. That is, they involve comparing one situation with another. Whether we are comparing and contrasting two different political situations or trees with people, we are identifying critical attributes of different phenomena and drawing conclusions therefrom.

The crucial aspect of developing a good argument on the basis of analogy is being able to identify those attributes or characteristics that appear similar, and those that make the situations different. Trees and people, for example, can both become old and diseased. But what other characteristics do they have that should be discussed in the chopping incident mentioned above? They are alive, but one is human and the other not; some trees live a great deal longer than people; trees have bark and people have skin; people have a soul and trees don't (?), and so on. The characteristics we identify will help us select those that are pertinent. Then, if we choose, we can analyze why these characteristics are the relevant ones.

Teaching Strategy. Irving Sigel of Educational Testing Service, Princeton, likes to pose this analogical question: "Consider the American Revolution, the Civil War, and the Vietnam War: Which two are more alike and why?" Notice what is required here:

> Knowledge of background information. What do we know about each situation?
> Ability to identify significant features or attributes of each situation. This will usually involve some assumed criteria. What are the characteristics/features worth noting or comparing here? Why these?
> Use of these characteristics to find similarities and differences, and then to discuss these to determine important relationships. How are the situations similar or different? Why are these significant relationships?
> What conclusions can you draw and why?

When I have engaged students in challenges like these, I have found that they often have difficulty with comparing and contrasting, just as the National Assessment of Educational Progress (1986) found. It seems as if a graphic organizer works well here, because we need to improve our ability to identify critical attributes and to discuss these in order to arrive at a conclusion.

Figure 10.3 has helped me work with teachers who have identified comparison and contrast as a particularly difficult problem for students. Most of what is presented to students is a listing of similarities or differences without much discussion of why these factors are important, how they relate one to another, what might have caused them, and what effects might result from such elements.

	Situation A	Situation B
Criteria/ Attributes		

DISCUSSION:
Reasons for Relationships or Priorities Among Attributes. Comparison of Information.

Conclusion _____ .

Figure 10.3.

We can use a framework like this (Figure 10.3), for example, to arrive at a conclusion about the American Revolution and Civil War. Our criteria might include location, kinds of weapons, political motivations, strategies, and results. Our discussion might examine how, for example, causes for these two conflicts were related: one party rebelling against another for political, economic, and social reasons. We can discuss how these factors might be different from (or similar to) the more contemporary foreign struggle, and then draw our conclusions, which might reflect the complexity of the situation: that although the two American conflicts seem much more similar, in each case we had elements of political rebellion, revolution, or civil war.

It appears evident that analogical reasoning is an area where our students can profit from more intensive work.

REACHING CONCLUSIONS

After considering the evidence, looking for assumptions and biases, considering others' points of view, and attempting to reason from them, we should be able to draw a conclusion. This means using the information we have to make a claim, such as "It will stop snowing here in a couple of hours," or "The Democrats/ Republicans are the best group of lawmakers to reduce the deficit."

As I noted above, we seldom spend a lot of time delving into assumptions or even other people's points of view. We do, however, hear in classrooms a great many conclusions. These come to us in the form of answers to problems, observations about content (facts, ideas, or concepts), feelings expressed in regard to classroom situations, and so forth. All of these, it seems to me, are ripe for further inquiry, *if they are significant enough to warrant taking the necessary time.* (See Chapter 7.)

Thus, any conclusion or claim should be supported by evidence, assumptions, and underlying beliefs or what some call values. Many of us can agree with Robinson (1967) when he says that "We very rarely consider . . . the process by which we gained our convictions. If we did do so, we could hardly fail to see that there was usually little ground for our confidence in them." Questions such as the following facilitate this process of determining how we arrive at our judgments:

"How did you reach that conclusion?"

"What evidence did you use?" ("Why *that* evidence and not *this?*")

"What assumptions have you made? Why are you taking that for granted?" (Invokes prior knowledge and how a person reasons from this knowledge base.)

"What criteria have you used to reach your judgment?" (Are there other you might have used? Opportunity for class discussion and evaluation.)

"What do you believe about people, situations, etc., for you to reason as you have?"

Teaching Strategy. Of all of these steps perhaps the one that teachers refer to more often than others is being able to use evidence to form general conclusions. How do we help students get better at it? Here is one way:

John Borchert teaches seventh and eighth grade science, and in his unit on fossils he gave each student a fossil and asked them to make accurate, objective observations of them. Students started by saying, "It's weathered." Whereupon John asked for more precise observations to support that conclusion. Eventually, students noted color, shape, length, kinds of indentations, position on the rock and so forth.

Then he asked them to describe what a fossil was.

"An imprint of an animal or plant from the past."
"When I dip my finger into plaster of paris, does it create a fossil?"
"When Vesuvius erupted and buried the people, did it create fossils?" (These questions provided rich opportunity for exploring alternative judgments.)

Next, he asked them to form a hypothesis about how they were formed:

"Layers of rock formed over it."
"Weathering, erosion."
"It fell into the mud which then dried."

These variations provided John with an excellent opportunity to play the role of facilitator of students' thinking—helping them figure out what a reasonable hypothesis would be and how to go about evaluating it. This hypothesis, then, became their tentative conclusion about fossil formation.

Finally, for homework John asked his students to write down any facts related to fossils they were curious about.

This simple, direct process used an inductive approach to arriving at conclusions. This is hard for seventh graders to do (some of them at least), because they must project themselves into the distant past, visualize leaves, rocks, mud, and so forth, and attempt to "see" the solidifying process over millions of years. We know that some have not developed their abstract reasoning abilities as yet, and therefore such a task will be difficult for them.

We can adapt such a procedure to figuring out the main idea of a paragraph:

List all the pertinent facts you observe.
Decide which facts are important by observing which are related to each other, and by noting which are highlighted by emphasis, repetition, etc.
Identify relationships among the pertinent facts/evidence.
Draw a general conclusion justified by the evidence.

Drawing conclusions is the kind of skill we seem to take for granted. That is, we assume students can do it without any direct teaching. Recently, another teacher of science told me that she had always just assumed that her biology students could draw conclusions. "I've got to teach them how to do it!" she observed with some excitement. And this she can now proceed to do, using the steps presented above or ones similar. It will take a fair amount of time, but she has determined that this process is vital for becoming better at thinking about the world from a biological perspective.

Now, becoming more reasonable in our thinking is not only a cognitive, intellectual exercise, but also an emotional one. The more I engage adults in some of the processes mentioned above, the more I become aware of the importance of feelings involved in asking someone else for reasons.

THE FEELINGS OF BECOMING REASONABLE

Traditionally, when speaking of "critical thinking," we read about healthy skepticism, an open mind, willingness to take another side of the argument, honesty, objectivity, and so forth. These are very important habits of mind, of course, but too little has been offered about the feelings associated with becoming reasonable. Most of us, I suggest, do not come by this enterprise very readily or easily, and I think it is because of prior training not to pry and explore another's thinking. Therefore, in this section I should like to share some observations about the often negative feelings associated with becoming more reasonable.

"I feel uncomfortable asking another for reasons."
"I have a difficult time keeping my own ideas out of this."
(Maintaining an open mind, objectivity, etc.)

"My Son Can't Stand My Asking Him for Reasons and Evidence. It's Ruining Our Relationship."

Have you ever engaged a friend, a spouse, or a colleague in conversation where you were attempting to explore that person's reasons for a belief or a judgment? I'm sure you have. What do you notice about your feelings during the process? Perhaps you recognize, as so many students have told me, that this is not a situation where you are at ease. You feel you must walk on eggs, phrase your questions with the utmost tact, and virtually apologize for asking them.

POINT TO PONDER: Why is this? What causes our feelings of discomfort in trying to foster more reasonableness?

Perhaps you feel that this enterprise of asking for reasons and supporting evidence is like prying into another's private affairs. Perhaps you also realized that for many such exploring is an entirely new undertaking; they aren't used to digging beneath the surface of someone else's thinking.

I have observed teachers probing with an overly aggressive style that really did put people uncomfortably on the spot, and this is to be avoided. But I have also witnessed expert questioning by one gifted teacher of a member of a class, gently and calmly, yet persistently, for one student's underlying reasoning processes. This so disturbed another member of the class that she later complained to the teacher about what he was doing to the poor student being questioned.

Teaching Strategy. So what do we do about it? Of course, there are no pat answers to this question as you know. But perhaps we can outline a few suggestions:

> Go easy when first attempting such a process with close friends or relatives.
>
> With students perhaps we need to realize that they will always have negative feelings when asked to find out what and why a friend of theirs thinks or believes something. Here modeling will help, of course.
>
> Acknowledge, privately and publicly, our own feelings of discomfort.
>
> Attempt to adopt the spirit of inquiry in which we are genuinely interested in how the student arrived at his or her conclusion. This requires that we attend very carefully to the tone of voice we use as we request this information. Tape-recording a few sessions will tell us whether we communicate genuine interest or aggressiveness.
>
> Naturally we must approach the task with genuine interest and open-mindedness to another's ways of thinking: "I am not trying to change your mind. I am only interested in learning about your approach here."

These are some suggestions and I'm sure others occur to you at this time. I think the open acknowledgment of our feelings in such situations will help us empathize with our students when we ask them to behave in a similar fashion.

"I Have a Difficult Time Keeping My Own Ideas out of the Process."

When I ask teachers to engage in an exercise where one person questions a small group about their reasons for making a claim (such as "Roosevelt [or any other person] was a great leader"), they often tell me afterward that it was difficult for them to keep their own biases out of the way. "I got frustrated because I kept wanting to give my own opinions."

Why is this so? It occurs to me that what Robinson (1967) has observed about our thinking is true: We want to believe what we want to believe, and very often our attempts at being reasonable result in merely confirming our previous convictions. Therefore, when engaging another in discussion, we often feel more comfortable putting forth our own views. We feel comfortable with our judgments—quite logically, because they are ours. And we do not wish to get rid of them, nor do we want to listen intently to another's way of thinking.

Here is where our being openminded and reserving judgments comes into play. This is where those habits of mind we wish to cultivate run smack into our emotional commitments to our own egos, and we must learn to recognize the conflict and be prepared to do something about it. What?

Teaching Strategy. Again, here are some suggestions:

> We can get better by consciously playing a different role, visualizing ourselves taking off the defender-of-my-views hat and replacing it with the "I really am interested in your thinking" hat.

This requires a script change, from "But, listen to what I have to say, and you'll be convinced!" to "Let's try to understand each other's ways of thinking."

To be openminded and objective, we must rewrite our scripts and practice these moves over and over again. Practice with our students as we engage in listening and quality responding.

Acknowledge to our students and friends that this may be difficult and ask them for an assessment of how well we are doing.

None of the above is likely to be quick and easy. Rather, it takes us time to acknowledge our feelings, determine their sources, unthink some of our preconceptions about our ideas and beliefs, and experiment with new and different roles with friends and in the classroom.

The importance of the foregoing, it seems to me, lies in relating the challenge to being reasonable quite closely to our feelings and attitudes about ourselves and our roles vis-à-vis others. Attempting to arrive at reasonable solutions and perspectives on issues is not solely a matter of intellectualizing; it is a process linked to or embedded within our psychological makeup. We cannot forget how egocentric most of us are when it comes to argument, debate, and even to listening to one another.

"I WONDER"

Continuing in the spirit of inquiry, we can appreciate the value of enhancing students' ability to question. By this I do not mean questioning authority primarily, but enhancing students' healthy wondering about why things are the way they are. Wondering about the world around us can and should be the first step in a process of inquiry.

Sandy Woodson's third graders have been asking "I wonder" questions, and some of their inquiries are very interesting. They were challenged to pose questions about nature, books, schools, themselves, the past, and the future using stems:

"I wonder about . . ."
"I am curious about . . ."
"What puzzles me is . . ."
"What if . . . ?"

Here are some of their curiosities:

"Why did men like George Washington wear wigs?"
"Who first saw space?"
"Why was I a baby?"
"Why do the outer planets have rings and the inner ones do not?"

"What if there were no school?"
"What if the sun didn't shine?"

These questions were part of a structured approach to questioning. Once they had their questions, they were encouraged to figure how to go about answering them. Nick, the student who asked about the sun, said, "Well, first I'd ask scientists, and if that didn't work, I'd look at a book, and if that didn't work I'd do an experiment." What kind? I asked him. He spoke of building a satellite with special metals that wouldn't burn and about the sun's being composed of gases that explode and how you could do that with baking soda and vinegar.

As students proceeded to answer their own questions, under Sandy's direction, they learned that it was often difficult, and sometimes you ended up by asking and therefore answering a completely different question.

The purpose of this "I wonder" experience was to pose questions that are meaningful, seek answers, and then, most importantly, reflect on the process to discover something new—not only about the sun (in Nick's case) but also about yourself and your own thinking. This is another way of fostering the inquisitiveness that Izzy's mother always sought in her child.

Perhaps a question we should always ask after every reading selection from first grade on upward is, "What does this make me wonder about? What am I now curious about? How could I find answers to my own questions?"

As I noted earlier in this volume, students come to school with billions of possible questions. We should do more to help them pose and resolve them.

INSTRUCTIONAL PLANNING

Instructional planning is that process wherein we translate long-range goals into specific objectives and strategies for Monday and the rest of the week. I would like to illustrate how two different teachers implemented some of these ideas, one at the elementary and one at the secondary school level. The former focuses upon the search for reliable evidence and the second upon recognizing others' points of view.

Searching for Reliable Evidence—Elementary

Skill to be introduced: searching for reliable evidence.
Subject area: fairy tales, fables and allegories (specifically "Chicken Little").
Objective: students will be able to identify good and poor reasons to follow someone else's direction.
Content (stuff): How we use evidence to draw conclusions.

Teaching Strategy

1. Prior to reading, show students the picture (if there is one) on the cover of the book and present the title. Ask what they think the book will be about. Elicit the students' hypotheses.

2. Ask them how they know when to believe what someone tells them. Elicit students' ways of determining believability.
3. Read the story of "Chicken Little."
4. As you read, ask questions like "Who is believing whom?"
5. Upon conclusion ask students if they notice anything curious about the story. See if students realize that animals followed Chicken Little for reasons that can be evaluated.
6. Following Chicken Little, review the criteria the students established prior to reading. Discuss good reasons for believing what someone tells you.
7. Ask students to summarize and apply lessons/generalizations to personal lives.

Kathy Skowron of Provincetown, Massachusetts, introduced this lesson to her first graders (Skowron 1987). She read the story to her students and then engaged them in analyzing what the animals believed:

S: They thought the sky was falling, but it wasn't really falling; it was an acorn that hit her [Chicken Little] on the head.

T: Was that her mistake?

S: She didn't look up. If she did, she would have known.

S: If she looked down, she would have known too. She would see the acorn and she would have known.

S: Well, maybe there was already an acorn there, so she wouldn't really know. . . .

T: You all have some really good ideas. What do you think the animals could have done instead?

S: She [Chicken Little] could have looked up or down.

T: Why do you think she didn't do that?

S: She was too scared. She was scared because she thought she'd get hit on the face.

S: She didn't notice she was near trees where acorns would fall.

T: What about the other animals? They all believed Chicken Little. What should they have done?

S: They didn't look up either. They were too lazy.

S: It was the way she said it; like it was really true.

T: That's interesting. It was the way that she said it that made them follow her.

S: They didn't have to go, but they were all scared that the sky was going to fall and wreck everything.

S: Maybe if the first one didn't go, then the second one wouldn't go.

T: What should [or could] they have done instead?

S: They should have gone back to see what was there.

T: Why do you think the animals believed Chicken Little?

S: Maybe one of them had gotten hit by something before.

S: That's not in the story, but it might have happened.

T: Do you think that they knew Chicken Little, or was she a stranger?

S: They knew her. The fox might have been a stranger.

T: So, you think that she was a friend and they believed what she told them. Do you usually believe what your friends tell you?

S: Sometimes, but not all the time.

S: Like a friend of mine said there's not really a Santa Claus, and there is!

During later discussions that day and during the week, Kathy explored further the issues of the reliability of sources:

> During the rest of the week we would dramatize the story with new endings, and most importantly, we would begin to relate the ideas they have been developing about determining reliability to their everyday lives. [Here Kathy builds in the transfer to childrens' lives.] In the follow-up dialogue about information they have heard from a friend, we would focus on questions about what they were told, who did the telling, why they were told, when they were told. As I write down their responses we will be beginning to develop a list of criteria for determining reliability of sources of information and for the reliability of the information itself. Of course, it's important to consider the experience and intellectual development of your students. I am working with first graders who are non-readers and who get most of their information from T.V., pictures, and word of mouth. (Skowron 1987)

This lesson has elicited several key aspects of the way we act upon what others say: Do we believe because they sound convincing? Do we check the evidence (by looking up at the sky or down to see if there is an acorn that has fallen?). When do our emotions (they were scared) affect the way we act? Do we usually believe our friends? The children have set up a set of criteria that can be summarized and displayed graphically around the room if this is a major concern. It might become of real importance if adults are worried about children wandering off with strangers. At one point Kathy asked, "Why do you think they trusted the fox?"

S: Because he pretended to be really nice, but he ate them instead.

T: Sort of like those strangers you're all supposed to watch out for? [Here is Kathy's transfer opportunity.]

S: Yes, like that.

Here is the social importance for youngsters of being careful about whom you believe and follow, and, of course, what they are learning is immensely important for us as adults. The curricular question is "To what extent do we follow up with a lesson like this, continuously returning to its theme and, as years progress, making the issue more complex and interesting so students reflect upon and revise their criteria for credibility?"

Recognizing Criteria and Others' Points of View—Secondary

Richie is a teacher of history who loves to work with the "average" and "below average" students in ways that challenge them to play the role of "history makers" (Barell 1980). That is, he places them in situations where they have to make decisions similar to ones made by Thomas Jefferson, Abraham Lincoln, and other significant American leaders. I have seen him create problematic situations that asked students to imagine themselves advising Jefferson on the wisdom of the

Louisiana Purchase, attempting to decide what to do with the "standing army" after the Revolutionary War, and trying to decide whether to free all the slaves if they were in Lincoln's shoes.

What Richie seems to be able to do is to find those moments in United States history where a momentous decision was made. How does he do this? I imagine he scans his subject matter and asks himself these kinds of questions:

What problems have confronted us in history?

Which of these problems are historically significant? Which have historically significant consequences? Which exemplify processes that are important for us to understand? Which reveal the thinking of major historical personages?

Which of these problems can we analyze and learn something about how historians think and how we think?

Which of these problems are suitable for the kinds of students with whom I am working? Suitable in their complexity/simplicity; historical significance, suitable for the developmental level of the students?

Which problems might help my students think productively about problems in their own lives? In other words, which seem to incorporate concepts, attitudes, conditions, and consequences that are significantly related to problems in students' lives beyond the classroom?

What would Richie's lesson plan look like for a typical problem-solving session?

Content: Identify the major concepts, ideas, principles, or processes: Emancipation; taking another's point of view and the process and feelings associated therewith.

Objective: Students will decide whether or not (and when) Lincoln should free the slaves.

Teaching Strategy

INITIATING ACTIVITY Confront students with a controversial and relevant situation; determine different points of view, and see if students can take the point of view opposite their own.

CORE ACTIVITY Have students review Lincoln's conduct of the Civil War up to 1863. Then take a class vote: "How many of you would free the slaves in 1863? How many would not?" Tally vote. Elicit students' initial reasons for making this judgment.

Form students into Side A and Side B and have them attempt to develop cogent reasons for their particular choice and to convince the other side. Or, have Group A figure out the reasons for Group B's decision and vice versa. Then share conclusions to see how well each perceives the other's point of view.

During ensuing discussion, attempt to elicit reasons why each side made its decision. Then ask Groups A and B to attempt to reason from the other's point of view. (At this point, if they have real difficulty, some direct teaching may be in order.)

METACOGNITION   Ask, "What was our problem? How did you go about marshaling your reasons? Figuring out how to argue from another's point of view? How difficult/easy was it? Why? What feelings did you have while engaged in this?"

TRANSFER   Ask, "How and where can we use this process of attempting to see another's point of view? How difficult/easy is it in your lives? Why?"

As I noted above, Richie is committed to working through such problems with his average students; he has communicated to them that he has high expectations of their ability to think through such situations logically, and they respond accordingly.

In Richie's case, this is not an isolated incident. He regularly thinks of his history curriculum as composed of nonroutine problems to be solved by his students. They regularly step in and out of various roles, acquiring thereby a sense that history is composed of problems to solve, decisions to be made that involve reasoning through very complex issues. As Newmann (1988) has noted, part of the challenge of social studies is "to see and to feel the world from another's point of view." To do this requires being able to empathize with those who lived in classical Athens, as well as those who suffered in the Holocaust. One of the results we hope to attain is, as in literature, an expansion of our domains of understanding—both intellectually and emotionally. Richie's entire curricular strategy is a movement in this direction.

CONCLUSION

In this chapter I have attempted to help us identify some important aspects of the search for reasonableness:

> The conclusions we draw are dependent upon a number of different but related processes: determining good reasons, based upon accurate information, data, or evidence, and unearthing our underlying assumptions, criteria, and belief systems.
>
> Together with these processes are those closely related, such as searching for counterevidence, taking another's point of view, and engaging in analogical reasoning. All the foregoing contribute to our arriving at reasonable conclusions.

Some of us, as English teachers, are always engaged in these processes when we ask students to write paragraphs and compositions. Others of us are familiar with it in making historical, artistic, mathematical, or scientific judgments.

Perhaps just as important is the close interrelationship between thinking and feeling when it comes to searching for reasons and supportive documentation. I tend to think this is a neglected aspect of our reasoning processes, at least our teaching of them. Our own difficulties with acknowledging and speaking about feelings in public probably play an important role here. In this chapter I have attempted not only to highlight this neglect, but also to help us figure out ways of dealing constructively with the difficulties, frustrations, and discomfort some of us feel when probing others for their reasons. This is certainly an opportunity for us to heed the elements presented in Chapter 5 to make our educational environments more invitational for thoughtful engagement—engagement that involves both intellectual processes and the feelings associated with them.

REFERENCES

Barell, John. 1980. *Playgrounds of Our Minds*. New York: Teachers College Press.

Goleman, Daniel. 1989. "Researchers Trace Empathy's Roots to Infancy." *The New York Times*. 28 March. p. C1.

Lipman, Matthew. 1988. "Critical Thinking: What it Can Be." *Cogitare* 2, 4:1–2.

McPeck, John. 1981. *Critical Thinking and Education*. Oxford, England: Martin Robertson.

National Assessment of Educational Progress. 1986. *The Writing Report Card*. Princeton, NJ: Educational Testing Service.

Newmann, Fred. 1988. "Higher Order Thinking in the Teaching of Social Studies: Connections Between Theory and Practice." In *Informal Reasoning and Education*, ed. D. Perkins, J. Segal, and J. Voss. Hillsdale, NJ: Lawrence Erlbaum.

Perkins, David. 1985. "Reasoning as Imagination." *Interchange* 16, 1:14–26.

Robinson, James Harvey. 1967. "On Various Kinds of Thinking." In *A College Treasury—Prose, Fiction, Drama, Poetry,* ed. Paul Jorgensen and Frederick Shroyer. New York: Charles Scribner's Sons.

Sarason, Seymour. 1982. *The Culture of the School and the Problem of Change*. Boston: Allyn & Bacon.

Skowron, Kathy. January 1987. "Is Chicken Little A Reliable Source." *Cogitare,* 2, 1:2–3.

Sternberg, Robert. 1985. *Beyond I.Q.: A Triarchic Theory of Human Intelligence*. Cambridge: Cambridge University Press.

Swartz, Robert. In press. "Structured Teaching for Critical Thinking and Reasoning in Standard Subject Area Instruction." In *Informal Reasoning and Education*, ed. James Voss, David N. Perkins, and Judith Segal. Hillsdale, NJ: Lawrence Erlbaum.

CHAPTER 11

Empowering through Metacognition

OVERVIEW

How do we empower students to take more control of their own learning, thinking, and management of life in and out of school? Research on metacognition provides some clues worth working with on many different levels—strategies involving instructional planning, use of teacher questioning, writing in Thinking Journals, and curricular planning.

Edith Wharton in her novel *The House of Mirth* describes a renowned family of New York City society, the Wetheralls, who conducted their lives in a quite distinctive fashion:

> The Wetheralls always went to church. They belonged to the vast group of human automata who go through life without neglecting to perform a single one of the gestures executed by the surrounding puppets. (1964)

The Wetheralls epitomize a way of living in this world that is all too similar to the way we educate students in our schools—keeping them thoroughly dependent upon other people's thinking. The Wetheralls are not in control of their own lives or their own destiny. They live for what other people think of and for them. They are totally other-directed and live their lives by marching and dancing to the same movements as all the other "puppets" that surround them. One wonders who is the puppeteer? Who pulls the strings? Who is in command?

In many respects the Wetheralls are very similar to Emily's tape recorder, merely taking in and repeating information without thoughtful consideration. The Wetheralls and Emily are treated in precisely the opposite fashion to the way we ought to treat people and our students. We should foster their control over their own lives, their awareness of their own emotional and intellectual processes. This awareness-and-control is the essence of the process known as metacognition. Derived from the Greek, *meta* means *after, amidst,* and *over and above*. In the case of our thinking processes, *meta*cognition refers to transcending our thinking, thinking about our thinking.

Emily appears to be more metacognitive than the Wetheralls, because she arrived at her conclusion about being a tape recorder as she reflected in her Thinking Journal (see below) about problematic situations in her personal life. Emily is, therefore, in a position to do something about her situation, whereas the Wetheralls might not even be conscious of acting like puppets.

METACOGNITION DEFINED

Cognitive

Usually we consider metacognition in terms of our awareness of how we think about a certain task or problem. Thus, we have thoughts about *the nature of the problematic situation*—for example, the detour or writing this book: What kind of situation is this? Is it related to any other I know?

Second, there are thoughts about the thinking process itself: How should I proceed? Should I just go ahead or should I attempt to reduce this problem to several parts and solve one at a time?

When these questions are posed before, during, and after the experience, we may have achieved "knowledge about, awareness of and control over one's own mind and thinking" (Swartz & Perkins 1989, p. 51). So metacognition focuses upon the mental processes we use within a specific situation. Marzano (1988) suggests that our awareness of our thinking can be further classified as declarative knowledge ("I know that books have a system of organization"), procedural knowledge ("This is how you go about organizing a book project"), and conditional knowledge ("I need to use my organizing strategies when I am working on the introduction to this chapter so the rest of it will be coherent") (p. 13). Knowing that, knowing how, and knowing when are crucial to reflective, metacognitive thought. As Pressley (1987) notes, "knowledge about when to use strategies is a particularly critical form of metacognition."

All of these aspects of metacognition are summed up in the illustration by a third grader from Salt Lake City, Dane Uriona, who drew his picture after he reflected on the meaning of wait time: "Wait time is a good idea I think because it gives time to imagine." (See Figure 11.1.)

Affective

Another aspect of metacognitive awareness and control is not always mentioned: knowledge of, awareness of, and control of the feelings that accompany certain situations. For example, some of us get very frustrated when confronting detours, examinations, or other complex problems. Such feelings are important, because they may reveal underlying and longer-term attitudes, dispositions, or habits of

Figure 11.1.

mind that help produce such self-talk scripts as: "I can't really succeed in situations like these. I'm not really very good when a problem involves numbers. I have a very hard time persisting in situations like these" (Hyde & Bizar 1989).

With such underlying attitudes, our immediate feelings of frustration and panic can take control of us and shut down our abilities to proceed rationally. It is important, therefore, to *recognize* our feelings when confronting a problematic situation (Chapter 8), acknowledge them, put them in the perspective of impediments to thoughtfulness, and thus take control of the situation. For example, Donna Sparacio is a young teacher who, after keeping a Thinking Journal (see pp. 232–233) for fifteen weeks, noted her progress in this regard: "One very important thing I have learned about my thinking, is that when I don't give in to panic, I am creative, and quite capable of solving most problems.''

Donna's reflection transcends Emily's because Donna has now asserted herself; she is not a slave or a pawn to her feelings and to those dispositions that might have told her, ''You're not very good at this sort of stuff!'' Donna has beaten down that negative attitude toward her own abilities and has reasserted herself. In this way she has become more of an agent controlling her own destiny and less of a pawn in an incomprehensible maze.

Thus, metacognition involves knowledge of ourselves (how we usually do or can perform in such situations) and of our task or problem (what kind it is and what sorts of strategies will help us resolve it). It is a ''crosscutting superordinate kind of thinking'' (Swartz & Perkins 1989, p. 51) that empowers us to act like the chief executive officer of a company when planning, monitoring, and evaluating our progress toward desired goals. Other metaphors or models that come to mind are an orchestra leader, a head coach, or a captain directing the movements of a ship through uncharted waters.

METACOGNITIVE PROCESSES

Several processes are associated with metacognition. First is the ability to reflect on our thinking before, during, and after our problem solving. This often involves planning, monitoring, and evaluating our thinking. Second is posing questions to ourselves as we are planning, monitoring, and evaluating. One seventh grader defined thinking as ''talking to yourself,'' and this is a significant observation, since some people have defined the essence of metacognition as that ''inner dialogue'' with ourselves as we are engaged in problem solving (Costa 1989). In Donna's case she found that the process of ''self-talk'' was the mechanism that empowered her to take control in the face of panic. She probably said things like the following to herself: ''You can do this. . . . You have succeeded in similar situations before, and you can here also with a good deal of persistence.'' In effect, Donna rewrote her self-talk script to reflect her now more positive outlook.

This ''self''-questioning, reflecting, and regulating may be the essence of metacognitive awareness and control, as Hyde and Bizar note (1989). We want students to conduct the inner dialogue and to become more self-directed and in control in the process. We do not foster such self-questioning by having students memorize rules and questions; this might even be counterproductive, since we want each of us to engage in thinking up our own questions, to create our own pathways of self-reflection.

Levels of Awareness

Swartz and Perkins (1989) have presented a very insightful continuum of ''levels of thought that are increasingly metacognitive'':

> *Tacit use:* We make decisions without really thinking about it.
> *Aware use:* Here we are conscious of our decision-making processes.

Strategic use: We organize our thinking by means of a selection of strategies for decision making.

Reflective use: Here "the individual reflects upon his or her thinking before and after—or even in the middle of—the process, pondering how to proceed and how to improve" (p. 52).

Let me illustrate how we might find students at different levels of awareness of their thinking in our classrooms.

I recently spent some time in Peter's high school sociology class. He was working with the students on the process of creating a questionnaire for distribution among other students. Peter and his class were interested in such things as how you become a member of a certain group (clique), what matters most to teenagers as members of one group or another, and how it felt not to be a member of one of the several groups within this particular suburban high school.

At one point Peter asked his students to write a question on a particular topic. After about five minutes, I noticed one student, Steven, in the back row had put down his pencil. I went over to the young man and asked him if he was finished.

"I don't know," he responded.

"How would you find out?" I asked.

"I don't know," he responded again without much enthusiasm for my questions.

After learning that he also did not know if he had done a good job or not, I tried to help him identify the resources he could use to help him evaluate completion of this task.

A bit later, Peter singled out another student, David, for his question, because it was exemplary. After class I approached David, as others were filing in and out of the room, and asked him if he could tell me about how he came up with such a wonderful, useful question.

"Well," he said not quite knowing what to make of this stranger who asked even stranger questions, "I guess it has to do with thinking about all the psychological tests I have taken . . . remembering the key words within these tests . . . trying to apply them to this kind of question. . . . It really takes a lot of *forethought,*" he said finally. "A lot of planning," he added, strolling out the door, appearing satisfied that he had passed another test or perhaps learned something new.

Now you can readily see that Steven and David are at different levels of awareness about their thinking.

POINT TO PONDER: How would you apply the Swartz/Perkins classifications to these two students?

Perhaps you thought that Steven is at the *tacit* level because he may be applying certain processes without knowing about it. It also seems to me that maybe he hasn't used any particular skills. Steven is not very aware of how well he performs; he does not know if he has finished a job at all, let alone finished it well. He does not seem to be in control of what he knows and does not know.

David, on the other hand, seemed well aware of exactly how he went about planning to generate a very good answer. "It takes forethought . . . planning," he said with much self-assurance. The fact that he could, with very little coaching from me, be very explicit about his thinking process, leads me to conclude that here was a student who was very much in control of his own thinking. David indeed seemed to be well aware of what he knew and didn't know. His self-confidence probably stemmed, to some degree at least, from this knowledge of his thinking processes. For these reasons he seems to be somewhere between the *aware* and *strategic* levels.

What does this tell us? Perhaps only that in all of our classrooms we most likely have students who are already conscious of how they go about figuring things out, how they solve problems. With a little instruction and coaching, David can become more reflective, and, one hopes, Steven can work toward more conscious use of specific strategies.

Planning, Monitoring, and Evaluating

What David exemplified was one element of metacognition: *planning* to carry out a task. The other two are *monitoring* your progress and *evaluating* the accomplishment of the task.

Planning

What is my problem or task? What am I asked to do, specifically? (Problem definition or location.)

Are there feelings associated with this situation to *recognize* and gain control of?

Can I *represent* this situation graphically, symbolically?

Can this problem be *reduced* to several parts and can I solve one part more easily than the others?

Is this problem *related* to any other I have solved?

What information is relevant and what is not important? *(Research.)*

How will I approach this task? What steps do I need to take? What other steps can I take to solve this problem? *(Strategy.)*

What *resources* are at my command and how should I use them?

How much *time* do I need to solve the problem?

What *results* do I predict?

Monitoring

How well am I doing? (Status report.)

What am I doing and why?

What steps have I completed? What do I still have to do?

Am I encountering any obstacles and how will I overcome them?

Evaluation

Have I completed my task? How do I know?
How well have I done? Did I do as well as predicted?
What did I learn by doing it this way? Might I have done it differently? Would
    I do it the same way again? Why?
What does the result mean?
How can I use this new knowledge? What does it relate to?

These are the kinds of questions that we can ask ourselves as we approach, engage in, and complete a task—any task from solving an algebraic equation to buying a house to entering the stock market. The questions I have used here are derived from an excellent study undertaken in Australia by Baird and White (1984). The best approach seems to be to try to have students pose questions like these for themselves, not for us to attempt to teach them directly. Some students, like David, already possess the ability to pose their own questions spontaneously; others, like Steven, do not.

STRATEGIES TO ENHANCE
METACOGNITIVE ABILITIES

There are several strategies I wish to discuss: assessing metacognitive potency; teacher planning, monitoring, and evaluating; teacher modeling; helping students plan, monitor, and evaluate (through goal setting and asking, "How did you solve it?"); students writing about their thinking in journals; and drawing your mind at work (Dane's strategy).

Assessing Metacognitive Potency

Mary Jane Fox of Shoreham–Wading River introduced a simple and direct means of assessing students' abilities to *plan, monitor,* and *evaluate* their own thinking. This strategy should be undertaken before any of those that follow, because it will provide you with pretest information with which you can then plan your own approach to improving students' control over their own thinking. Following a workshop on metacognition, she went back to her classroom and realized that her students had just done very poorly on an examination given by the Social Studies teacher with whom she team-taught in a humanitieslike course. Mary Jane decided to find out why students had done so poorly by posing a series of questions which students were asked to respond to in writing:

1.   How did you prepare for this test?
2.   What did you do during the test?
3.   How did you think you had done after the test? Why?
4.   What was your grade? How do you feel about it?
5.   What do you plan to do differently for Friday's test?

6. What will you do differently during the test?
7. How well do you think you will do on Friday's test? Why?

As you can see, Mary Jane's questions follow the *planning, monitoring,* and *evaluating* model of *metacognition* presented in this chapter. When she read the students' responses, it became evident to Mary Jane that something very significant was occurring. Here are a few responses to question 1:

"I made lists of all the stuff I knew. . . ."
"I looked over the questions and kept looking them over. . . ."
"I reviewed over the questions I didn't know. . . ."
"Underlined what was important. . . ."
"Mostly memorized. . . ."
"Wrote all the information I could think of. . . ."
"Made outlines."

What surprised Mary Jane was the paucity of intelligent strategies, such as outlining and reviewing what you don't know. She was also taken aback by the presence of memorization strategies, especially among the highest achievers in the classroom. "Wrote all the information I could think of" came from a student whose grades heretofore had been exceptional.

Here are students' responses to her fifth question: "What do you plan to do differently for Friday's test?" Next to each student's response I have listed the grade on the previous test:

"Fully study every little detail. . . ." [52]
"Study more. . . ." [60]
"Take as many notes as I can and study hard. . . ." [45]
"Pay great attention to the movie. . . ." [77]
"Take notes . . . compare them with Jen to see if Mr. R. said one thing in Period 5 and another in Period 6 . . . summarize the entire story. . . ." [63]

These are the responses that Mary Jane and I became most fascinated with. They tell us a great deal about what students' think is important, about how they are taught (the hidden curriculum), and how much control they have over their academic destiny. Take a few minutes to analyze students' responses to Mary Jane's question.

POINT TO PONDER: What do you think these responses indicate?

I'm sure that you have observed many of the same kinds of things that Mary Jane noted.

"They have no control over their own learning!" she exclaimed in a meeting with other teachers at her school. What did she mean by this? Perhaps that even the "best and the brightest" students seemed mired in a memorization mentality. "Fully study every detail" is the kind of "mind-forged manacle" indicative of memorizers. What disturbed Mary Jane more than anything was that people who can only think of swallowing everything have little control over their own lives. "They're totally outer-directed," she observed. "No internal locus of control at all!" This is in line with Goodlad's finding that students seem to exercise little independent control over their own academic destiny (1984).

I have shared these findings with many teachers in various parts of the country. What strikes some people like a blast of frigid air in winter is the force of the "hidden curriculum": We have taught these students that to attain academic success, they must master "every little detail." How else to explain the predominance of memorization strategies? We have been successful in communicating the message: If you want to do well on Friday's test, then master more facts. This is nothing new. I am convinced that I got through a history major in college with exactly the same strategy. Beyond that I am also rather certain that my qualifying exams for the doctoral degree demanded a very high degree of regurgitating factual information I had swallowed whole. We say we want people to think, but do our examinations really call for anything more than repeating back all the information we had to master earlier?

My colleague at Montclair, Rob Gilbert, would look at Mary Jane's results and compare her students to those athletes he coaches toward a winning philosophy. "It's not working harder that's important," he would say. "It's working smarter." That means having a strategy to improve your performance. No one becomes a winner or an Olympic gold medalist simply by doing more of the same; you must exert your energies toward a goal with a specific strategy you think will improve your performance. Just running, swimming, or swinging a bat harder will not help you improve. What we need to do is examine what successful athletes have done to break their own personal barriers. I can still remember reading about how Dr. Roger Bannister planned to break the four-minute mile: He calculated with some exactitude where he needed to be at each quarter mile, how he would achieve these objectives, how he would monitor his progress along the way.

Mary Jane's students will not improve until they begin to think of themselves as athletes preparing for an important race or match: Work smarter, not just harder. Plan, monitor, and evaluate continuously.

Now, here are some developmental approaches to help us deal with what we find by using Mary Jane's strategy:

Teacher Planning, Monitoring, and Evaluating

Make very explicit before, during, and after a lesson exactly what strategies will be used:

Prior to any learning activity, teachers will want to take time to develop and discuss strategies and steps for attacking problems, rules to remember, and directions to be followed. . . .

During the activity, teachers may invite students to share their progress, thought processes, and perceptions of their own behavior. Asking students to indicate where they are in their strategy, to describe the "trail" of thinking up to that point, and to define alternative pathways they intend to pursue next helps them become aware of their own behavior. (It also provides teachers with a diagnostic cognitive map of students' thinking, which can be used to give more individualized assistance.)

Then *after* the learning activity, teachers can invite students to evaluate how well the rules were followed, how productive the strategies were . . . and what some alternative, more efficient strategies would be used in the future. . . . (Costa & Lowery 1989)

This is a grand strategy, one that encompasses the whole learning experience, and should be, therefore, part of everybody's repertoire.

One teacher I know gives us a practical need for such a strategy. When she presents a problem-solving process to her high school math students, she is confident they understand it. Why? "When I ask them if they understand, they say, 'Yes, I understand it when I see you do it, but I have difficulty doing it on my own.' " This should suggest to you that this student might not understand what he is hearing from the teacher. One antidote to this is to pause occasionally and ask the *monitoring* question, "What do you understand about this process? Tell me what you are thinking as we work through this topic or problematic situation. Who can describe for us the strategies you are using up to this point." Some call this a "comprehension check," and when I have used it, I often find that some people were really struggling to understand concepts, such as "mass" or "metaphoric thinking."

Some teachers have made their expectations very clear at the beginning of a lesson with *planning* statements: "Today we will be listening to and commenting upon each others' answers. We will be trying to understand someone else's reasoning processes."

Others, like Mary Mulcahy in first grade, have asked *evaluating* questions like these after a particular learning experience (Chapter 4): "Have we been good thinkers today? Who can tell us about his or her thinking and whether you believe you did well today?"

At the high school level we can ask: "How well did we do? Who can analyze and evaluate our ability to work through these problems? To understand the concepts? To use the strategies we have practiced? What do we need to work on now to improve?"

This overarching structure to our instructional practice is, then, the same structure we can foster in our own and our students' thinking: "What do I want to do? How will I do it? How well am I doing? How well have I done?"

Teacher Modeling

I noted in Chapter 5 the efficacy of our own modeling. Costa and Lowery (1989) note the value of using the language of thoughtfulness. This involves identifying the specific strategies we wish students to become immersed in as we work through a problem. For example, we model by thinking aloud, "What is my problem and how will I *represent, relate, reduce* it? How do I feel about such problems?"

One teacher, Victoria Bell, instructed her students in how to create a haiku. She first identified some strategies: "By discussing the strategies I would use to help solve the problem (create a poem) I was helping my students keep them in mind for their own use, and helping them to evaluate the performance (both theirs and mine) afterwards." (1990) Then she modeled the creation process. Subsequently, her students were able to discuss their own thinking, using her modeling as an example: "I visualized a birthday party to see what was there" and "We were talking about work in school, and I related that to work at home." Then Victoria asked what strategies they had used, and her students responded with more of the language of thoughtfulness: using your own experience, researching, and making associations. "These are all words that I used when I created my poem, but I had not formally instructed the students to use them." The teacher has successfully made thinking visible and her students were able to apply the strategies she modeled to their own creative process.

Helping Students Plan, Monitor, and Evaluate

One of the general strategies we can use is to make the thinking visible. By this I mean we can begin to ask students like Steven and David to think more broadly in terms of planning, monitoring, and evaluating.

Planning Processes.   This is an excellent place to begin breaking away from the Right Answer Syndrome. Challenging students to think, not about their answers but about their planning to get answers, may help move them from mindlessly doing things to what Swartz & Perkins (1989) call more reflective use of thought processes.

Goal Setting.   Let me return one more time to the process of students' identifying a goal and working toward it, because this process involves planning, monitoring, and evaluating. In Doreen Guzo's English class, we asked students how they went about arriving at the goals she regularly asked them to set for themselves:
    Jeff wrote:

> The most effective way of choosing goals I can achieve is first thinking were [*sic*] I am now. Second I will think of where I want to be. I will decide on whether or not the goal is achievable and whether I'm willing to put in the time and hard work needed to achieve the goal. . . .
>
>   The kind of thinking I use in achieving goals is I don't set universal goals because these goals will seem too big to achieve. I break my goals down into smaller parts and eventually I will accomplish my universal goal.
>
>   The main part of working toward a goal is knowing how long it will take to accomplish. Many of my goals may take ten years, a few may take a lifetime. I must not try to accomplish a goal too fast. I must take the time and put in the work.

    Sarah wrote:

When I was thinking about my goals I thought about some of the most craziest things that I would really like to do. I thought out what some things other people did, that I used to admire now. Some of the goals that I wrote were things that I knew I wanted to do, like live in N.Y.C. I also wrote down little things that I have talked about with my friends.

It doesn't take too much analysis to see that Jeff has given goal setting a good deal of thought. When I asked him where he learned how to set and work toward goals, he said, "My dad taught me."

What is important here is that he learned some sophisticated ways of defining his goals for himself. When I showed Jeff's response to my colleague Hope Hartman, she noted how many "executive processes" (Sternberg 1985) were present in his thinking: knowledge of present and desired states, objectives, time and effort required to reach goals, different kinds of goals, and goal analysis. The second student, by contrast, uses her imagination and is strongly influenced by models and differentiates between long-range and short-term goals.

I used to admire only Jeff's thinking, but I have grown to see value in Sarah's less methodical approach. We can imagine learning something from both students. Using the planning and self-monitoring forms presented at the end of Chapter 5, we can challenge students to become more self-directed about just about any activity, from getting to school on time and paying attention, to becoming a better physics student and listening to others' arguments in class.

In Problematic Situations. Planning how to go about solving a problem is really the essence of the Seven R strategy outlined in Chapter 8. We want students to reflect on their feelings, the nature of the problem, and its relationships before they jump to generating solutions, and emphasizing the planning is another way to go about it. Research (Sternberg 1985) indicates that more intelligent persons spend more time in "global planning," because here they think about the important concepts and issues at hand. Novice thinkers spend more time with the surface characteristics of situations and fail to plumb the depths of the important stuff that you find in any dilemma.

Here there are several approaches we can use:

1. Help students with their own planning processes by asking them to think aloud through the same questions: "What is my problem and how do I think I will go about solving it? or What do I want to do and how will I go about doing it?"

    For example, Connie Short teaches her middle school students to ask good questions—ones that call for factual recall, inferential thinking, and evaluation. In one of her lessons, she focused entirely on inferential questions. She told the story "Jack and the Beanstalk" and then asked her students to write down one or more questions beginning with "Why?" that they did not know the answer to. This element was important: They must not know why something happened in the story. Once the question was asked, then the directions were to try to find evidence within the story to support one or another hypothesis.

When we role-played this situation with teachers, Tina asked, "Why did Jack go back to the Giant's dwelling a second and third time?" Several students offered suggestions using evidence from the story.

Then Connie asked Tina: "Now, how could you go about answering your own question?"

This was the metacognitive question, calling upon Tina to plan a strategy for investigating her curiosity further. It is the same strategy Sandy Woodson's students used to further their inquiry. It is a metacognitive strategy, because it calls upon the student to think before acting, to plan a course of events that can then be monitored, just as if we were solving a physics or aesthetic problem: "How am I going to do this?"

2. Work with students in small groups to allow them time to pose planning questions for themselves. Give them a problem, dilemma, or issue to work on and for the time being just have them focus upon how they will go about doing it and why they think these approaches will be productive. John Borchert challenged his eighth graders to identify ways they would go about determining how fossils had been formed: "What questions do you ask yourself and how will you answer them?" His emphasis was upon their planning how they would answer their own questions.

3. As we noticed in Chapter 7, there are many opportunities for students to think ahead about the kinds of learning they wish to pursue. This can be part of an overall metacognitive approach. For example, Kathy has used a variation on this metacognitive strategy to improve students' levels of involvement in a second grade unit on dinosaurs. She asked students to pose questions they wished to answer before they commenced the unit. There were many questions, such as "What did they eat? Which was the biggest? What colors were they?" But there was one question that caught everybody's eye: "What are the dinosaurs like that we haven't discovered yet?" Consider that this second grader—who had been classified as having a learning disability—imagined what had not yet been uncovered.

Kathy, of course, used these questions to guide students' inquiry and to create challenging activities, like making charts to compare and contrast the different kinds of dinosaurs. This strategy is very similar to what we might do in planning, monitoring, and evaluating our own reading. Show students titles, pictures, or first sentences of a story, and ask them to generate questions they wish to answer while reading this passage. This strategy is fully developed by Jana Mason in her recent book (1985). We can also ask students to make predictions and create images about the nature of the story on the basis of the evidence they see so far. This prediction process is then monitored as we read, for we are progressively confirming or disconfirming our original hypotheses. In this way, reading text becomes a more reflective process of inquiry, creating meaning, pursuing a purpose we establish for ourselves. We are constantly, therefore, answering our own questions.

Monitoring Questions.   Once we have a plan, of course, we begin to execute it. Whether in small or large group instruction, we should encourage students to watch their thinking closely, to track it closely. Research on intelligent behavior indicates that monitoring one's progress through a problem—looking back to detect errors made and forward to choose a strategy—are necessary for successful performance (Costa 1984). They know what their goals are, how they are pursuing them, and how well they are doing at any given point. Palincsar and Brown (1989) include monitoring as one of several strategies that promote reading comprehension: "using monitoring activities (e.g., paraphrasing, self-questioning) to determine if comprehension is occurring" (p. 20).

Here are some monitoring questions for our large group presentations:

> "Let's stop here. Would you please share with us your thinking up to this point, David?"
>
> "Jennifer, would you please tell us how you are following my thinking at this point? Tell me in your own words what I am doing and what you are thinking about it."
>
> "Sarah, if you had to teach this process right now, what parts would you focus upon? Would you do it the same way I have? Why/why not? Let me hear you start teaching me what we have been working on, please."
>
> "Since very few of you have followed me up to this point, let me ask you where did I lose you? Where did you reach a dead end?"

Wayne Bond uses the latter strategy (Barell 1988) when he notices what he calls the "glaze of the eyes": Students are lost or paying attention to other matters. When he notices this phenomenon, he says, "When I see you drift out, you've got to tell me what you're thinking about" (p. 43). He wants to know when they left the discussion, why, and where they went. Perhaps they are daydreaming: How can I keep myself awake here, or, What would it be like to be a farmer in the Cotswolds? Sometimes, though, I think the destinations students go to at these moments can be very revealing of productive thought. For example, we can be discussing romanticism, revolution, and rebellion, and students often will naturally begin making connections that are meaningful to them: their rebellion against parents, friends, and teachers. These connections may be important to identify and dignify because they help students make the abstract more meaningful.

As noted above, if we have followed research-tested approaches in reading (Palincsar & Brown 1989), we will be asking students to track their progress in answering the questions they generated during prereading activities. During the monitoring phase we can also find out what strategies they use when they do not understand a certain word (do they stop and give up, or do they explore the text to figure out its meaning?), what new questions are they generating as the result of their reading. Such self-monitoring can be, and often is, perceived as the heart and soul of becoming aware and in control of our own thinking.

How Did You Solve It?   The exploratory question "How did you get that answer?" may be the most significant metacognitive strategy. Here the emphasis is upon thinking processes, not the solution. We are looking for students to identify the processes they used to arrive at a solution.

Miriam's Social Studies students began keeping Thinking Journals recently. They conducted an activity and then responded to these questions: What was the problem? How did you solve it? Did you solve it well? What would you do differently next time? Here are some of their first stabs at "thinking about their own thinking processes" in response to a problem Miriam presented: Should the Concorde be allowed to land at JFK airport? The issues here related to the Constitution's reserve clause (Tenth Amendment) and federal-state conflicts over such difficulties. Here is what some students wrote in their journals:

> "How did we solve it?"
> "By thinking of alternatives to this problem . . . by discussing it with other group members, and by asking questions of the validity of our solutions." [Good opportunity here to look for reasons and criteria—see Chapter 10.]
> "By taking the positive and negatives of landing in a state-owned airport. I had to consider the reasons for the state's opinion and the federal opinion." [Again, looking for reasons and criteria.]
> "Used knowledge we learned in class, looked at possible solutions, gathered info. Different points of view." [Use of prior knowledge, generating alternatives, and considering alternative points of view.]
> "I had to base it on the evidence. I had to think about what was said and come to a conclusion." [Search for good evidence.]
> "I used prior knowledge and the information given. I also gathered new information to find the rights of each side. I also used my own feelings." [I wonder what those feelings were?]

The last comment about feelings is intriguing, because we often omit mention of our feelings about how a problem might be solved. What is our gut reaction? This is evidence of our need to invite students to *recognize* the feelings they have in such difficult and perplexing situations as the Concorde's landing in our country. Such feelings may stem from attitudes (one way or the other) toward our country or from a felt need to protect the environment.

What we are striving for is best summed up by Tejal, one of Rosemarie Liebmann's students, who reflected on her thinking process in her journal:

> I do not want to be dependent on others to help me solve my problems. My dad usually helps me by asking me questions about problems. I guess what I should learn to do is ask myself similar questions. Writing about my problems helps me to see what I don't understand so I can ask better questions.

Tejal has realized that one of the key factors in becoming a more intelligent person is asking ourselves good questions, just as Izzy's mother demanded of him so many years ago. As she has expressed it, one of our objectives in probing students' thinking is for them to become more self-directed in their learning. This strategy can also be used in conjunction with what is called semantic mapping, a process whereby students visually outline sets of expected relationships before commencing to read a selection.

Now that we have explored a number of strategies for fostering students' growth toward more reflective use of their thinking, I will share some of what I have learned from students' maintaining their own Thinking Journals. It has been my conviction, based upon my own experience as a writer, that writing can be very beneficial in figuring out how to solve problems. I think as I write, and the writing conditions how I think.

There are three varieties of Thinking Journal we shall deal with: Double Entry Journals, Open Ended Journals, and Problem Solving Journals for awareness and transfer.

Students Writing about Their Thinking

Double Entry Journals.   Karen Dalrymple (1987) has long used a writing strategy with her young students, a strategy that helps them become autonomous questioners, persons capable of charting their own course through a situation where there are no obvious paths to follow.

Here are the kinds of questions we might pose for our writing while engaged in problem solving:

> *Prior:* What is my problem? How do I feel about it? How do I start? What do I need to do? How will I get to where I want to go?
> *During:* How am I doing? Do I know what I have completed so far? Was my original way of going about this a good one?
> *After:* Am I finished? How do I know? How well did I do? Were I to do this over again, would I follow the same steps? Why? Why not? What have I gained by finishing this task? How will it help me?

Rosemarie Liebmann has experimented rather extensively with Double Entry Journals. Her math students draw a vertical line down the middle of the page; They do the math on the left, and on the right they record the questions and thoughts they are experiencing as they work through the problem. One particular entry is quite remarkable, because the student, Rich, continued to find this a usable strategy for problem solving after he left Rosemarie's class. Here are his observations generated in response to an algebra problem that gave him considerable difficulty:

> This problem scared me while reading it. It got better after I read it six or seven times. I just took it step by step. First assign variables.
> This took time to figure out, but I remembered doing a similar problem in class. [Use of prior knowledge.]
> Success in the last problem builds my confidence for this one. This is the same format, just slightly altered. [Planning and classification of problem type.]
> When reading the problem I almost got thrown with the word "area." Thinking of the idea to square y—but it's wrong. [Monitoring progress and strategy selection.]
> Again the problem is very similar to the last one. The hardest part is organizing the variables. [Planning again; analysis of problem type.]
> They are trying to trick us by using square roots. [Monitoring your analysis of the problem and your understanding of what is important.]

The best thing to do is to square both sides. Simplicity. [Identifying best solution.]

This part is tricky! [Monitoring, observing/evaluating your progress.]

I thought I ran into a problem when I calculated the left side to be one. It's
Cake! [Final evaluation.]

What strikes me as I commit Rich's thinking to paper is that right off the bat
he *recognizes* his emotional state: fear! But with rereading he gains some com-
posure, and perhaps then he is able to think back over his performances during
the past few days and recalls a problem with similar characteristics. Many of us
feel this initial surge of despair; but if we are more reflective than impulsive, and
do not give in to the fear or the panic that Donna mentioned above, we gain
control of our thinking.

You might be interested to know that Rich got the right answer. His com-
panion Dave did not. Here is Dave's record of his thinking:

Saw inversely proportional. Plugged numbers into equation $xy = k$. Found constant—Found New Signs.

Rosemarie saw this as an example of "rote, mechanical" thinking—just plug
numbers into a formula as quickly as you can (1987). Research on good problem
solvers in sciences (Mestre 1987) indicates that novice problem solvers respond
primarily to the surface characteristics of a problem, while more expert students
are able to identify the major concepts within a problem and respond accordingly.
Obviously, Rich has taken much more time with this problem in an attempt to
understand what he is being asked to do and to figure his way out of "doubt,
uncertainty, and difficulty."

This Double Entry strategy is not only useful in mathematics, but it could
also be used in any classroom where there is a task to perform that requires some
extended thinking: writing a term paper or a poem, completing a science lab
experiment, preparing a group report on a novel, finishing a painting or ceramic,
etc.

Open-Ended Thinking Journals.   A far more open-ended strategy has been attempted successfully for quite a while by Doreen Guzo. She has developed a
writing journal based upon an idea by Youngblood (1985). In this journal she has
students record what they think about a novel, before they discuss it in class.
Students write down their thoughts as they read about the characters, about the
situations, about the author's purposes, about their own thinking and their wonderings while reading. Here are a few excerpts from the thinking journals of
Doreen's students as they read Edith Wharton's *Ethan Frome*:

Stephen: "I wonder why the author named the characters Ethan Frome, Zen-
obia Frome and Mattie Silver. The author is always speaking about the crash-
up. I wonder if this is going to be the climax of the story. This scene reminds
me of another scene I've read were [*sic*] they started off in the present and
they go back to old memories to tell a story. I really dislike her mentioning

of the crash-up because you already know then the stories [*sic*] climax."
[Notice Stephen's wondering about names and where the story will proceed;
he is setting up his own projective schema as good readers do. Notice also
his comparison/contrast with prior knowledge.]

Sue: "One of my favorite phrases from this Chapter [1] is when Ethan is describing Mattie's face. He says it "always looked like a window that has
caught a sunset." p. 35. I think an important thing to consider is what the
author was trying to say about Mattie's personality. It seems Mattie may
develop into a very interesting character." [Here Sue is also reflecting and
projecting future possibilities, ones that will guide her reading of subsequent
chapters.]

Ted: "I wonder if Zeena couldn't go to sleep because she thought something
was going on between her husband and Mattie." [Ted is speculating upon
cause and effect in Chapter 2.] "When the author said Zeena carried the
cracked pickle-dish as if it were a dead body, was she foreshadowing?" [Ted
is speculating about Wharton's technical skills as a writer.]

John: "Mrs. Hale's ability to judge people intrigues me. I have begun to feel
lately that I have a similar ability. I feel that I often let this "aloofness" get
the better of me and for this reason I try to supress [*sic*] it. However, I can
see from the story that this ability, when properly used, can be a positive
thing." [John here relates his own experience to that of one of the characters.
He is expressing his empathy for Mrs. Hale perhaps by feeling himself into
her character.]

Stephen: "The tragedy of this story is showing itself. Ethan constantly knows
what to say and do; he just doesn't do it. The feeling of 'what might have
been' is felt throughout the story." [Here Stephen is finding recurrent themes
by relating events with common attributes.]

Doreen told me that, after completing these reading and thinking logs, students enjoyed the discussion of *Ethan Frome* more than any previous class. She
also noted that the logs allowed them to deal productively with the factual knowledge of plot, setting, and character, and that they could spend their time discussing
problems students had identified within the book, such as cause and effect relations, character analyses, and symbolic meanings. Here is another way in which
students have taken *control of their own learning* and set some of their own
directions. When you read journals like these, you find a lot of speculating, another
testament to the marvelous potential all our students have for wondering.

Journals of these kinds are facilitated by providing students with stems such
as the following ones used by Karen Nichols of Salt Lake City: I learned that; I
wonder about; What really surprised me; What I am feeling right now; I agreed/
disagreed with . . . because; It makes me think of/reminds me of; The big idea
is; I changed my mind about . . . because; What I think is important is; My thinking
and feeling are. Students gradually become comfortable expressing their ideas
and feelings.

Reflection of Feelings. Another element that comes forth, especially from John's
entry, is that the journal has provided a forum for the expression of feelings
associated with the novel. John's empathy for Mrs. Hale is coupled with the
always wistful feeling of "might have been" that we all experience now and then.

Notice how he *relates* his own experience to Mrs. Hale's, thereby establishing that crucial and meaningful connection. Expressions like these indicate a class environment that is highly invitational to students' thoughtfulness. Very often students will reserve their feelings for a private vehicle such as the journal, but Doreen has established such a warm, supportive atmosphere, through her gentle encouragement of students, that feelings like these can eventually be brought from the private pages of John's journal into open discussion, where others would share their emotional responses to the novel. *Once again, we must realize how important the expression of feelings is for establishing the thoughtful classroom.* Often it comes easier for students than expressing their thoughts. Thus we are not only interested in cognitive operations; we are also interested in the expression of students' feelings about a subject.

The Stuff to Think About

As I noted in Chapter 7, I am just as interested in understanding the concepts and ideas within the subject as I am in fostering the thinking processes that make these ideas productive. Doreen's use of Thinking Journals fosters this kind of understanding, because she can closely monitor students' identification of significant ideas within the novel. We can use students' writings as diagnostic tools to answer questions like these:

> Can they locate significant concepts?
> Do they understand them?
> Can they *relate* these concepts to prior knowledge?
> Can they use concepts to form significant ideas? (E.g., Ted's perception of
>   foreshadowing.)
> Are they asking good questions about the text? *(Research.)*

With students' writings to guide us, we can proceed to reteach where necessary or build upon students' understanding toward more complex thinking about ideas.

Thinking Journals for Problem Solving and Transfer of Strategies

Figure 11.2 represents a Thinking Journal format I have developed to enhance students' metacognitive awareness and control as well as to foster transfer of significant concepts and processes to other "messy, indeterminant" situations.

You will notice that it is much more structured than Doreen's more open-ended format, but it does provide opportunities for students to search their lives for situations to reflect upon. It was in Part 2 that Emily was moved to reflect on her life in classrooms (Chapter 1) and to analyze the situation as one of being like a tape recorder.

Over the past several years, I have collected journal entries from several students that I believe suggest that they might be becoming more aware of their own thinking, more in control of how and when they solve problems.

THINKING JOURNAL

NAME

CLASS/GRADE

DATE

CONTENTS

1. **Problems You Have Solved:**

   a. What was the problem you had to solve?

   b. How did you solve it? (Identify thinking strategies, not solutions.)

   c. Did you solve it? Well? How did you feel working through it? Why?

   d. What would you do differently next time? Why? What did you learn about your problem-solving abilities? About your feelings?

   e. What other kinds of problems (in school and personal life) can you solve using these strategies? Where else are the strategies applicable? When could you have used these strategies in the past? When can you use them in the future?

   f. What are you learning about your thinking and feeling?

2. **Problem Finding**

   a. Identify a problem/dilemma/conflict of interest you have. It might be a situation out-side of school if you wish.

   b. What questions do you have about this situation? Generate as many different kinds of questions about the situation as you can. Each week look over the list of questions posed last week and see how many more you can generate.

   c. How can strategies learned in class help you solve this problem, resolve the conflict or dilemma?

   d. How are your feelings and dispositions affected in this situation?

   e. What are you learning about responding to life situations as a result of recording your thinking/feeling processes in this journal?

Figure 11.2. Helping Students Achieve Metacognitive Awareness.

Second Grade.   Lois Granito (1990) was determined to help her second graders analyze word problems to get to their meaning and not just look for the words *more* or *less*. This key-word strategy she found very detrimental to students' understanding of what they were doing and to their being able to develop effective problem-solving strategies. Too often they gave up within a few seconds of seeing the problem. Here is Vanessa's journal entry for the following problem: "Lynn has 80 cents. She buys a new assignment pad for 55 cents. How much money does she have left?"

First, see if you need to add or subtract. You have to subtract because you are spending money. Then decide if you need to rename. This problem you need to rename because the bottom number in the ones place is bigger than the top number. First, rename like this

$$
\begin{array}{r}
710 \\
\cancel{8}0 \\
-55 \\
\hline
\end{array}
$$

Then take the five away from the ten like this

$$
\begin{array}{r}
710 \\
\cancel{8}0 \\
55 \\
\hline
5
\end{array}
$$

You should get 5. Last take the five away from the seven like this

$$
\begin{array}{r}
710 \\
\cancel{8}0 \\
55 \\
\hline
25
\end{array}
$$

So your answer is 25. 25 makes sense because you have less money now.

Many students were not as explicit as Vanessa, but here Lois saw her students attaining improved awareness and control over their own thinking. Vanessa understood the problem and did not act impulsively.

Sixth Grade.   Regina Kamlet engaged her sixth graders in a wide variety of scientific enterprises in order to improve their problem solving. She did not use the format in Figure 11.2, but we devised a variation that asked these questions about a particular "mystery moisture" experiment:

What could be a possible source of moisture in your system?
Describe your plan for testing your ideas.
Check yourself: How well am I doing?
Is my plan working?
How can I tell?

After four days of experiment, Regina asked these questions for their journals:

What did you find out?
Did your plan work? How do you know?
What did you learn about reasoning in science?
What did you learn about how we prove things in science?
What did you learn about your own thinking?

When asked "What did you learn about reasoning in science?" one student replied, "I learned that first you have to make a plan. Next you have to ask yourself questions. After you do that the whole thing makes sense." I'm sure you notice, in this student's response, the way in which things begin to become meaningful: by planning and posing questions.

"I learned that not all experiments work and to use your mistakes to learn." What interests me here is the student's recognition of the value of mistakes. She reminds me of the truth of Jacob Bronowski's observation that progress in science is made by this continual process of pushing the boundaries of the known into the unknown "where we shall make mistakes." Discovery, he notes (1978) "is made with tears and sweat . . . by people who are constantly getting the wrong answer. . . . Progress is the exploration of our own error" (p. 111 ff). We should spend far more time with students helping them work through their mistakes and thereby learning the value of error.

Another student wrote, "If you really think about all of the steps in our plans, then we can figure out why the plans succeeded or why they did not succeed." Here the observer realizes the essence of metacognition: becoming aware of strategies that work and ones that do not in a given situation. This leads to the strategic and reflective uses of our thinking mentioned above.

When asked, "What have you learned about how we prove things in science?" one student noted, "To make a plan ahead of time and to try your own thoughts out."

Does this remind you (Chapter 2) of the essence of thinking: trying out promising "tracks" which might prove fruitful and might not? This experimental element is of utmost importance because we want students to take a risk or a chance in order to find out.

When students were asked to reflect on what they had learned about their own thinking, several responded with comments that reflect the self-questioning and self-generating nature of good thinking:

"That I can ask myself questions and I can make my own plan. . . ."
"That I work better when there is a task and I ask questions and make a plan. . . ."
"You can figure things out if you define your task, make your plan and monitor what you've done."
"That if I think of the idea, I feel that I made an accomplishment, but when someone [else] thinks of it and tells me it, I feel like I'm not even participating."

You may recall one of Mary Mulcahy's first graders saying his thinking was not good because he was sort of copying other people's ideas. Good thinking for these youngsters has something to do with creating your own pathways.

High School—Mathematics.   In Rosemarie Liebmann's classes we spent many months experimenting with the Thinking Journals with students at all ability levels: slow, average, and advanced. We used the format in Figure 11.2, and as noted above, Emily was responding to Part 2 when she wrote about the tape recorder.

Rosemarie eventually got to the point where these journals became part of the assessment process, amounting to 30 percent of the students' grades.

In Part 1 of the journal, students are attempting to become more conscious of how they go about figuring something out. Shannon faced a problem in algebra, and here is her analysis of the strategies she used:

1. Identify kind of problem.
2. I underline the exact direction for better understanding.
3. "Rewrite" all the facts (2d = time)
4. Identify a variable ($\times$ = others time)
5. Write basic equation (rt + rt = 1)
6. Apply facts to equation (   )
7. Solve the (fractional) equation
8. Check or evaluate answer

As you can see Shannon was very methodical in her analyses of problems. What impresses me here is her first step: "Identify the kind of problem." As I noted in Chapter 8, unless students correctly identify problematic situations they are confronting, it will be very difficult for them to proceed. We can also recall Rich's Double Entry Journal, where he had to reread the problem several times in order to understand it.

We do not have Shannon's self-evaluation of her thinking, but we can see how she responded to question (1e) in Figure 11.2: "Where could I have used these strategies effectively?"

> I don't think you can get anywhere in a problem if you don't identify it! After doing that and organizing all the *facts* [underlined twice] one should ask questions which would maybe lead to possible solutions. After thinking up solutions, one should apply them (solutions) to the problem. Imagine the result or outcome and evaluate which path or "equation" is the easiest to take.

On another occasion, after analyzing how to study for her math examination, Shannon listed "Strategies for Life":

1. Analyze problem and break it down so it doesn't look so big.
2. Take one step at a time.
3. Be curious about confusing things.
4. Don't procrastinate—the more gradually a goal or problem is attacked the better the solution will be.

After item 3 Rosemarie wrote in the margin "Izzy."

High School—Art.   Marilyn Kuhlmann is an art teacher, who has introduced her students to the Thinking Journals in high school. At the end of a semester's work, which involved not only drawing and studying color, but also examining how they were thinking and feeling about their projects, one student wrote:

> The writing helped me with the drawing. It showed me what I was doing and why. *I thought it just comes out, and the way it comes, it comes.* It will tell what I was doing wrong and how I can make it look better. It helped me while I was

drawing with what I should add to balance it off. It helped me in shaping while drawing it first and then fixing it after. *I thought I'd never even ask myself questions until you pointed them out to me.* It will help you out and if a drawing comes out good you will know what to do if you want it to happen again. [Emphases added.]

Perhaps this student became so articulate about her own thoughts because Marilyn modeled this journal-writing strategy for the whole class:

The first step was to keep a written log of my thought process when initially describing drawing to myself. Second, by actually drawing and writing directly on my paper, I became aware that I was asking myself an internal question, making a decision, and finally evaluating the success of the decision (metacognition).

Before the use of keeping a journal, it never occurred to me that there were decisions being made about the very subtle aspects of artistic technique.'' (Kuhlmann 1989)

Marilyn's discovery is obviously beneficial for her art, but perhaps it has personal rewards as well, such as knowing that she can share with others her continual exploration of how to improve. Once this is modeled for students, the whole tenor of the classroom can change.

Seeking the Transfer Connection

Students were often asked to complete Part 2 in Figure 11.2 and transfer the strategies learned in one subject to the same subject, to different subjects, or to experiences beyond school.

Within the Subject.   Candy completed her journal entry in math by analyzing her own thinking: "I was able to answer all my questions and find my mistakes." What would she do differently next time? "I think when I study maybe I'm only looking at the surface of things. In other words, only what we've done. I should go into more depth whether I like it or not." As for transfer, she noted:

I'll study more in depth for final exams. . . . Next time I complain about something, I'll turn around and question myself and solve my complaint. . . . I will try not to blame anyone for anything because I now know I am able to fix things myself and if I have a problem, I better do just that! Well, wait. I think I better change this statement to . . . I can fix things that I cause but if others do give me grief I don't know what can fix that!

Candy's remark about studying "in depth" is very reminiscent of studies of "expert problem solvers" who are not satisfied with the surface characteristics of problems; they persist, in order to disclose the underlying concepts and meanings of problems, to discover the "kind of problem" they are working with. We can also see that her approach differs from those of Mary Jane's students, mentioned earlier.

Transfer into Other Subjects.   Transfer into other subjects was often on the minds of Rosemarie's students. For example, Shannon was having particular difficulty understanding *Romeo and Juliet,* so she listed her strategies:

1. Take "foreign" words and translate them [e.g., thy, thou, thee].
2. Complete the vocabulary list.
3. Read synopsis of the plot.
4. Read questions and try to answer them completely.
5. After every scene discuss the major points with a friend.
6. Reread sections I don't understand and if I still have problems—*Get help!*
7. Get movie version for visual help.

Shannon finished this entry by transferring these operations into life, where she realized she should "always identify what I don't understand and try to tackle it alone first." But if this doesn't succeed, Shannon has become aware of the value of getting "another person's opinion" because maybe she missed something. Finally, she realizes the importance of another way of learning or thinking about something—in this case, getting visual aid in the form of a movie, making a picture, "color-coordinate people or use word associations." Shannon is using a wide variety of *representations* and *resources* in order to figure out the meanings of difficult situations.

Transfer into Personal Life.   Finally, students became very good at transferring some of their strategies and awarenesses into their personal lives. For example, we have already (Chapter 8) seen where Mark helped a girl friend "break down her problems into small ones [over the phone], so that the sum of the problems that she had made would not seem so overwhelming—like an incredibly hard algebra problem, where you take it one step at a time rather than all at once. . . ."
    Toward the end of Mark's entry he notes:

> I got her to use a little metacognition, which I think is understanding and recognizing one's problems. She realized that she needed to be a little more positive about herself and much more confident. . . .

What do you think of Mark's analysis? Do you agree with me that, in the process of thinking through his own thinking, he has exemplified the nature of thoughtfulness defined earlier in this book: being considerate of others' feelings and ideas as well as pensive and deliberate? Mark has given us an example of how thinking about our thinking also involves *recognizing* feelings—our own as well as those of others.
    Other students, like Marisol, saw their Thinking Journal as a resource for tackling just about any problem:

> Often when I come across a difficult decision that I have to make I break down my problem so as to comprehend what my choices are and what results will come about from my decision.

In today's teen world where peer pressure is becoming increasingly difficult, I often resort to my journal thinking skills in making decisions on drinking and smoking. . . .

So many students have found connections between what they do in school and what they want to do in their lives that it seems as if all the strategies described here serve as one pathway toward breaking down that barrier that so often exists between the content of our courses and the personal meanings students create in the world beyond.

Dane's Strategy: Draw Your Mind At Work

After writing about our thinking, we might follow Dane's example (Figure 11.1) and create a picture of how our mind is, or has been, working. Writing about wait time perhaps gave Dane the idea of drawing the picture of being confronted with a problem, the picture of the inner workings of his mind at work, and finally the picture of sheer delight. Let us draw pictures of how our minds wrap themselves around an idea or problem.

Metacognition and Personal Meaning

It has become evident to me—and I hope to you as well—that the students who have spoken through these pages are learning not only about science, math, and Shakespeare, but discovering personal meanings about themselves. Here I define "personal meanings" as those concepts, ideas, facts, and feelings that directly relate to our sense of self, and to our general attitudes, dispositions, and habits of mind.

Emily, Shannon, Candy, Mark, and Marisol are all embarked upon those explorations that end up with discoveries about themselves as well as about the subjects they started writing about. Annie Dillard is a writer who has reflected upon her craft to note (1989) that:

> When you write, you lay out a line of words. The line of words is a miner's pick, a wood carver's gouge, a surgeon's probe. You wield it, and it digs a path you follow. Soon you find yourself deep in new territory. Is it a dead end, or have you located the real subject? You will know tomorrow, or this time next year. (p. 3)

I think our young writers and thinkers may have discovered, within the new territories of the self, attitudes and dispositions that, if nurtured, may be with them for some time to come.

CONCLUSION

How can we use these strategies in our year-long planning of the curriculum? There are several ways of proceeding:

1. Have students keep Thinking Journals. During long-term projects on ecology Beth Friedman asked her students to keep the kind of open-ended

journal mentioned above. Doreen Guzo has done this in English class, at the end of units of writing short stories and poetry. I have sat in on the discussions students have conducted during these occasions to hear students talk about overcoming problems with "voice" and "point of view" in their writing. In other words, the metacognitive challenge is reflected in the processes students explored and discovered as they figured out what and how to express their thoughts and feelings in story and poetic form.

2.   As mentioned in Chapter 7, design our curricula around problematic situations for students to think about, so they are continually engaged in problem solving. Engage them in working through these situations early in the year, and then use Mary Jane Fox's diagnostic strategy to gauge awareness and reflection.

3.   As students solve difficult problems or resolve complex dilemmas, ask them, as Mary Mulcahy did continually, "How did we do this? Tell me about your thinking processes" and display the results around the room as she did.

4.   Use cooperative groupings—whether small problem-solving groups or "think aloud" dyads—as forums to elicit more awareness of thought processes. Instructional strategies should be woven into the entire year's fabric. Encourage groups to reflect on their thinking, not just in journals. For example, with fourth graders engaged in researching the local problem of why crossing guards who are women must wear skirts and are not allowed to wear ear muffs in winter time, Marie Curry was in a position to challenge this group to reflect: "What do we want to do? How are we going to go about doing it? How well are we doing? What have we done? Have we done it well? What have we learned about our problem solving abilities? About working together? About the kind of problem we have been researching? Where else can we use this kind of information?" (1990).

5.   Finally, there is one other long-term strategy that I have used. This is for students to summarize what they have learned about themselves at the end of a semester. Let me return to Donna Sparacio's reflections in her journal at the end of a semester's work in teacher education. This is her journal summary and the questions concerned: "What have you learned about your own thinking? What have you learned about reaching your own personal goal [Chapter 5]? How has your problem solving been affected by considering the Seven R strategy?"

One very important thing I have learned about my thinking, is that when I don't give in to panic, I am creative, and quite capable of solving most problems. . . .

After some metacognitive work, in which, more than anything, I *evaluated* my thinking, I became more aware of my behavior when a problem would arise. Knowing, then, that I was prone to panic, and to getting "locked in," I would immediately "catch" myself, and do some self-talking. . . .

[After receiving a particular setback in her college career.] I didn't allow my anger, or panic over the idea of extended time in school . . . to rule my thinking.

I immediately decided to appeal and I instantly thought of different alternatives. Not only did I try to think of alternative ways to get the decision overturned, but I also started to think of alternative solutions in case the decision was upheld. . . . Thus, once again I attempted to put into practice what I had learned about being a good thinker, and my progress became evident after awhile.

I noticed great improvement in my thinking strategies, especially with regard to persistence and the use of different alternatives. It became apparent to me when we did the triangle problem [with six straws, create four congruent equilateral triangles]. Uncharacteristically, I didn't panic. . . . First of all, I had gained enough confidence from having practiced strategies that I felt comfortable with the situation. Second of all, I related this problem to the bagel one [cut a bagel into twelve pieces using three straight slices, without folding] and decided the solutions were probably similar in some ways. Another facet of my improvement was that I didn't get tunnel vision. Instead of thinking the problem had a one-dimensional solution only, I envisioned, and attempted, a three-dimensional shape. . . .

[Describing a decision about whether to hire movers.] I *researched* by calling different movers to get prices and dates. Next, I used some *reflection*. I challenged assumptions I had about the capabilities of professional movers. . . . *Reducing* the problem I realized the crux of my dilemma was a concern over asking my friends to do such difficult work in the first place. Finally, by *relating* this to other moving experiences, I remembered all the times that I helped some of them.

Therefore, I have used the heuristic approach in solving problems, and the use of these skills, in addition to my progress in other areas of critical thinking, will help me in teaching. (Sparacio 1989)

In summarizing one of her experiences in asking probing questions, Donna shows us how this has also affected her personal life, how she has transferred this process into life with people beyond the classroom:

I find myself asking probing questions during normal conversation with family and friends. I mean, whereas before I would simply accept what I was told, now I find myself asking, "Well, how do you know that?" Or I'll ask them (in a subtle way, of course) to relate some experience or produce some evidence. I can't help it I feel compelled! (Sparacio 1989)

In conclusion, what we are striving for is for students like Emily to transcend her own self-recognized image of the tape recorder and solve those ill-structured, nonroutine problems with strategies she has been using in school. We want students like Tejal to conclude that there is something to be gained from asking herself questions and not always relying upon her Dad, and for Candy to summarize her learnings in this fashion: "From now on I'll look before I leap. If I question my actions before I actually go through with them, I'll be better off."

Unlike the Wetheralls "who always went to church" because they never failed to do anything that was performed by "the surrounding puppets," Candy is more like Isabel Archer in Henry James's *Portrait of a Lady:*

I try to judge for myself; to judge wrong, I think is more honorable than not to judge at all. I don't wish to be a mere sheep in the flock; I wish to choose my fate and know something of human affairs beyond what other people think it compatible with propriety to tell me.

That is the challenge—nothing less will do.

REFERENCES

Baird, J., and R. White. April 1984. "Improving Learning through Enhanced Metacognition: A Classroom Study." Paper presented at the annual meeting of the American Educational Research Association, New Orleans.

Barell, John. 1988. *Opening the American Mind.* Upper Montclair, NJ: Montclair State College.

Bell, Victoria. 1990. "Analysis of My Own Teaching." Unpublished manuscript. Montclair State College.

Bronowski, Jacob. 1978. *The Origins of Knowledge and Imagination.* New Haven, CT: Yale University Press.

Costa, Arthur. 1984. "Mediating the Metacognitive." *Educational Leadership* 42, 3:59–62.

Costa, Arthur, and Larry Lowery. 1989. *Techniques for Teaching Thinking.* Pacific Grove, CA: Midwest Publications.

Curry, Marie. 1990. "Skirting the Issue: A Fourth Grade's Experience with Problem Solving." Unpublished manuscript. Montclair State College.

Dalrymple, Karen. 1987. Personal communication.

Dillard, Annie. 1989. *The Writing Life.* New York: Harper & Row.

Granito, Lois. 1990. "Initial Research on Metacognition in Mathematics." Unpublished manuscript. Montclair State College.

Hyde, Arthur, and Marilyn Bizar. 1989. *Thinking in Context.* White Plains, NY: Longman.

James, Henry. 1963. *The Portrait of a Lady.* New York: New American Library.

Kamlet, Regina. 1989. "Report on the Culminating Activity." Unpublished manuscript. Montclair State College.

Kuhlmann, Marilyn. 1989. "Creative Success Enhanced through Critical Thinking." Unpublished manuscript. Montclair State College.

Liebmann, Rosemarie. Personal communication.

Mason, Jana, and Kathryn Au. 1985. *Reading Instruction for Today.* Glenview, IL: Scott Foresman.

Mestre, Jose. 1987. "Why should mathematics and science teachers be interested in cognitive research findings?" *Academic Connections.* Princeton, NJ: The College Board. Summer, pp. 3–11.

Palincsar, Ann Marie. 1984. "The Quest for Meaning from Expository Text: A Teacher Guided Journey." In *Comprehension Instruction: Perspectives and Suggestions*, ed. Gerald Duffy, Laura Roehler, and Jana Mason. April. White Plains, NY: Longman.

Palincsar, Ann Marie, and Ann Brown. 1989. "Instruction for Self-Regulated Reading." In *Toward the Thinking Curriculum: Current Cognitive Research,* ed. Lauren Resnick and Leopold Klopfer. Alexandria, VA: Association for Supervision and Curriculum Development.

Pressley, Michael, et al. 1987. "What Is Good Strategy Use and Why Is It Hard to Teach? An Optimistic appraisal of the Challenges Associated with Strategy Instruction." April. Paper presented at the annual meeting of the American Educational Research Association, Washington, DC.

Sparacio, Donna. "Final Thinking Journal Summary." Unpublished manuscript. Montclair State College.

Sternberg, Robert. 1985. *Beyond I.Q.: A Triarchic Theory of Human Intelligence*. New York: Oxford University Press.

Swartz, Robert, and David Perkins. 1989. *Teaching Thinking—Issues and Approaches*. Pacific Grove, CA: Midwest Publications.

Wharton, Edith. 1964. *The House of Mirth*. New York: New American Library.

Youngblood, Ed. 1985. "Reading, Thinking, and Writing Using the Reading Journal." *English Journal,* September, pp. 46–48.

CHAPTER 12

"Thinking Gives Me a Headache!"

OVERVIEW

The best plans do not always bring outstanding results;
therefore, in this chapter I shall explore various elements that
might account for our difficulties: students' inexperience,
teacher preparedness, the school and community culture.

A teacher in Newark once observed that, when she challenged her students to think in ways described in these pages, her students would try, but then one student would say, "Please stop asking those questions!"

"Why?" she asked in some dismay.

"Because this thinking gives me a headache!" he responded, clutching his head in his hands.

LACK OF PRACTICE

This does illustrate one particular idea: Our students know when they are being asked to do more than they have usually done, and sometimes these unusual assignments cause physical strain. It's similar to what happens after years of inactivity when we suddenly decide to play golf, swim, or run. For several days thereafter we might have aches and pains in many places. Such physical discomfort makes us recognize that we have possibly over stretched long-unused muscles. We then exercise with a little more restraint for a few days, being mindful that we want to develop those muscles with care and concern for damage.

In the same way, we must take it easy when we introduce thoughtfulness, initiating the change from passive listening to active engagement slowly, incrementally, a little at a time. This is especially important if students are in the upper grades and are not used to this kind of intellectual challenge.

Another alternative is possible: more active listening to our students if and when they speak of such difficulties. How do they feel? Do they know why? Can they think of ways to overcome the problems identified? By asking such questions, we respond to them as persons and continue to design and develop the environment so that it invites thoughtfulness. We also begin to share some control with students through our attending to their problematic situations.

THE HIDDEN CURRICULUM

When Rosemarie Liebmann began asking more challenging questions in one of her high school classrooms, Heather exclaimed: "Stop! Why are you doing this to us?"

"What?" Rosemarie asked.

"Making us think! No other teacher asks us to do this!"

And here you have the evidence of the quality of expectations of those around us. Evidently Heather had learned what Emily had: that some of us demand that our students play the role of a recording device, whose only responsibility is to reproduce what we have said. A few other expectations that we will want to challenge include the following:

The teacher "teaches" and the students "sit and listen" or "learn" passively.

There is one "right answer" to any question, and it is in the book to be read.

The answer to most questions can be given in one or two words, and no one will challenge you to go much deeper.

Books and teachers are always "right," and we learn only from them, not any other resource in the room, such as our friends.

If we wait long enough, a teacher will answer her own question, and we won't have to do much work. The teacher is the only one worth listening to.

If we ask enough questions about a difficult assignment, we can get the teacher to make it a lot easier and less demanding.

"Thinking" is not something we talk about.

If I memorize enough stuff, I can get a good grade.

Most tasks and tests will demand recall of isolated pieces of information, and I will not have to show how concepts and ideas are related or how facts illustrate underlying principles.

You can add many more to this grim list, but its grimness does not mean that these elements of the hidden curriculum—or what students learn just by being in school for so many years—cannot be attacked and altered within a well-designed invitational environment. In the next chapter I shall present one of the best ways of dealing with these factors—that is, the peer group strategy that involves changing the entire school culture.

However, if you are working by yourself, there are things you can do until the school catches up to you:

1. Again, listen to students' justifiable observations that you may be the only teacher presenting them with nonroutine challenges involving thinking.
2. Ask them if they believe in what you are asking them to do. In other words, "Is it important to know how to think in this world? In the twenty-first century? In life beyond school?"
3. As suggested in Chapter 5 (creating an invitational environment) we can begin working on those attitudes and dispositions as well as pedagogical practices that will gradually wear away these elements that seem embedded in granite.
4. Help them grow into the expectations you are making by taking it slowly and by using the personal life strategy introduced in Chapters 5 and 6. Here we use our own personal life experiences as examples of the various processes we use to solve problems. Most of my students become rather adept at using the Thinking Journal format for analyzing their own thinking. Once again, here is a simple way of beginning this kind of operation:
   a. Model your own thinking using personal life examples to identify kinds of thought processes and attendant emotions or dispositions. (See Chapters 3 and 6).
   b. Invite students to reflect on problems, conflicts and decisions in their own lives and begin to identify the kinds of mental and emotional activity they engage in.
   c. Make Thinking Journals a regular learning experience.

It is difficult for one teacher working alone to be successful in combating the rigidities some of our students come to school with; it is much easier if we are working collaboratively with each other. But with relatively few exceptions, most of the teachers mentioned here are working without too much support, and they have made the differences noted, for example, in their Thinking Journals.

LACK OF KNOWLEDGE

I recently asked my students how they decided whom to vote for in a gubernatorial election. Someone noted that you often had to compare one candidate with the other, and when I asked how you did that, I got answers like these:
    "You look at their record."
    "Well, I want to know about their stand on certain issues."
    And so on. What no one gave me was a clearly stated set of processes used to make a comparison, and this made my students similar to those surveyed in the National Assessment of Educational Progress's (1986) *Writing Report Card* that found most students in grades 4, 8, and 11 could not make adequate comparisons and contrasts in their writing.

The answer was to do some direct teaching of this skill. For this we used the visual organizer presented in Chapter 10. Repeated use of such graphics plus practice are bound to enhance students' abilities.

COGNITIVE STYLES

Some of us admit to having a propensity toward impulsive actions whereas others tend to be more reflective. Schrag (1988) refers to Brodzinsky's (1985) definition of such tendencies as "preferential modes or strategies of adapting in a problem-solving situation" (p. 150). We can see such modes in terms of other and perhaps false dichotomies:

    Concrete———Abstract
    Analytic———Intuitive
    Visual———Linguistic
    Cognitive———Affective

Sometimes these words become labels attached to different teachers or students and defining their learning and/or thinking styles—this one is "abstract random," that one an "intuiter"—and this bothers me. However, such concepts can be helpful if used to help us *broaden* the ways we perceive students and our teaching strategies.

For example, I found geometry rather easy, perhaps because I'm a good visual thinker. I seem to create representations of situations very rapidly and to be able to manipulate them around in my mind with some ease. Others tell me that this is much more difficult for them; they attend to words much more consciously and report difficulties with visualizations.

When we encounter student difficulties with some of the strategies and concepts mentioned herein, we may be encountering stylistic or preference differences.

The best remedy is not to label students but to do the following:

Ensure that our teaching strategies offer opportunities for a wide variety of modes of interaction: physical, visual, auditory, tactile.

Learn from our students how they think: "How do you relate this information in your mind? How are you figuring it out [if it is a problem]? How do you make connections [if they are seeking meaning]?"

Ensure that each person's ways of processing and using information is acknowledged, so we can all become better at those processes we are not good at. Those, for example, who claim not to be good visualizers will perhaps benefit from the use of visual organizers. (Jones et al. 1989)

For me, the enriching aspect of cognitive styles is the knowledge that each of us creates his/her own pathway toward understanding. We must learn from all of them by making the thinking more visible.

COGNITIVE/AFFECTIVE DEVELOPMENTAL DIFFERENCES

Earlier (Chapter 5) I mentioned Cliff's class in seventh grade science where Pam asked the question, "How can you tell how old the galaxies really are?" Cliff redirected the question to his students, who then engaged in a spirited debate about the origins of galaxies.

The tape, however, reveals that some students were not participating. Even though they had the same small photos of different kinds of galaxies in front of them, they were not sharing their hypotheses about origins and relationships to the Big Bang.

Some of the nonparticipants may have had a difficult time reasoning about something that was invisible to them—the origin, that is. The enthusiasts were able to combine multiple relationships—time, space, explosive force, and light— into abstract hypotheses.

We know that some students are going to become better thinkers about abstractions, and some sooner than others. Some, even as adults, are never going to be able to manipulate several elements, project into the future, and see multiple nuances of meaning (shades of gray)—in certain areas of their lives. But effective teaching can narrow the gap. At appropriate ages—for example middle school years—we can provide students with challenging, nonroutine, and complex issues where they can begin to develop more facility in dealing with abstract reasoning.

ADULT DIFFICULTIES AND PROBLEMS

Instead of always pointing fingers at our students, we need to recognize that we, the adults in the classroom, might be the ones with the most difficulty in inviting and enhancing students' thoughtfulness. Our problems and anxieties might stem from a number of different causes:

Our own *lack of knowledge* about our own thinking. This will naturally inhibit our willingness to ask students about their thinking.

Our own *lack of experience* with questioning and problem-solving strategies. Without some experience of this sort we will be reluctant to jump in and experiment with various inquiries and approaches.

The *rigidities of our own ways of thinking*. Some of us have difficulty being open to multiple possibilities, tolerating ambiguity, and responding empathically to others' feelings. Such fixed dispositions and embedded ways of behaving will make it hard for us to model and present students with problematic situations that lend themselves to various perspectives and meanings.

Our *fears of losing control*. If we believe that opening discussions to multiple perspectives, intellectually far removed from "the right answer," risks near-chaos in the classroom, we will be reluctant to attempt this strategy.

Our realization that *we may be alone* in this experiment. Such a realization will discourage some of us from venturing into unknown territory. We need support from friends while exploring new, untried pathways, and without the knowledge that our supervisors will back us up, many of us will be loath to undertake the expedition.

Our realization that *"all real change involves loss, anxiety and struggle"* (Fullan 1982, emphasis added). Who likes to struggle with the doubts, difficulties, and uncertainties? Only some of us—for the thrill of being the first or for the satisfaction of exploring new ways of teaching, thinking, and living with our students.

All these, and probably many more, might be reasons we would be reluctant to start creating the invitational environment. We might not want to play host to all the new, and sometimes radically different ideas and ways of thinking that will emerge once students begin sharing their thoughts and feelings with us.

What to do? Face ourselves and some of these realizations and feelings. This is the beginning of awareness and ultimately of control. Beyond this level of consciousness, there are the first phases of experimentation:

Identify an immediate, concrete need: For example, students have difficulty with providing more than one-word answers to complex questions.

Set a modest objective: Practice inducing students to broaden their understanding with probing questions such as, "Why do you think that? Can you give us a reason? How did you figure that out?"

Monitor your progress weekly and evaluate results.

I shall present a more fully developed strategy in the following chapter, but that relies more upon groups of teachers getting together to bring about change. Suffice it to say here that the difficulties listed above are very real, but everything doesn't have to be changed all at once. We start in small, incremental steps, just the way we learn to walk or ride a bicycle. Most successful change starts this way, and many organizational failures result from attempting too much all at once.

SCHOOL-BASED HEADACHES: "WHAT ABOUT YOUR ANTICIPATORY SET?"

I once had the pleasure of working with a teacher who had developed several strategies for engaging her students in thinking reflectively and productively about her subject matter. One day the superintendent visited the classroom, together with her supervisor, for the purposes of observation. After the class the teacher described why she had used various strategies to get the students to be more metacognitive, how she had been successful in helping them analyze and describe their fine products, and the thinking that went into it. Afterward, teacher, supervisor, and superintendent conferred.

The supervisor loved everything she'd seen and heard, but at the end of the conference, the superintendent had only one comment: "I think you ought to work on your anticipatory set."

POINT TO PONDER: What is the nature of this situation?

Perhaps you thought of the superintendent's having one set of values and priorities, and the teacher and her supervisor another. Perhaps you inferred from this that here was a system with conflicting goals, and how difficult it must be for the teacher to have a significant impact. Or perhaps you wondered why I even wrote this, because every lesson needs an anticipatory set (an introduction linking the current lesson with past learning) and maybe she didn't have one? I don't know if she did, but what occurs to me is that the superintendent and the teacher need not be in conflict; that is, all the strategies mentioned herein can coexist with, or build upon, direct teaching (Barell 1985).

What distressed the teacher was the superintendent's lack of support and inability to see value in what she was doing. How do we work within such conditions? Many of you have evidence of conflicting cultures within the school (Sarason 1982). Here are some suggestions:

Don't give up in despair. Resolve that you will continue your good work.

Begin to search for allies who might see situations as you do.

With your friends, find opportunities to communicate with the superintendent (or others who reflect the predominating cultural values in the school) what you are attempting and why. The best way to begin this dialogue may be with your assessment of needs. (See Chapter 4.) All sound change begins with a rational diagnosis of a need and the development of a clear and practical strategy to meet that need (Fullan 1982).

Try to see the school situation from the perspective of the superintendent. Why is her/his indication of the anticipatory set so important? Acknowledge its value, and perhaps work toward integration of both ways of analyzing classroom interaction. We always have something to learn from others.

Reach out to others beyond your school with whom you can network, parents as well as other teachers. There are so many networks to join, electronic and traditional varieties, that we can certainly find support through one of them, their meetings and newsletters. (ASCD Network on Teaching Thinking.)

It can be most distressing to feel alone and think no one supports us, that we are "bucking the tide" or "fighting city hall." The worst strategy is to give in, but I realize how agonizing it can be to feel that you are an island unto yourself. If the above strategies fail to help build mutual support and a sharing of viewpoints, then we always have our students, and this is always our greatest reward.

"I WANT MY CHILD LEARNING THE FACTS, PLEASE!"

In Chapter 9 I referred to the teacher who asked his students to write stories about intriguing problems in science. He thought this was a wonderfully adventurous learning experience, one that would stimulate the kind of inquiry Izzy thrived upon. When students are identifying what puzzles them, they can be initiating an exploration into wonderful lands of unknown discoveries.

Several parents disagreed. "Why are you teaching story telling? That's not science—it's kid's stuff. I want my child to learn the facts, please. That's the only way she'll pass the tests and get into college."

So, unfortunately, my friend stopped asking students to use their minds in adventurous ways. The teacher and parents missed a good opportunity to see just how effective embedding information within a story, or other self-generated framework, can be.

POINT TO PONDER: What alternatives are there to giving up?

I'm sure you've thought of several good alternatives, such as meeting with the parents who complained, discussing the situation with the students, and engaging them in thinking about the rationale for such experiences. You probably also thought of working collaboratively with colleagues to share with parents your intentions and the reasons for them. Once again, collective action can be very powerful.

Perhaps you also thought of the strategy Rosemarie Liebmann used with parents of her students when she decided to make the Thinking Journal 30 percent of the grade in high school mathematics. She designed a set of criteria for A, B, and C grades and explained them, outlining her purpose—one or two sentences summarizing the research about writing and thinking and learning (see Romberg 1989, p. 213) in mathematics. When parents expressed misgivings about the value of writing in a math class, Rosemarie sent them a letter cosigned by her department chairperson. This strategy effectively clarified parental misgivings and worked well for students.

Another strategy that various elementary schools have used is for teachers who are familiar with the strategies to conduct workshops for parents. These can do a great deal to communicate expectations, share powerful strategies, and enlist the support and assistance of the parents in working toward your goals.

CONCLUSION

I have attempted to take the preceding chapters out of the realm of glittering ideals without any blemishes, warts, or pitfalls. There always will be ways in which students themselves find thinking difficult, ways in which we ourselves are somewhat reluctant to venture forth on such unknown paths, ways in which our school culture will not support us, and neither will the surrounding community.

But there are ways of dealing with such real problems. The best might be to use some of the problem-solving strategies outlined earlier. It will make a world of difference if we can do this with our colleagues, and this is the dimension to which I now turn.

REFERENCES

Barell, John. 1985. "You Ask the Wrong Questions." *Educational Leadership* 42, 8:18–23.

Fogarty, Robin, Coordinator, ASCD Network on Teaching Thinking. Illinois Renewal Institute, Suite 250, 200 East Wood St., Palatine, IL 60067: Publisher of *Cogitare*.

Fullan, M. 1982. *The Meaning of Educational Change*. New York: Teachers College Press.

National Assessment of Educational Progress. 1986. *The Writing Report Card*. Princeton, NJ: Educational Testing Service.

Jones, Beau, Jean Pierce, and Barbara Hunter. 1989. "Teaching Students to Construct Graphic Representations." *Educational Leadership* 46, 4:20–26.

Romberg, T., et al. 1989. *Curriculum and Evaluation Standards for School Mathematics*. Reston, VA: National Council of Teachers of Mathematics, Inc.

Sarason, Seymour. 1982. *The Culture of the School and the Problem of Change*. Boston: Allyn & Bacon.

Schrag, F. 1988. *Thinking in School and Society*. New York: Routledge.

CHAPTER 13

Envisioning the Thoughtful School

OVERVIEW

In this chapter I shall use examples from a number of different schools to illustrate several points about effecting change: Positive school change results from acknowledgment of needs and development of strategies to meet those needs. In such a collaborative problem-solving venture, teachers are adventurous, reasonable, reflective within core groups or whole faculty groups, and can realize a vision established by all participants—a vision of thoughtfulness.

INITIATING THE CHANGE PROCESS

David is the principal of an elementary school in a district where an important innovation has been mandated from the superintendent's office: Bring everybody "up to speed" on thinking skills in the next four years. Together with two of his teachers, David attended a summer workshop for one week in preparation for this massive change, and he identified several problems he was concerned with.

POINT TO PONDER: What do you think his major problem might be?

As he described it to me that summer, "We're supposed to implement this thing, and I don't know how to start." He listed several other difficulties that you might have thought of: Why the rush? Isn't it dangerous to bring about change from the top down? Don't we need to work on how to get others involved? What do our students need? Is this going to work?

Perhaps you also have noted that focusing narrowly on a curriculum of "thinking skills" might be a dilemma. "Thinking skills" is not what thoughtfulness is all about, even though they are included. We have to be wary of staff development projects that focus too minimally upon a direct teaching of skills without considering the attendant dispositions—the invitational environment as well as the curriculum.

David's situation is typical of how change comes about: from the top down without too much input from those who are supposed to implement the change. His situation had an urgency to it, because he was to be responsible for initiating, within two months, a change he did not necessarily have a lot of experience with. As others (Sarason 1982) have noted, this is too often the way important changes are brought about: quickly and without reflection about ramifications and possible consequences.

So what does he do? There are many options, from being rather disengaged and allowing things to happen to him and his teachers to taking a much more active leadership role, where he becomes a sharing partner in learning what needs to be done to effect such a change. The latter possibility offers the best potential for success. It involves a collaborative process of assessing needs, setting goals, designing strategies, evaluating progress, and reflecting upon what has been learned. The peer-group strategy uses all the mental processes and dispositions suggested in the preceding chapters on a larger, schoolwide scale.

Let me contrast David's real situation with what occurred in four widely separated elementary schools early in a staff development process:

As new principal Esther Fusco convened her first faculty meeting in Babylon, New York, she brought out a pendulum toy for teachers to play with. One ball is swung out and let go to strike the next one, which then strikes the next; eventually they are all in motion. Before doing this, she asked the teachers to predict what would happen. She wanted them to reflect on their own mental processes before studying students' thinking.

In the Wasatch Elementary School in Salt Lake City, Sylvia Mathis spent portions of a faculty meeting modeling wait time, and then she visited classrooms to provide more modeling and support. Teachers shared with others their discoveries and feelings about attempting to help their children spend more time thinking about an answer.

One of the first things teachers and John Erickson in Hopkington, Minnesota, did was to volunteer to work with a colleague in a peer observation and sharing experience focused upon analyzing the kind and quality of questions used in classroom discourse. Each person made a videotape to share with a partner.

Peter Johnson, of Whittier Elementary School in Waukesha, Wisconsin, formed his core group of teachers, and one of their initial activities was to audiotape their own teaching in order to understand not only the kinds of questions they asked, but also the length of wait time and the quality of their responses. Teachers worked in pairs and then all participants congregated to share their findings and set personal goals.

POINT TO PONDER: What do you see as differences between David's situation and those of the four individuals mentioned above? How are they similar and how are they different?

Well, you have noticed that David is being told what to do by the folks downtown and to do it with all deliberate speed. He might or might not believe in what is going on; he might or might not have diagnosed students' needs; he might or might not have concluded there were areas for improvement.

You have also noticed no doubt that Esther, Sylvia, Peter, and John started with teachers within one school. Why is this important? Because massive, across-the-district changes like David's are not as likely to succeed. We need smaller changes over time in order to experiment with alternatives.

And I'm sure you noticed that, in each case, the principals, teachers, and supervisors were starting with very limited objectives, most of which reflected pedagogical elements mentioned within Chapter 5: questioning, wait time, and responding. In Esther's case the major focus was upon the teachers' ways of thinking—how they analyzed and figured out a complex phenomenon.

Finally, it was probably evident to you that there was a degree of volunteerism, especially in Peter's and John's situations. They started with core groups of teachers who *wanted* to examine their own teaching, reflect on their strengths, and set personal goals for improvement.

Thus, a local focus is a strong plus: concentration on the school as the unit of change, limited teaching changes, and teachers who are interested or committed to the innovation. These are significant elements in the schools that have become invitational environments for thoughtfulness.

There are several other elements in bringing about school change that I wish to explore. The very best situation (Fullan 1982; Joyce 1990) occurs when the principal is not only an advocate of the innovation, but also participates in its design, implementation, and analysis. I am presenting the change model from the teacher's point of view because that is the perspective used throughout the book, but it is to be hoped that those with leadership responsibilities will actively support teachers who are interested in effecting change.

Establish a Core Group of Colleagues

A core group of colleagues is what we need for mutual emotional support and for intellectual stimulation. It can be several persons or the entire faculty under the principal's leadership. How do you go about identifying friends who will share ideas and perhaps join in collaborating with you? Here are some suggestions:

Find friends who share your concerns for the quality of thoughtfulness within the classroom. Be specific about what you see and do not see.

Speak to your supervisor and/or principal to see if they share your interests and desires for experimentation. Very often we make assumptions about peoples' lack of interest that turn out to be invalid.

Contact friends in other schools.

Join professional organizations, such as ASCD, NCTE, and NCTM to find like-spirited persons.

Decide upon Time and Place to Meet.   Assuming you can find friends within your school, then you will want to get together to share ideas. Meetings should occur on school time. This is professional work. This, of course, is an ideal, and many times we have to meet after school. Eventually, however, we should begin to create budgets that provide for substitutes, release time, and perhaps consultants. This is why it is so important to have the principal's support and sanction.

Identify a Limited Set of Goals.   Some possibilities include assessing students' needs (Chapter 4), reading more about nature of thinking and strategies to enhance it, reflecting on teaching practices that foster thinking and inhibit it.

Decide upon a Limited Set of Experiments and Strategies.   These could encompass some of the pedagogical processes mentioned in Chapter 5, developing the invitational environment: for example, questioning, waiting, and responding.

Meet Regularly to Reflect and Set Goals.   Use such experiences to acquire more knowledge about our own thinking, students' thinking, effective classroom practices (the fundamentals), and the nature of thinking.

Share Experiences with Other Faculty.   Find ways (faculty meetings, newsletters, memos, etc.) to share with others not in the core group the rationale, goals, strategies, and results of investigations. Even if there is no sanctioned core group, it is a good idea to talk with others about your work. Very often this is the best way to enhance the quality of support within the school community. You will find out that others on the faculty notice the same things you do and have tried some of the strategies you are working with. It doesn't always succeed, of course, because some will perceive your efforts as "too much work," as "stuff we did twenty years ago," and/or as not within their job description: "I teach, and it's their job to learn!"

But sharing can be very important for another reason: You want, at all costs, to avoid being perceived as elitist by those working in other areas. It can be damaging to the entire school climate if one group is seen as secretive, uncooperative, and above the level of everyone else.

Now, let us explore the various ways such an adventure can be brought to fruition.

The Core Group Strategy

Every teacher can, on his/her own, challenge students to become more thoughtful. The core-group strategy that I outline here is designed for concerned teachers to work on together as part of a long-term staff development effort. This, it seems to me, is the best, most effective way of bringing about change: on a small scale initially, with a group of friends/colleagues who can give support. Someone has called such core groups the champions of thoughtfulness in the classroom. The rest of the faculty could be divided into those who will take a wait-and-see attitude and those who will probably resist the change. Both groups should be kept informed of your progress, because the whole change effort is predicated upon the rational problem-solving model: identify needs, set goals, design strategies, implement, and evaluate continuously. Research (Fullan 1982) indicates this is more effective than changing because it is someone's pet idea, or because there is some money to spend and why not use it here?

Let me now make a little more specific some of the concepts in this model:

Assessing Students' Thinking.   Within our group we should collect information about how well our students solve problems and make decisions, whether they are impulsive, good listeners, comfortable with ambiguity, and are cooperative, etc. For this we can use student products, standardized tests, and some of the informal measures identified in Chapter 4. We need to become very good observers of how our students approach life situations: from losing their lunch and resolving fights on the playground to figuring out how to write a report on the Big Bang or identifying an ecological problem worth solving.

A way to begin is suggested by Brendan Desilets of the Bedford, Massachusetts, school system. Rather than identify a set of skills—one for each grade level—his core group in the John Glenn Middle School reflected on this question: "Shouldn't we just ask them [the teachers] about solvable problems that the kids have and then build our plan around those problems?"

> If we could identify student difficulties, then we clearly had . . . an answer to the question, "Difficulty in doing what?" It seemed that the answer to that question might imply a way of organizing the whole scope and sequence so that it would make sense. For example, we might find that Jane's second graders need better fluency and originality in order to overcome difficulties in doing large-scale thinking tasks like solving problems and making decisions. If we could agree on those large-scale thinking tasks, we could organize large parts of the scope and sequence around models of those tasks.

And they did reach agreement on three different models: one for problem solving, one for decision making, and one for reasoning from effects to causes. One teacher noted that these three models "were not really a burden for teachers in self-contained classrooms. They're actually resources, which the teacher can use with issues ranging from what causes the wars we study in Social Studies to what approaches to decision making might avoid fights on the playground." What convinced other teachers, then, were what Desilets called "these reality-based insights," stemming from the core group's examination of "real difficulties in student thinking and teaching to those observed problem areas" (1988).

Assessing Our Thinking.   In addition to assessing our students' needs, we need to reflect on our own thought processes and those dispositions that support them. Unless we are prepared to model our own strengths and vulnerabilities, our talking to students about being better thinkers will not be very effective.

There are a number of ways of beginning. I have attempted in this text to model the use of our personal life experiences as good data from which to learn about how we think. Within the core group, we should find it more comfortable to use a set of criteria such as those suggested in Chapter 4 and set goals for the development of our ways of thinking. In working with teachers over the years, I have discovered a number of intriguing problems that I share with them for this purpose:

> The Bagel Problem: Cut a bagel into twelve pieces using three straight slices—no bending, folding necessary. This problem is good for seeing if participants do the following: *Reflect* on assumptions (that the bagel must remain flat on the table, for example); *represent* the problem and its various parts visually or graphically. See Chapter 8 for a useful heuristic for most of these problems.
>
> The Nine Dot Problem: Connect all nine dots using four straight lines without lifting pen from paper.
>
> The Six Straw Problem: Using six straws create four congruent, equilateral triangles.
>
> Any puzzle of this nature: "A man goes to work, gets on the elevator, rides to the third floor, gets off and walks up to the twelfth floor where he works all day. At 5 P.M. he gets on the elevator and rides down to the ground floor and goes home. Why does he follow this pattern every day?" This activity is based upon the kind of puzzle thinking Richard Suchman describes as an inquiry strategy (Joyce & Weil 1982). The exercise proceeds like this: You, the participants, can ask me any question about this situation that I can answer with "yes" or "no." The intent is for participants to explain this rather unusual situation. It is a good one for determining if problem solvers do the following: *Represent* the problem; *reduce* it to several different parts; *relate* this to prior knowledge; *reflect* on assumptions; and *generate* varied hypotheses on the basis of others' thinking.
>
> Any problem from Whimbey and Lochhead's *Problem Solving and Comprehension* (1982) or one not printed in that book that I use every time: "What will be the day after the day after tomorrow, if the day before the day before yesterday was Monday." This is good for analyzing peoples' *reducing* problems to parts, *representing,* setting an intermediate goal (e.g., determining "today" in the problem context) and using a strategy.

These are lots of fun to try to figure out, and if we use the Thinking Journal format (Chapter 11), we can begin to analyze our own thinking and set goals for its further development. Sharing our own foibles and idiosyncrasies communicates to students not only our vulnerabilities but also our openness to experimenting, taking risks, and above all, learning.

Knowledge of Thinking.   We need to know how philosophers regard thinking as well as what cognitive psychologists think thinking consists of. We should consider such philosophic definitions as Gilbert Ryle's that thinking is more like "path finding than path following," and we should consider Lauren Resnick's observations of thinking as "nonalgorithmic" processes that are complex, nuanced, and given to multiplicities of meanings. (See Chapter 3.)

We need to know about developmental differences between the thinking of younger children and adolescents. This means consulting such persons as Sigel (1984) and his work with children, and it means considering Piaget's work with this age group and with adolescents and their development of formal thinking. (See Mosher 1979.)

We can acquire this knowledge by selecting specific readings for each meeting of the core group from the following list:

- Jonathan Baron. 1985. *Rationality and Intelligence*. New York: Cambridge University Press.
- Arthur Costa, ed. 1991. *Developing Minds*. Alexandria, VA: Association for Supervision and Curriculum Development.
- Arthur Costa and Larry Lowery. 1989. *Techniques for Teaching Thinking*. Pacific Grove, CA: Midwest Publications.
- John Dewey. 1933. *How We Think*. Boston: D. C. Heath.
- Ellen Langer. 1989. *Mindfulness*. Reading, MA: Addison-Wesley.
- Robert J. Marzano et al. 1988. *Dimensions of Thinking*. Alexandria, VA: Association for Supervision and Curriculum Development.
- David Perkins. 1981. *The Mind's Best Work*. Cambridge: Harvard University Press.
- Lauren Resnick. 1987. *Education and Learning to Think*. Alexandria, VA: Association for Supervision and Curriculum Development.
- Gilbert Ryle. 1979. *On Thinking*. Totowa, NJ: Rowan & Littlefield.
- Francis Schrag. 1988. *Thinking in School and Society*. New York: Routledge.
- Robert Swartz and David Perkins. 1989. *Teaching Thinking: Issues and Approaches*. Pacific Grove, CA: Midwest Publications.

After reading each we can ask these questions:

What are we learning about the nature of thinking?
Which aspects of thinking do we see evident in our students? Which seem to be underdeveloped?
What other aspects should we try to notice?
What do our students think about their thinking? Do they think it's important? Why? How do they want to improve?

Strengthening the Fundamentals.   At these early stages we need to spend time examining all of the elements described in Chapter 5. We might begin by studying with our students the classroom's physical environment. Ask them if they think it is conducive to their learning and thinking. If not, allow them to play as much of a role in the restructuring as possible—they need and deserve to know what is occurring and will become, if so informed, our best supporters (Fullan 1982).

After spending four years developing an excellent model for teaching thinking processes within social studies, Jane Rowe of Provincetown, Massachusetts, schools offered (1989) this advice: "I wouldn't start with specific thinking skills at all. *I would start with such teaching behaviors as questioning.* I've seen too many teachers try to do lessons on critical thinking as they have always taught the multiplication tables. You can't do it that way!" The evidence suggests that Esther, Sylvia, Peter, and John would agree with her analysis.

Model of Intelligent Behavior.   The model of intelligent behavior this book is predicated upon sees human beings as persons engaged in problem posing and resolving:

> A human intellectual competence must entail a set of skills of problem solving—enabling the individual *to resolve genuine problems or difficulties* that he or she encounters and, when appropriate, to create an effective product—and must also entail the potential for *finding or creating problems*—thereby laying the groundwork for the acquisition of new knowledge. (Gardner 1985, p. 60)

As we have already noted in Chapter 3, thinking itself is a problem posing and resolving process. The model of intelligent behavior is informed by the realization that we as human beings have for millennia been growing intellectually as the result of encountering real dilemmas, conflicts, difficulties, problems, and perplexities in life.

But beyond having such a model of how the mind functions, we might also consider other kinds of "models." For example, Art Costa (1989) has developed a three-stage model focusing upon input, process, and output. Such a model of intellectual functioning helps us organize instructional practice by focusing upon the kinds of questions we ask. (See Figure 5.3, The Three Story Intellect.)

Goal Setting.   Goal setting, especially by a collaborative team of teachers and administrators, is the heart of any good staff-development effort. Too often the goals are set by the folks "downtown" and handed to those who must implement them. This may have been the situation in David's district mentioned above. We know from research (Fullan 1990) that where this strategy of posing problems and resolving them has been used, districts are more likely to implement and institutionalize desired innovations. Goal setting requires, of course, designing strategies, and this is where our deliberations will reflect exactly what we are fostering in the classroom: There are many different ways of accomplishing the same objective. We need to be open to diversities of approach.

Notice, once again, how the goals implied by Esther, Sylvia, Peter, and John concentrate upon a very limited set of processes: questioning, waiting, and responding. We should also set goals for the development of our own thinking, much as we might help our students set goals for the improvement of their thought processes.

Reeducative Experiences: The Problem-Solving Process.   Once goals are set, we ask, "What kinds of experiences will help us achieve our goals?" You may choose from among varieties of experiences that include the following:

1. Experiment in class with questioning, for example.
2. Record your teaching, using audio- and/or videotape for self-reflection and possible sharing with others.

3. Visit other classrooms and other schools.
4. Identify teachers with expertise in desired areas to act as resources, for direct teaching in your classroom and to observe your students and provide you with feedback.
5. Attend meetings of organizations specializing in the kinds of instructional strategies you wish to learn more about.
6. Read, read, and read some more.
7. Discuss the results of your inquiries and experiments with your colleagues.
8. Engage in joint lesson planning with colleagues.
9. Meet with consultants.

I prefer to work with a small group of persons who are committed to the process, but I have also found that there are some schools, like Esther's and Sylvia's, where the whole faculty forms the core group.

Program Purchase.   There are many excellent programs on the market that can be of immense help in providing us with strategies and approaches. These can be most useful if they help us get started and, subsequently, help us address questions like these: "How do these meet our needs? What processes or dispositions are emphasized and which are overlooked? How do they affect the roles we play in the classroom? How do they help us design and implement the invitational environment? How might we improve upon or modify these materials?" Questions such as these place us, teachers and administrators, at the wheel of the ship, in control of our own destiny. They provide us with more than a skills approach; they provide us with a balanced approach that includes not only teaching strategies, but a consideration for the classroom environment and the roles we play in it.

Core Experiences as the Stuff for Reflection.   In addition to being an efficient and challenging way to acquire information, the core group's meetings also offer a unique opportunity to engage in problem solving and reflection. The meetings offer excellent opportunities to learn about our own thinking, our own strengths, possible biases, and the kinds of assumptions we perhaps make before considering all the relevant information. If we consider the core group's deliberations as opportunities, we have experiences ripe for metacognitive awareness and enhanced control. Here are some questions you should pose after each discussion or problem identification and resolving session:

What have we done here? How well did we do?
What have we learned about our thinking processes?
How do these learnings affect what we do in classrooms to foster thinking?
What would we do differently next time and why?
Where else do we use these processes and attitudes? (E.g., outside school.)

Responses to these questions can be recorded in the core group's journal of its progress, which affords excellent possibilities for reflection upon our collective growth and development. By engaging in these processes, we will be exemplifying the research of many (Lieberman 1986, Sarason 1982) that suggest we need to create a new social setting that supports the alternative values of open inquiry, experimentation, risk taking, and learning from mistakes. As these processes become part of our way of viewing ourselves, we will find it easier to implement them within our classrooms. We will gain sustenance from this peer group and become more empowered to change our roles—from information disseminators to facilitators and hosts to students' thoughtfulness.

Core Group Meetings

Before moving on to consider briefly how the core group works toward school restructuring, I would like to take you to a core group meeting of teachers from Whittier Elementary School in Waukesha, Wisconsin. Led by principal Peter Johnson and Joan Radecke, a staff developer at Whittier, volunteer teachers used a self-devised observational system to examine their questions, wait time, and kinds of responses. (See Chapter 5.) They used the design three times, with the objective of seeing how different their instruction was under varying circumstances. Each teacher audiotaped her lessons in order to get objective information about her teaching. Here is part of the discussion in Peter's group. As you read, see what elements you think make for a productive staff development process. Note that "open" refers to questions with multiple possible responses; "closed" refers to those asking for short (one- or two-word) or predictable responses.

> JOY: We were wondering about the nature of some of our questions. Were they open or were they closed? And we thought if you had some little phrase starters such as "How do you feel . . . ?" That's the kind of thing we couldn't decide. . . . We also found it very interesting to listen to each other's lessons. . . . We were able to say, for example, "Oh, here you were really clarifying, there you elaborated. Look how you encouraged." Even though we focused on the questions, we also looked at the student responses and teacher responses to student answers.

> PETER [THE PRINCIPAL]:   Another thing you just touched upon is the value of peer coaching . . . how in fact that might be a focus of a way of finding our strengths and weaknesses. . . .

> DIANE: It was an introductory reading lesson. . . . Where kids had to learn to write a character study from looking at a picture. I found the first lesson extremely boring, I didn't use a lot of open questions.

> PETER: Boring.

> DIANE: Flat.

> JOANNE: That's an interesting observation. You had an unexciting lesson with good questions.

> JOY: See, I didn't think it was unexciting at all. She asked each child to imagine a hypothetical picture that had to do with the story. She then asked each child to go back to his or her image and describe it. It wasn't concrete at all because each child had a different picture. . . .

> PETER: When we look at an artist at work . . . you shouldn't judge flatness with—

> JOANNE: Would you think of doing responses now to see what you did?

> DIANE: I also listened to the questions the kids generated, and there was a lot they didn't know about, but they were able to do it.

PETER: Any comments about the peer relationships?

DIANE: Oh, it was great! We work well together.

Next round of peer observers:

JEAN: The first lesson was a reading lesson. Just from the nature of the subject it was so structured, I did a lot of closed questions. When we got through I asked some summary questions. . . . Then I did a lesson on Dr. Martin Luther King, and it was a lot of getting the students to understand the concept of what prejudice is. It was a very open ended kind of discussion and the kids' feelings came out; when I played that back, I found myself asking a lot of open ended questions to help them restate something and evaluate what they wanted to say. As we got going I ended up doing very little talking. Then the kids started to interact and ask questions. . . .

JOANNE: Did you improve because of the subject matter or because you thought more about what you were doing?

JEAN: I think a little bit of both. I think it really had to do with knowing about the questioning strategies. . . . Also with wait time . . . there wasn't as much with the first lesson. . . . Did you want us to tally this? I didn't know you wanted us to do that.

PETER: Yes, just so we have some data. Just to show change if change occurs. . . .

JOANNE: We wanted a tally [of questions] on each of the three tapes to see which direction you are moving in.

PETER: You might also think about the nature of the instrument as well—positive and negative.

MARY: We began the baseline tape with more closed questions. . . . We made a positive move from closed to open questions.

PETER: Any change in attitude or behaviors on the part of the students as you changed?

MARY: I'm not sure I changed . . . we were having so much fun doing this.

SHIRLEY: One thing you could add is a student question category because that keeps coming up here.

JOANNE: What I think some of you are finding is that, even though we were focusing upon the questioning, you wanted to look also at wait time and responding.

PETER: That was to make it easier, to focus upon one variable. It's really interesting to note that you wanted to look at the other areas.

POINT TO PONDER: If you were listening in on this conversation as a teacher or principal from another school, what observations might you make about this core group's deliberations?

Well, there are many different elements you might have noticed here that would contribute to a productive staff development process. Compare your list with mine:

The principal played an active role.

The principal's comments were constructive, supportive, and nonevaluative.

Teachers seemed free to express their strengths as well as areas they have improved upon or wanted to improve upon.

All participants shared ideas about questioning, wait time, responding in a nonjudgmental environment that invited openness, risk taking, and sharing.

For at least one teacher (Jean) there was a direct relationship between the
student-to-student interaction and question asking and the kind of teacher
questions posed.

Some teachers have realized the significance of their follow-up responses or
questions—for example, the probing questions that challenge students to
clarify or elaborate.

The leaders (Peter and Joanne) were interested in growth and change and in
teachers' documenting and working toward that for themselves, not imposing it by fiat as might have occurred in other schools.

Teachers found ways of improving the observational format they had created—in terms of students' questioning. This seems to have arisen as they
examined the relationship between closed and open questions.

And, finally, Peter seems very interested in peer coaching as a model to foster
more teacher-teacher sharing and problem solving.

What strikes me in listening to this tape is the collegiality, the sense of sharing
an inquiry process where people explore new territories, new kinds of behaviors.
It isn't quite clear whether or not they have yet seen the close relationship between
kinds of questions and the teacher's instructional objectives. One teacher later
on indicates that she asked a lot of closed questions, but it was appropriate for
the subject, such as typing or any introductory phase of learning.

Finally, what one hears is the enthusiasm of the participants: "We were
having so much fun!" This is the fun of exploration, the fun of inquiry, the fun
of Izzy's asking good questions and of Richard Feynman's "puzzle drive." This
excitement is also attributable to a strategy we see far too little of in schools:
peer observation, coaching, and reflection. Teaching is such an isolating profession that whenever we have opportunities to work with others in a risk-free environment toward common goals, it is positively exhilarating.

You can imagine where Peter and Joanne were able to take this core group
meeting: into ever more complex explorations of questioning, instructional strategies, personal goal setting, and analyses of teacher growth and metacognitive
awareness of their own thinking. Because he was the principal, Peter was able
to set a tone, a mood, and work collaboratively toward empowering strategies
with his faculty. Let us turn now to whole-school considerations that might grow
from our core-group strategy.

The Core Group and School Restructuring

Up to now, I have been discussing how the core group of teachers, administrators,
and perhaps parents can identify needs, set goals, and begin working to effect
change within the classroom. Significant school change can emanate from this
core group. But more as well. If we take seriously some of the above comments
about reflecting on our own thinking as adults and becoming more metacognitive,
these personal self-reflections can be extended to the entire school. Thus major
changes can be initiated.

For illustration purposes I shall refer to one school in this discussion, the
Wasatch Elementary School in Salt Lake City, Utah. This is the school where

Sylvia Mathis has done so much modeling within classrooms, conducted so many after-school meetings with teachers, and in general brought most of the students (K–6) to the point where they can talk knowledgeably about wait time, different kinds of thinking processes, and different programs that challenge them to use their minds and hearts productively. Dr. Corrine Hill is the principal, and it is primarily as the result of her leadership that Wasatch embarked upon such a thoroughly integrated approach in 1985. Her school is one of twenty-seven elementary schools in the Salt Lake City School District, and its student population was at this writing (Hill 1989) 615. Of these students 88.1 percent are white, 2.8 percent black, 4.2 percent Hispanic, 3.9 percent Asian, and 1 percent American Indian. There are twenty-two teachers, two special education teachers, two teacher aides, one P.E. instructor, and one librarian/media specialist.

Let us examine several of the well-integrated components of this school, including its philosophy and goals, the instructional program, social-emotional relationships, staff and professional development, and decision-making processes. Systemic elements comprise any organization, and if we wish to work toward a vision of the thoughtful school, the leadership must enlist the assistance of all constituents—students, teachers, and parents—to work cooperatively.

Educational Philosophy and Mission Statement.   Developed over a five-year period of time, the school philosophy states that

> All students can learn—in different ways and at different times.
> It is important to understand leadership styles and learning styles.
> Students need to be systematically taught thinking skills.
> A safe school climate to take risks must exist. (Hill 1989)

In another collaborative effort among teachers and parents, this mission statement was crafted:

> It is the goal of Wasatch Elementary School to create a cooperative atmosphere where teachers can effectively teach and students are engaged in activities that provide for optimal learning. Our mission is to foster the development of thoughtful, responsible students who appreciate the unique differences of all individuals, who are well equipped with academic and problem solving skills and who possess confidence to meet the challenges of real life situations.

The elements of thoughtfulness that we have been discussing throughout this book are present in these two statements: an emphasis upon problem solving and the importance of the feeling of self-confidence—all within an environment that challenges us to take risks.

It is also important to note that the above two statements were developed by parents, teachers, and students working with each other to fashion a vision for the school.

School Instructional Program.   Philosophic visions must be translated into an instructional program if they are to become a reality. So where do we see the Wasatch vision implemented? Dr. Hill tells us that problem solving and decision making "are taught as part of the thinking skills program at all grade levels" (p. 23).

In Language Arts students engage in problem solving as they create their own plays, design their own spelling programs, and create dioramas from favorite books using a variety of arts methods. "One class of sixth graders is following the preparation of this document [a nomination proposal for school recognition] as their teacher participates from research, rough draft, editing, rewriting and proofing to final copy" (Hill 1989, p. 13). "All of Bloom's levels of thinking must be addressed" in the students' writing: recall and review of information, translation into speech and print, organizing ideas, constructing a framework toward a focus, and then evaluating and editing the product. Katherine Gardner, a fourth grade teacher, reports that before the emphasis on thoughtfulness in her classroom, children would respond to a writing assignment with minimal effort and then ask, "Is this enough?" Now, after several years of focused staff development that threads sequentially through all grades, students are more willing and eager to state an idea and then develop and substantiate it.

In Mathematics, problem solving is reflected in the selection of textbooks (the Addison-Wesley math series and problem solving experiences) and in the teachers' emphasis upon "estimating, analysis, prediction, problem solving, finding alternatives, graphing, patterning, classifying, and metacognition. . . ."

In Science students participate in an Invention Convention, where they design such items as cookie-jar locks, socks with pockets for house keys, heated windshield wipers, and a device that allows handicapped individuals to play golf.

In third grade Karen Nichols presented problematic situations within an economics program called Mini-Society, where students established and ran their own business. Obviously they posed and resolved many different problems while engaged in this complex operation.

In art, the parents sponsor four creative-thinking workshops in visual arts, literature, music, and photography, and every student is able to participate. In addition, "art is taught as a combination of visual, creative and critical thinking skills. Aesthetic appreciation and expressiveness and openness to new ideas "are considered essential to the teaching of thinking as well" (Hill, p. 16).

There is a program for the gifted and talented students at Wasatch, and a future problem solving model is followed "as teams of students systematically address problems such as the arms race, vanishing rain forest, and poverty" (Hill, p. 19). In many schools only those students designated as "gifted" participate in future problem solving. In Wasatch, all fifth graders engage in this program. Similarly, competitions, such as designing thinking-related T-shirts and slogans, are open to the entire school.

Thoughtfulness further applies to areas such as discipline and school management. Bright yellow posters declare "Think Before You Act" and are posted throughout the school (accompanied by school rules). "Open discussion or class meetings involve students in solving behavioral or communications problems that impact the class. Students might analyze an incident, define problems, look at cause and effect, suggest alternatives, and plan for more effective ways to resolve such issues in the future" (Hill, p. 22). These problem-solving skills are taught as part of the instructional program at all grade levels and are used in rethinking such significant problems as the school's being known as the Warriors. The students identified the problem (the name "signifies making war") and generated alternatives, using their own criteria for an acceptable alternative.

Instructional Strategies.   Problem solving is one major instructional strategy that permeates the curriculum at Wasatch. For example, in Karen Nichols's third grade a traditional activity of making a gingerbread house turned into something different recently. "After students covered their milk cartons with brown paper, several of them sat down and on their own began planning what they would do the following day as they finished their creations" (Mathis 1989). This may be a spontaneous and transferred-from-prior-instruction example of metacognitive planning, monitoring, and evaluating. At least it shows an awareness of planning and goal setting.

Among the many and diverse strategies teachers use in Wasatch, those involving peer interaction seem very appropriate to fostering the school's progress toward its overall goals. A high priority seems to be placed upon collaborative work. "Children are encouraged to help each other read and write in peer tutoring programs. Sixth graders read to kindergartners and help the first graders write dictated stories which are beyond their ability to encode" (Hill, p. 13). Fifth graders write their own stories and read them to kindergartners, thus providing them with the satisfaction of a real audience for their endeavors.

You can imagine the extensiveness of peer cooperation when students are involved in the Invention Convention and future problem solving experiences.

School Organization and Collaborative Decision Making.   With all this emphasis upon problem solving within the students' curriculum, how would it seem if the principal, Dr. Hill, insisted upon abrogating to herself all decision making? If she felt she was the only one who could solve problems adequately? What would that say about the vision of the Wasatch Elementary School?

I'm sure you can see that the vision would fade from anyone's mind rather quickly. But this is not the case at Wasatch. Far from it. The teachers at several levels are involved in collegial problem identification and decision making:

A teacher serves on the School Improvement Council, a body found in every Salt Lake City school because of the district's belief in "shared governance." This body "shares the responsibility of setting policy and determining school goals and activities."

The Instructional Leadership Team operates collegially and focuses upon such instructional issues as discipline, for which a plan was "developed, implemented and modified by the faculty, along with input from the parents . . ." (p. 9). Members of the team, the teacher leaders, are selected by the principal after an interview and input from the faculty.

The principal is described as a "walk around" kind of leader, often in classrooms, conducting informal as well as formal observations. "She encourages discussion and ownership by all members of the staff when deciding school direction. . . . She has empowered the faculty to make curriculum and school decisions . . ." (p. 11). One sixth grade teacher, Margaret Lane, indicates that Dr. Hill treats her staff "like clear-thinking adults and, together with Sylvia Mathis, has created an atmosphere where teachers feel safe to 'risk.' "

"Parents at Wasatch are involved as formal decision-makers through participation in School Community Council. These open meetings with previously announced agendas provide for a Shared Governance form of policy-making giving the community view equal weight with that of the School Improvement Council" (p. 25).

It would appear as if the statement's call for "increased involvement, support and ownership" as well as "sharing responsibility for and implementation of the decisions" has more than a little substance to it.

Social-Emotional Environment.   Among the factors that contribute toward "favorable staff working conditions" at Wasatch are cohesiveness and professionalism. "The staff cares about one another. They are friends. They are compatible, both professionally and socially. The teachers on this staff teach one another—the feeling is one of *cooperation* rather than competition!" (Hill, p. 11.)

In reading letters from the students and teachers at this exemplary school, I come away with the feeling that there is a great deal of caring on the part of all participants. Margaret Lane reports that "the tone in the building is very professional, but warm and loving at the same time." Barbara Sharp, who teaches first grade, attributes some of what she calls "dabbling in each others' approaches" to the faculty's knowledge of different learning styles: "We understand one another's styles so much better and realize all are valid" (1989).

Karen Nichols indicates that wait time has played an important role in creating a risk-free environment within her third grade classroom: "When I was introducing double-digit multiplying on the board in the spring, I had the class work the problem as far as they could on paper at their seats. When I felt that enough time had elapsed, I demonstrated the answer on the board. As I began a solution, Beth called out, 'Don't do it yet, I'm not finished!' " Both Beth and her classmates felt she was "entitled to sufficient time to perform her own calculations" (Nichols 1989a, p. 10).

It is really not possible to overemphasize this element of organizational health and productivity. We do not need experts like Tom Peters and Robert Waterman to tell us that, when we feel comfortable in a group, when we feel as if we belong and people respect our contributions, we are more likely to work harder and be more creative and productive. No one likes to work in the kind of environment where fear, lack of respect for your ideas, intimidation, or distorted communications prevail.

Physical Environment.   What we say ought to be reflected in what we see around us in the classroom and building. In various parts of the building you can see the language of thinking words—*wait time, metacognition,* and *impulsivity*—emblazoned on banners. "A display case near the office elaborates on some aspect of thinking and invites onlookers to become cognitively involved" (Hill 1989, p. 17).

Rewards and Acknowledgments.   No one is going to work toward a goal unless her/his efforts are ultimately rewarded, and at Wasatch these rewards take the form of Blue Ribbon Thinking Awards given to various students on a weekly basis. Karen Nichols, a third grade teacher, describes how two of her students received these awards:

John's award "had been presented because he questioned something an author wrote in a book. In a book entitled *Stories from the Greek Myths*, the god of the sea was called Neptune (the Roman name) instead of Poseidon. John exhibited good critical thinking skills when he questioned an obvious inaccuracy. In another example, Bob earned an award by transferring knowledge gained in one area to another. In Math we had learned about Roman numerals and practiced using them in that setting. A few days later, Bob noticed that the spelling games in third grade use a combination of Roman and Arabic numerals to denote unit and week" (Nichols 1989a, p. 11).

Too often grades in schools are based upon Emily's criterion: acting like a tape recorder, repeating information passed down from the teacher. We need many more opportunities to show that thoughtfulness is valued.

Staff Development Restructuring.   In order to bring to fruition a vision such as that stated by Hill and her teachers, what kinds of staff development opportunities would be most effective?

How effective, for example, would an unconnected series of one-shot deals be in helping Wasatch reach its vision? These, you know, are the norm in many places—workshops developed to fill a slot in the calendar without much relationship to needs or problems.

Well, as you can imagine, what goes on at Wasatch is quite different from a top-down program, where those in power tell teachers what they think they need. A wide variety of staff development opportunities are available at Wasatch, one of the most important being the leadership provided by teachers themselves. "Teacher Leaders and Career Ladder Specialists, whose job descriptions reflect the goals of the school, are chosen each year by the staff. They become 'experts' in their assigned areas and work to help teachers in planning the educational programs of the school" (Hill, p. 9). During the year of this writing (1990) specialists focused upon thinking skills, Social Studies, Language Arts, and walking wellness.

One of the specialists, Sylvia Mathis, has provided the students at all grade levels with a wide variety of experiences designed to introduce them to such pedagogical practices as wait time (Chapter 5), key words and their meanings such as *metacognition,* and de Bono's Six Thinking Hats Model. In her role as a specialist, Sylvia has visited all of the K–6 classrooms to model thoughtfulness and help teachers and students relate significant processes to their subjects.

One teacher of sixth grade, Margaret Lane, noted that when Sylvia first introduced the concept of wait time, she "thought 'No way do I only allow 2–3 seconds for an answer.' Well, the first time I asked a question and counted to 10—it was unbearable." But now she notes how students have changed: Their responses "are more thoughtful and of a much higher quality. Our students are also very comfortable asking for more time to think—or 'please come back to me' " (1989).

Staff development in thinking processes has been extensive: "Teachers have been bombarded with research data, lectures, videotapes, observations, demonstrations, practice with feedback from peers, and opportunities to attend workshops featuring nationally recognized speakers on the subject'' (Hill, p. 10). Faculty meetings are often used to discuss some of the work introduced to the students, for example, the concept of wait time. Instead of having teachers sit and listen to materials they can read themselves, Sylvia organized presentations, where teachers spoke of their classroom experiments and what they were learning about their own teaching. What a refreshing departure from all the administrivia we have all had to listen to over the years.

In-service work is also extended to parents, who can attend monthly workshops at noon and in the evening, ''dealing with ways to extend and document thinking in the home'' (p. 18). How can we neglect those people whose influence upon our children can be so powerfully positive?

In one parent workshop, a mother told Sylvia her son was much happier in Barbara Sharp's first grade where ''his thinking is so much more valued'' than in his previous school. And another parent related how the content of the workshops was helping her support her younger children when they engage in brainstorming (a process learned at Wasatch) and to teach her older children (who did not attend Wasatch) to ''defer judgment'' when they hear their siblings' creative ideas.

Finally, what kind of impact has all of this staff development had upon Wasatch teachers? Here is a reflection from one teacher:

''I am getting better at problem solving. I'm more confident that I can [solve most problems]. . . . I look at a wider range of alternatives. . . . I'm more of a risk taker. . . .''

This is the essence of thoughtfulness.

CONCLUSION

What seems evident in the descriptions of these schools and their exciting work on thoughtfulness is that, when we make a commitment to work toward a vision, we can succeed—if we have confidence, if we persist, and if we work collaboratively so that everybody's problem-solving skills and dispositions are drawn upon.

David's school might not succeed as well as the Wasatch Elementary school—unless it creates an environment that invites everyone's mindful participation. For an example, note Peter Johnson's staff development meeting quoted above.

Finally, the efficacy of a problem posing and resolving approach seems validated by some of these reports. If problem solving is important in the classroom, it is equally important in helping us restructure the traditional school from one where one person, the principal, makes all major decisions, to one where we experience the joys and, yes, the hard work of shared governance. I believe that the schools described herein reflect those characteristics of ''healthy'' organizations identified by Matthew Miles (1979): clearly stated goals, communications adequacy, in which people discuss matters openly and without distortion, problem-solving adequacy, in which problems are not swept under the rug but are dealt with cooperatively and openly, and adaptability, the ability to effect change.

The entirety of the school dimension we have been exploring in this chapter seems best summed up by Karen Nichols of Wasatch:

> What a long way I've come in four years! Thinking skills in the curriculum sounded great but I had no grasp of what was really involved those many months ago. From a fumbling, questioning beginning, our faculty has defined, [and] formulated a program and moved forward. It's amazing to reflect on this journey. Our students have benefitted as we've added wait time and higher level questions to our teaching strategies. I have begun to value my students more as I recognize the quality of thinking and questioning of which they are capable. I have begun to realize the value of flexibility because as children think and question, the curriculum I've envisioned takes some interesting detours. (1989b)

Karen has identified one more element to be discussed: how we as teachers grow and change, how our roles become expanded as we develop more flexibility as educators. This is the final chapter of our journey: teachers' reflections on their own personal growth as the result of journeys described by Karen.

REFERENCES

Baron, Jonathan. 1985. *Rationality and Intelligence.* Cambridge: Cambridge University Press.

Costa, Arthur, and Larry Lowery. 1989. *Techniques for Teaching Thinking.* Pacific Grove, CA: Midwest Publications.

Desilets, Brendan. 1988. "An Experience in Empowerment: The Bedford Model." *Cogitare* 3, 2 (November): 2–4.

Dewey, John. 1933. *How We Think.* Boston: D. C. Heath.

Fullan, Michael. 1982. *The Meaning of Educational Change.* New York: Teachers College Press.

———— 1990. "Staff Development, Innovation, and Institutional Development." In *Changing School Culture Through Staff Development,* ed. Bruce Joyce. Alexandria, VA: Association for Supervision and Curriculum Development.

Gardner, Howard. 1985. *Frames of Mind: The Theory of Multiple Intelligences.* New York: Basic Books.

Hill, Corrine. 1989. "Nomination Package for 1989–90 Elementary School Recognition Program." Unpublished manuscript. Salt Lake City, UT: Wasatch Elementary School.

Joyce, Bruce, ed. 1990. *Changing School Culture through Staff Development.* Alexandria, VA: Association for Supervision and Curriculum Development.

Joyce, Bruce, and Marsha Weil. 1982. *Models of Teaching.* 2d ed. Englewood Cliffs, NJ: Prentice Hall.

Lane, Margaret. 1989. Personal communication.

Lieberman, Ann, ed. 1986. *Rethinking School Improvement: Research, Craft and Concept.* New York: Teachers College Press.

Mathis, Sylvia. 1989. Personal communication.

Marzano, Robert, et al. 1988. *Dimensions of Thinking*. Alexandria, VA: Association for Supervision and Curriculum Development.

Miles, Matthew. 1979. "Healthy Organizations: Figure and Ground." In *Organizations and Human Behavior: Focus on Schools,* ed. Thomas Sergiovanni and Fred Carver. New York: McGraw-Hill.

Mosher, Ralph, ed. 1979. *Adolescents' Development and Education: A Janus Knot*. Berkeley, CA: McCutchan.

Nichols, Karen. 1989a. "Integrating Thinking Skills into the Curriculum." Unpublished manuscript. Salt Lake City, UT.

Nichols, Karen. 1989b. Personal communication.

Resnick, Lauren. 1987. *Education and Learning to Think*. Washington, DC: National Academy Press.

Rowe, Jane. 1989. Personal communication.

Ryle, Gilbert. 1979. *On Thinking*. Totowa, NJ: Rowman & Littlefield.

Sarason, Seymour. 1982. *The Culture of the School and the Problem of Change*. Boston: Allyn & Bacon.

Schrag, Francis. 1988. *Thinking in School and Society*. New York: Routledge.

Sharp, Barbara. 1989. Personal communication.

Sigel, Irving, Carol Copple, and Ruth Saunders. 1984. *Educating the Young Thinker*. Hillsdale, NJ: Lawrence Erlbaum.

Swartz, Robert, and David Perkins. 1989. *Teaching Thinking: Issues and Approaches*. Pacific Grove, CA: Midwest Publications.

Whimbey, Arthur, and Jack Lochhead. 1982. *Problem Solving and Comprehension*. 3d ed. Philadelphia: Franklin Institute.

CHAPTER 14

Our Personal Journeys toward Thoughtfulness

OVERVIEW

In order to create the invitational environment that will eventually result in students and teachers becoming more thoughtful within their classrooms and schools, we all must undergo a change process, one that involves not only learning new strategies, but expanding our roles, examining our beliefs and commitments, and experiencing a wide range of feelings from doubt and despair to elation.

Karen Nicols of Wasatch looked back upon four years of change in her school and noted "What a long way I've come in four years! . . . From a fumbling, questioning beginning, our faculty has defined [and] formulated a program and moved forward. It's amazing to reflect upon this journey."

POINT TO PONDER: Why should such a journey be "amazing"? Why do you think Karen sounds surprised at what she uncovers as she reflects on the past four years?

Your answers to these questions might include some reference to the following:

That it has taken four years to get where they are.

That Karen started out "fumbling" and moved to a position of "flexibility" in her teaching repertoire.

That she sees her students now in a different light, as playing different roles in the classroom. Evidently her students now question more than they did in the past.

That she is perhaps more open about exploring uncharted areas within the curriculum as students question more.

Finally, the fact that she is now "reflecting." Many of us go through changes without engaging in this kind of reflection. Life passes us by, and we are unaware of why we are where we are, what we did to bring ourselves to such a point. Without a certain amount of reviewing the tracks we have made and where they lead, our lives are less under our direct control. Karen's reflections are the stuff of the examined and self-aware life and the essence of successful staff development processes in schools.

Another notion that occurs to me after rereading Karen's statement is that she started out with an inquiring mind and the disposition to follow her curiosities. In order to answer the questions she posed for herself, Karen obviously had to muster courage. Even working within the supportive environment provided by Dr. Hill, the principal, Karen and her colleagues had to be willing to take some risks.

But what impresses me most about Karen's reflections is that she has changed her role in the classroom, made it more flexible. She seems to have rethought how she thinks of herself, her students, the role of the curriculum, and probably the nature of education in general. She has done a lot more than bring into her classroom several discrete skills and exercised the students toward mastery of them.

These reflections on our roles and the emotional journeys that accompany our inquiry are important, because too often we don't realize that for successful, significant change to occur, we engage not only materials and strategies, but also our *belief systems, our values, and the whole range of our emotions and attitudes*.

Too often the improvement in our thought processes is ill-conceived as requiring little more than drill and practice in specific skills, such as generating alternatives and uncovering assumptions. Nothing could be further from the realities. Every significant change—and enhancing thoughtfulness is certainly a significant change effort—will involve our attitudes and beliefs about ourselves and others as well as the development and improvement in our cognitive processes. If we as teachers and administrators fail to plan for these changes, our efforts to create the thoughtful classroom and school will be less successful than they might.

To conclude our journey that commenced with Emily's reflections on her high school experiences, I should like to share with you two other reflections, this time of teachers who have made journeys similar to Karen's. My purpose is to let them tell us what they have learned about their students and themselves.

The major principle we shall discover within their reflections is *sharing control* with students (Chapter 5). The reason for this commonality is because, as Karen realized, when we challenge students to become more thoughtful, we open their intellectual spaces. Where there is more collaborative effort, there will be more joint decision making about what is important and how to make it meaningful.

TWO CLASSROOM EXPERIMENTS

Jill Dommermuth is a kindergarten teacher who became dissatisfied with a prevailing pattern within her classroom (Sarason 1982, Chapter 6). Math consisted of her doing a demonstration, students' doing workbook pages, and then grading the papers, all within twenty to twenty-five minutes. She identified this pattern as unsatisfactory and then asked two questions: "Why does this pattern exist?" and "What alternatives might serve our purposes better?" In response to the first question, she noted that this pattern served the needs of efficiency, control, predictability, and accountability: "Teachers and administrators find papers to be 'proof positive' of learning or learning difficulties" (Dommermuth 1989, p. 3). She then generated a number of alternatives and selected one: to broaden the curriculum to include many more manipulatives that would be developmentally appropriate and would enhance students' abilities to reason mathematically.

Jules Palmieri is a teacher of foreign languages at the high school level, and he became dissatisfied with the high degree of student passivity. He did all the talking and questioning, and students spent far too little time trying out the language they were supposedly learning. He posed the same questions as Jill did: "What is the pattern I am uncomfortable with? Why does it exist? What are several alternatives?" Consequently, in his Italian IV class he decided to engage in several different experiences designed to facilitate students' speaking and thinking in Italian.

Jill's Role Changes

Jill realized the truth recently stated (Romberg 1988) that children "enter kindergarten with considerable mathematical experience," but they "begin to lose their belief that learning mathematics is a sense-making experience. They become passive receivers of rules and procedures rather than active participants in creating knowledge" (p. 15). In other words, children too quickly become doers of workbook pages, where what counts is the correct answer. As Jill noted, the results of this approach were "boredom and distraction" during math.

One of her first innovations was to encourage children to explore and play freely with the manipulatives they would be using. Boredom tended to dissipate, because "they [were] directing their play." In the course of such explorations, disputes arose and "at this early stage I was already beginning to feel my role shift," because she modeled good negotiation strategies and allowed students to make and live with their own decisions.

As the units in math commenced, Jill had to teach patterns and pattern recognition, and here is where her instructional role began to shift. She noticed that when a student had a problem with a pattern "several of his classmates worked together to help him. . . . I asked them, 'How did you realize there was a problem?' and I listened to them. This is another role shift for me, because in the past I would have told them there was a problem and why it existed. Now I wanted the children to do the thinking. Another question I asked frequently was, 'What can you do to solve the problem?' By being open to their thoughts, I was learning about their thinking processes'' (Dommermuth 1989, p. 8). And becoming less directive!

In subsequent units on classification and counting, Jill noticed more inquiry and collaborative problem solving. ''The children had new confidence about directing the problem-solving and most weren't consulting me at all. I realized the children had made a major shift in their role perception'' (Dommermuth, p. 9).

Jill was realizing the truth of Fullan's (1982) observation, based upon cumulative research on school change efforts, that ''implementation actually comprises a change in the *role relationship* between teachers and students'' (p. 157). Management of small groups was being left to the children. ''They decide how and where to place the groups. They discuss among themselves where an [attribute] block will go. . . . I am a facilitator and guide during these lessons.''

Through strategies such as free exploration, small-group problem solving, and relating the content of mathematics to the children's experiences at home and on the playground, Jill was enriching their sense making, empowering them to take more control of their own inquiry, and allowing them to have a lot more fun.

Why was Jill successful in enhancing students' thoughtful engagement with patterns, classes of objects, and counting? She noted, ''I [was] willing to reassess my role and my perception of my role as a teacher to facilitator.'' And part of this role reassessment involved experimenting with students' decision making about subject matter: ''The kids are deciding what categories to use—shape, size, color, thickness. They are negotiating among themselves about placement of the shapes. My role is to compliment [*sic*] [or mediate] their thinking skills, question to get them verbalizing, and ease management of supplies and groups'' (Journal entries).

Almost as an afterthought, Jill noted something quite significant: ''It is interesting to note that my perception of my role as a teacher has shifted, but the children's roles have remained the same. Children are active participants in their learning and view themselves as doers. They know no other way at age 5. So, while I'm going through this major shift in my occupational identity [Fullan 1982, p. 29], the children go along their merry way—learning as naturally as always'' (Journal entry).

Jules's Experiment—High School

Jules's strategies consisted of rearranging the room so all students sat in a circle and could listen to and observe each other. Gradually he encouraged the students to express themselves more openly and not pay so much attention to grammatical errors in midspeech. He offered them more choice in they wanted to do in Italian: read Dante, converse about life situations, or play ''Jeopardy.'' Thus they were empowered to help design their own learning experiences.

While deep within discussions of Dante's portrayal of Ulysses, Jules discovered students' expressing an interest in more self-direction: ''They veered the discussion to a theme they found relevant and opted to follow this course'': the contemporary experience of cloning and test-tube babies. In both medieval and contemporary societies, there have been and are concerns about limiting the pursuit of knowledge.

Of course, Italian IV is an elective, and this afforded Jules more freedom of expansion than might be found in other classrooms; however, the principle his students discovered still applies in all classrooms: When people are involved in decisions that affect their lives, their commitment is strengthened. We all feel a sense of ownership for that which we create.

Jules insisted that all conversation be conducted in Italian. "I witnessed for the first time students expressing opinions, changing opinions, asking questions, and challenging each other in a foreign language. Placing value on another's opinion . . . leads to stimulation and interest" (Palmieri 1989, p. 6).

For the next project, the class created and enacted their version of the game "Jeopardy." The significant change in my role was apparent during this exercise. I was no longer the main actor in the class. In fact, with my function having been reduced to helping with certain technical questions about grammar and syntax, I was almost excluded from this particular activity. My satisfaction at the self-direction which characterized the class's preparation of this project was tempered by a slight feeling of being unnecessary—a feeling which must make many teachers hesitate from employing exercises dealing with cooperative learning. (p. 7)

Just as Karen saw students exploring pathways within the curriculum hitherto overlooked, so too did Jules find that he could cover some essentials within the language curriculum, such as grammar and historical episodes, by having students take charge of preparing newspapers reflecting events from the thirteenth and fourteenth centuries and preparing talk shows with an Italian/historical basis. Once students realized they were being taken seriously, it seemed, their creativity knew few boundaries. Their willingness to experiment with roles far different from their usual passivity led into many diverse directions. Students assumed roles hitherto only experienced by the teacher.

Jules's experiment with sharing control extended to students' self-reflections upon how they should be evaluated. "Allowing students [some] control over evaluation does not result in lessened demands. The students are always at least as demanding as the teacher in an authoritarian role might be." One thing that definitely changed was the means and criteria for evaluation; students wanted other projects, such as a Renaissance bulletin board, included in their final evaluation, and this provided another forum for individual decision making.

How effective was this experiment in terms of learning to speak Italian? By listening to students' voices more attentively, by providing a more supportive and risk-free environment, Jules succeeded in inviting students to express a wider variety and complexity of thought in their new language.

"In a recent discussion of some of da Vinci's writings and paintings, I saw a change from answers [in Italian] restricted to the repetition of data such as when the artist died and what the artist painted to what the student believed beauty was and to what he or she considers to be the most expressive art form."

What kinds of feelings did Jules experience during this adventure?

"The fears that I experienced in allowing for a redistribution of power in the class were predicted in the comments of the critics. ['All you do is play games?'] They had to be tolerated in order to achieve the goal of turning more power over to the students and thus give them the opportunity to have more vocal domination of class time. Errors in grammar, timing, and pronunciation had to be overlooked at times to foster an atmosphere conducive to cooperative efforts involving not only the students but the teacher" (p. 13).

His fears "of loss of control" were just as real as any teacher's who embarks upon these new territories, where we listen to students' voices and encourage them to think for themselves.

"The redistribution of power was simple and resocialization and redefinition of roles were achieved with a minimum of anxiety, although this feature was present" (p. 16).

One observer of change (Fullan 1982) notes that all real changes involve "loss, anxiety and struggle." Both Jules and Jill experienced some of this as they struggled with loss of the dominant role—teacher as disseminator of truth and right answers—and experimented with teacher as facilitator of students' own thoughtful engagement with real problems.

"Praise, respect for opinion and an atmosphere in which authority can be shared and accepted rather than imposed are the hallmarks of a positive learning environment, that is, an environment open to change" (p. 18).

PLANNING OUR JOURNEYS OF ADVENTURE

How do we take Jules's and Jill's journeys into account if we are working alone or in collaboration with others? One way to begin is to ask ourselves some questions derived from the problem-solving model (Chapter 8) such as the following:

Search for Meaning

How do I feel now about changing my routine, my classroom organization, my teaching strategies, etc.?

How would I represent the role I play now? As the one who pours information into a container, as one who coaches along the sidelines?

How can I relate this challenge to any other? What did I learn the last time I tried to bring about change?

Who can help me? Who are my colleagues and sources of emotional support?

Am I assuming too much? That I can change things overnight? That students will be committed to the same experiments I am? That this will not involve my role, my feelings, my sense of self?

Where do I wish to start? At some small task not too complex at first: kinds of questions, wait time, responding, peer interaction, goal setting, etc.?

Being Adventurous

How will I go about effecting a modest change? What different strategies can I think of?

How can I involve my students in thinking constructively about the desired change?

Being Reasonable

Which alternative makes most sense? Is most doable? Is likely to ensure success? These are some evaluative criteria.

This is one way of planning for the kinds of journeys Karen, Jules, Jill, and many others have undertaken. If we attempt to make the journey meaningful in our own terms from the outset, we stand a better chance of being in control of the pathways we traverse.

LEVELS OF USE AND AWARENESS

Robin Fogarty (Fogarty & Bellanca 1989) has developed a meaningful way of analyzing how some of us undergo the change process. As the result of her studies, she has identified several levels of use and awareness that can act as guidelines to the inner journeys we will experience. She presents her levels metaphorically in terms of birds that move from outright rejection of the innovation to being fully integrated.

Bird	Level of Use
Ollie the Head in the Sand Ostrich	Overlooks entirely
Dan the Drilling Woodpecker	Duplicates through drill
Laura the Look-alike Penguin	Replicates in similar content not new content
Jonathan Livingston Seagull	Integrates within existing repertoire
Cathy the Carrier Pigeon	Maps strategy into new areas
Samantha the Soaring Eagle	Innovates in new realms

What these birds do for our understanding of the explorations we are about to embark upon is to suggest the following:

Some of us will get on board at different intellectual and emotional stages. Ollie doesn't get on board at all, and Cathy takes a strategy rather easily into new areas not previously explored. Karen Nichols seems to typify what Fogarty means by mapping into new curricular domains.

For each level of use there would appear to be a separate level of emotional awareness and involvement as well as varying role orientations. Ollie is totally uninvolved and perhaps rejects the innovation, perhaps because it isn't clear or because of fear and anxiety over movement away from the familiar or fear of loss of control. Dan begins to do exactly what he has seen modeled, is willing but perhaps tentative because of the above emotional states. Laura is moving ever so slightly into similar content areas and probably feels some of the anxiety over stretching beyond the known. Jonathan is feeling more confident, because he is making connections within his own experiences, territory he already knows. Cathy is even more confident about her new role and is able to create many different kinds of association within a wider variety of subject matter and territory not previously covered. Samantha is fully in command of the innovation and has expanded into a new role definition.

It seems to me that Jules and Jill, without their telling me, probably started out as Lauras and ended their journeys somewhere between Cathy and Samantha. They started tentatively at first, and as experiences grew, they felt less discomfort and more confidence in their ever-expanding roles. Karen probably is now accepting her classroom experiences:

"I'm feeling much more comfortable incorporating thinking into the curriculum now. I have a grasp of what thinking skills are about and can now see ways of integrating them into existing units."

POINT TO PONDER: Where do you think Karen's reflections place her now? At which level? Why do you think so? Would you agree that she is probably a Jonathan or a Cathy?

Why are these levels important? Simply because we ought to know before commencing these journeys of exploration that some of us will expand into new roles with greater ease than others. Some may advance to a certain level or enter at that level, and not be able to move easily toward more complex levels of awareness and self-discovery.

Knowing this, it is even more vital that we attempt to involve ourselves in a peer-group strategy to provide a core of emotional support as we attempt to stretch ourselves from a limited role, what one teacher called his "tunnel vision," to become ever more flexible in our repertoires of teaching strategies.

CONCLUSION

In this chapter I have explored an aspect of enhancing thoughtfulness that is too often overlooked: the personal journeys we all embark upon when we change our roles in the classroom. These changes inevitably involve a wide range of emotional responses to experimenting with new behaviors and, in some cases, leaving the familiar to explore the unknown.

It is not uncommon for us to feel nervous about the prospect of sharing control with our students; for some it even suggests losing control, although I have never seen this actually happen. What I think most of us are apprehensive about is being confronted with questions for which we have no answers. But the concomitant rewards of working with students to inquire about common problems is a thrill all educators deserve to experience.

Jill concluded her comments about her mathematics experiment by comparing change in the classroom with change in her personal life:

> The most important concept I was reminded of was that change is a process, not an event. . . . I learned very quickly that both my changes had to be made in small steps that acted as building blocks. As I made small shifts, I was able to reflect upon their success or failure and refine and move along to the next challenge. I quickly learned that my attitudes and beliefs would not change in one step. . . . Although I was highly motivated to accept the change in my personal life and the change in my math program, I was still afraid of giving up the familiar. Each step forward meant gaining new knowledge which meant I couldn't go back. . . . Acceptance of the loss, anxiety and struggle were important in the success of the changes. . . . Acceptance of the fact that change takes time was important to success. At times when I felt unsuccessful or a lack of confidence, I reminded myself of the *process* of change. When I realized that I would not always feel that way, I was able to accept the discomfort I was feeling and learn from it. I began to expect progress, not perfection. The process of change has been slow but steady which has allowed me to make the most meaningful shifts from within. Because these shifts affect my attitudes and beliefs, they are lasting changes. (Dommermuth 1989, p. 12)

Many journeys begin with some kind of recognition of discomfort with the present condition, such as Emily's recognition of her life as a recording device. Jill is well along on her journey of exploring new roles in her personal and professional life and accepting the realities of such journeys: We hope for progress, not perfection.

REFERENCES

Dommermuth, Jill. "An Analysis of a Personal Change." Unpublished manuscript. Montclair State College.

Fogarty, Robin, and James Bellanca. 1989. *Patterns for Thinking: Patterns for Transfer.* Palatine, IL: Illinois Renewal Group.

Fullan, Michael. 1982. *The Meaning of Educational Change.* New York: Teachers College Press.

Palmieri, Jules. 1989. "Effecting Change in the Fourth Level Foreign Language Class." Unpublished manuscript. Montclair State College.

Romberg, T., et al. 1989. *Curriculum and Evaluation Standards for School Mathematics.* Reston, VA: National Council of Teachers of Mathematics.

Sarason, Seymour. 1982. *The Culture of the School and the Problem of Change.* Boston: Allyn & Bacon.

CONCLUSION

"We Are a Summons and a Challenge."

In *Leaves of Grass* Walt Whitman spoke of humankind as a "summons and a challenge." I submit that this challenge is forever to heed the advice of nuclear physicist Isidor I. Rabi's mother to ask "good questions." His mother, whose origins lay in Eastern Europe, knew the essence of our humanity: posing thoughtful questions about our lives and pursuing with much persistence the universe of alternative answers. As a result of such persistence, Rabi was awarded the Nobel Prize in Physics in 1944 for his work on the resonance method of recording the magnetic properties of atomic nuclei.

Emily is embarking upon her quest for good questions and answers. At the end of her high school years, she again reflected on her life and noted that her "tape recording instincts" were still strong. She worried that "colleges would stop relying so heavily on standardized testing before it was [her] turn to apply." Because of schools' heavy reliance upon such testing, Emily doubted that she possessed much "real world" knowledge. But she was gaining confidence, and her self-image has changed in the two years since her "Beam me up, Scotty" journal entry:

"Now, instead of feeling like a tape recorder, spitting back what someone told me, I feel as if someone handed me a box full of jigsaw puzzle pieces that I'm supposed to fit together. Some of the pieces don't fit anywhere, and I'm not sure what the puzzle is supposed to look like or how big it is. The best I can do is pick out the corner pieces and work out the edges. Maybe what I would have liked was more reassurance that I was getting someplace. . . ."

Emily doesn't quite see how all the pieces fit, but that doesn't bother her:

"I'm graduating now, and I'm a little nervous, but pretty excited. I think I'll be all right. I've realized, you see, that no one is going to expect me to know

274

everything after graduation from high school and that I can always learn how to do things. Someone told me that this was the most important function of school—it teaches you how to learn."

Thus, Emily's questioning is developing beyond the mechanical process of "spitting back" what someone told her and trying to remember it all. She is moving toward the search for meaning and being in control of her own destiny. She is creating her own picture puzzle, which she assembles in ways that are meaningful for her.

Teachers like those mentioned in this book deserve a lot of the credit for creating the environments where Izzy and Emily could develop their thoughtful curiosities and wonderings. This is our continual challenge: to pose good questions for ourselves and our students; to commence a process of inquiry about the ways in which we live in our classrooms. To locate those patterns of behavior that might be inimical to establishing an invitational environment and to change them, gradually and purposefully. Emily has given us reason to pause, reflect, and set our sights higher than perceiving our students as tape recorders.

Tennyson wrote a poem about the aging hero Ulysses wherein he frames the journeys we are embarking upon:

> Yet all experience is an arch wherethro'
> Gleams that untravell'd world, whose margin fades
> For ever and for ever when I move.

Every experience we have is potentially an arch leading off to those untraveled worlds worthy of exploration if we but pose the question about meanings, alternatives, or potential consequences.

> How dull it is to pause, to make an end,
> To rust unburnish'd, not to shine in use!
> As tho' to breathe were life. Life piled on life
> Were all too little.

Emily and the other students and teachers I have written about are explorers and adventurers into the domains of thoughtfulness. They have chosen not to pause or to rust unburnished in their careers. They are risk takers pushing back that margin of the unknown as they inquire and pause to reflect on their experiences with children and adolescents and young adults.

> Come, my friends,
> 'Tis not too late to seek a newer world.
> Push off, and sitting well in order smite
> The sounding furrows; for my purpose holds
> To sail beyond the sunset, and the baths
> Of all the western stars, until I die.

And for all those who have not yet embarked upon the journeys of change and challenge, we who have experienced the thrills of seeing our students in newer, more open roles urge you to join us on this momentous adventure.

> *that which we are, we are;*
> *One equal temper of heroic hearts,*
> *Made weak by time and fate, but strong in will*
> *To strive, to seek, to find, and not to yield.*

This is our summons and challenge—nothing less will do as we are poised on the margin of the twenty-first century.

REFERENCES

Rowe, F. J., and W. T. Webb. 1938. *Tennyson*. London: Macmillan.

Afterword

If, in the future, we desire a more cooperative world society, rational approach to resolving conflicts, and compassionate attitude toward our fellow human beings, schools will need to be redesigned to become more thoughtful places. Children, our legacy for the future, demand new educational goals. The achievement of these goals requires different instructional strategies, fresh school organizational patterns, and innovative curriculum. It also requires alternative and varied forms of assessment—we cannot measure process-oriented goals with product-oriented assessment techniques.

While we might subscribe to this lofty vision of the transformed school, the most challenging aspect of change is the one to be effected within ourselves. Giving up our timeworn traditions; enlarging the expanse of our cultures; replacing our obsolescent beliefs; relinquishing our outmoded behaviors—all can be difficult, if not excruciatingly painful.

John Barell eases us into a new form of schooling which fosters thoughtfulness. He presents a composite view encompassing the rational and analytical capacities of critical thinkers, as well as the concern and empathy of compassionate and cooperative human beings.

By providing helpful examples, vivid vignettes, real-school descriptions, and specific directions, John has eloquently presented a refreshing, inspirational, and practical strategy for developing thoughtful schools, teachers, and curriculum orchestrated to produce a more thoughtful generation.

ARTHUR L. COSTA

Teacher Resources

The teachers and administrators whose names are listed below have been mentioned in the text and they have generously given their permission to be listed as resources. I encourage you to write them on your own.

John Borchert
Rye Middle School
Rye, NY   10580

Carol Cutrupi
Cherry Hill School
River Edge, NJ   07661

Brendan Desilets
John Glenn Middle School
MacMahon Road
Bedford, MA   01730

Jill Dommermuth
Westmoreland School
Fairlawn, NJ   07410

Mary Jane Fox
Shoreham-Wading River High School
Route 25A
Shoreham, NY   11786

Beth Friedman
Rye Middle School
Rye, NY   10580

Esther Fusco
Principal
Babylon Elementary School
171 Ralph Ave.
Babylon, NY   11702

Doreen Guzo
Whippany Park High School
165 Whippany Road
Whippany, NJ   07981

Karen Guidera
S. A. Roberson School #7
Andrew Street and Avenue C
Bayonne, NJ   07002

Corrine Hill
Principal
Wasatch Elementary School
30 R Street
Salt Lake City, UT   84103

Peter Johnson
Principal
Whittier Elementary School
1103 South East Avenue
Waukesha, WI   53186

Marilyn Kuhlmann
West Orange High School
West Orange, NJ   07052

Rosemarie Liebmann
Assistant Principal
Voorhees High School
Route 513
Glen Gardner, NJ   08826

Sylvia Mathis
Wasatch Elementary School
30 R Street
Salt Lake City, UT   84103

Mary Mulcahy
Richard Byrd Elementary School
640 Doremus Avenue
Glen Rock, NJ   07452

Karen Nichols
Wasatch Elementary School
30 R Street
Salt Lake City, UT   84103

Mary Ellen O'Donnell
S. A. Roberson School #7
Andrew Street and Avenue C
Bayonne, NJ   07001

Jules Palmieri
Belleville High School
100 Passaic Avenue
Belleville, NJ   07109

Ken Schopp
Franklin Avenue Middle School
755 Franklin Avenue
Franklin Lakes, NJ   07417

Viola Stanley
Richard Byrd Elementary School
640 Doremus Avenue
Glen Rock, NJ   07452

Sandy Woodson
Wiley Elementary School
Hutchinson, KS   67502

Index

Absenteeism, teacher (example), 140, 147, 164, 186
Abstract reasoning, 47–48, 49, 50, 240
Acknowledgments/rewards, 260–261
Adventurous thinking. *See also* Experimentation/
    exploration; Imaginative thinking
  and alternatives, 150–151
  assessment of, 48–50
  and assumptions, 150–151
  and conclusions/solutions, 150–151
  and the definition of thoughtfulness, 2, 7–8,
    10–11, 12, 16, 17
  and experiences, 150–151
  and meaning, 150–151, 270–271
  and obstacles to thinking, 243
  planning journeys of, 270–271
  and reasonableness, 271
  and reflection, 150–151
  and relationships, 150–151
  and representation, 150–151
  and research, 178
  and teaching thinking, 25
  and the thinking process, 16, 17
  and unit plans, 125
Affective domain. *See* Feelings
Age, 103–106, 109, 200–204, 225–229, 240, 251
Alternatives
  and adventurous thinking, 150–151
  and assessment, 35–36, 44, 51, 52
  and control, 71
  and the definition of thoughtfulness, 10
  and the environment, 67–68, 71
  and feelings, 28
  and instructional processes, 81–83
  and meaning, 150–151

  and modeling, 67
  and posing problems/questions, 81–83
  selecting, 153–154
  and teaching thinking, 24, 25–26, 27, 28
Ambiguity, 13, 14, 34, 38–39, 45, 52, 240, 241. *See
    also* Disclosure model
Analogical reasoning, 183, 193–195. *See also*
    Metaphoric thinking
Anticipating results, 152–154
Arendt, Hannah, 9, 15
Art (discipline). *See* Humanities
Arter, J., 47, 51
Assessment. *See also* Evaluation; *name of specific
    method*
  of adventurous thinking, 48–50
  and alternatives, 35–36, 44, 51, 52
  and ambiguity, 38–39, 45, 52
  and brainstorming, 55, 56
  and change, 249–250
  classroom episode about, 32–33
  and cognition, 47–48, 51
  and comparisons/contrasts, 52
  and complexity, 38–39, 50, 52
  and content, 52
  and control, 53
  and cooperation, 37–38
  and creativity, 48–50
  criteria for, 33–34, 36–38
  and critical thinking, 51
  and decision making, 34, 53
  and the definition of thoughtfulness, 33
  and the disclosure model, 128
  evaluation of, 34
  and experiences, 46, 50

6. Please identify those portions of the book you find most meaningful:

7. Specific strategies you have used in your own classroom, and results:

8. Suggestions for improvement:

9. Other comments:

Please return to:

Naomi Silverman
Senior Editor, Education
Longman Publishing Group
95 Church Street
White Plains, NY 10601

Reader Response Survey

The author and editors of *Teaching for Thoughtfulness* would like to know what you think of the ideas presented in this book and how useful you find them. Your comments will be used to improve future editions of the text, and can also be used to initiate a reader network if names and addresses are provided. Please do not feel compelled to comment on the entire text. Thank you very much for your interest and commitment.

1. Name (optional): _____

2. Address (optional: _____

3. How did you learn about this book? _____
_____

4. If you are a *preservice student:*

    a. What is the name of the course in which this book was assigned to you?
    _____

    b. Is this an undergraduate or a graduate course? Circle one.

5. If you are a *school practitioner:*

    a. Was this book assigned to you in a course you are taking?

    (Yes/No)   If yes, which course? _____

    b. What is your role in the school? Circle one:

    Teacher (grades taught___)   Administrator/Supervisor   Parent   Other

(over)

Cut along dashed line.